THE FIRE
NEVER DIES

Critical Acclaim for Richard Sterling

Travelers' Tales Books

Country and Regional Guides
America, Australia, Brazil, Cuba, France, Greece,
India, Ireland, Italy, Japan, Mexico, Nepal, Spain,
Thailand; American Southwest, Grand Canyon, Hawai'i,
Hong Kong, Paris, San Francisco, Tuscany

Women's Travel
Her Fork in the Road, A Woman's Path, A Woman's Passion
for Travel, A Woman's World, Women in the Wild,
A Mother's World, Safety and Security for Women
Who Travel, Gutsy Women, Gutsy Mamas

Body & Soul
The Road Within, Love & Romance, Food,
The Fearless Diner, The Gift of Travel, The
Adventure of Food, The Ultimate Journey, Pilgrimage

Special Interest
Danger!, Testosterone Planet, There's No Toilet Paper
on the Road Less Traveled, The Penny Pincher's
Passport to Luxury Travel, The Fearless Shopper,
The Gift of Birds, A Dog's World, Family Travel,
Shitting Pretty, The Gift of Rivers, Not So Funny
When It Happened, 365 Travel

Footsteps
Kite Strings of the Southern Cross, The Sword of Heaven,
Storm, Take Me With You, The Way of the Wanderer,
Last Trout in Venice, One Year Off, The Fire Never Dies

Classics
The Royal Road to Romance, Unbeaten Tracks in Japan,
The Rivers Ran East

THE FIRE NEVER DIES

*One Man's Raucous Romp
Down the Road of Food,
Passion and Adventure*

Richard Sterling

TRAVELERS' TALES
SAN FRANCISCO

Travelers' Tales and Travelers' Tales Guides are trademarks of Travelers' Tales, Inc., 330 Townsend Street, Suite 208, San Francisco, California 94107. www.travelerstales.com

Portions of this book appeared in *Dining with Headhunters: Jungle Feasts & Other Culinary Adventures,* published by The Crossing Press, 1995. "Male of the Species" used by permission of Lonely Planet Publications, *World Food Vietnam.*

Cover Design: Stefan Gutermuth
Cover Illustration: © Owen Smith
Interior Design: Melanie Haage
Page Layout: Melanie Haage, using the fonts Berthold Bodoni and Sabon.

Distributed by: Publishers Group West, 1700 Fourth Street, Berkeley, California 94710.

Library of Congress Cataloging-in-Publication Data
Sterling, Richard.
    The fire never dies : one man's raucous romp down the road of food, passion, and adventure / by Richard Sterling.
        p. cm.
    ISBN 1-885211-70-8
    1. Food--Anecdotes. 2. Travel--Anecdotes. I. Title.
    TX357 .S78 2001
    641.3   2001034740

First Printing
Printed in the United States of America
10 9 8 7 6 5 4 3 2 1

To Laurie, Tammy,
and Susan.

Richard Sterling

Contents

P r o l o g u e

Iᴛ ɪs ᴀʙᴏᴜᴛ ᴏɴᴇ ᴀ.ᴍ. ᴏɴ Jᴀɴᴜᴀʀʏ 1, ᴀᴛ ᴛʜᴇ ʙᴇɢɪɴɴɪɴɢ of a new century. A fire crackles on the beach next to the thatch-roofed Cafe Almeja. I am the only man in town wearing a tuxedo, and likely the only one barefoot at the moment, wriggling my toes in the sand. The Baja California town of Mulege (MOO le hay) has just observed the passing of the year, in typical form. There was no countdown to midnight. At about ten minutes after, somebody noticed the time and announced it to all the revelers. Then, as we do every year in this faraway little town, we embraced each other, drank a toast, and carried on. Some of the folk have gone to the plaza where the local mariachi band will play and people will dance till dawn. They will eat and drink. They will talk and laugh. For those who wish to sing, the band will play their requests. And they will dance and dance till they can dance no more.

I contemplate the glowing fire. In the past people thought of fire as a thing—something sacred and mysterious, often worshipped as the manifestation of a god. Today we know that it is not a thing, but a process. The reduction of compounds to elemental carbon. The dancing flames are merely the release of gasses, so hot that they glow. All very simple, really. Easily explained. And yet it still has the power to evoke the sacred and the mysterious. And how not? Without this process there could be no life, only cold nothingness. Most of what is in the universe is fire. Just look up in the sky, day or night, to the nearest star or to those farther away. Or look inward, into our bodies. A chemical fire, quite literally, burns. And how should we not burn? We are stardust. And in us deeper still lies the passion. That which we say burns. And how should it not? Without passion we are as cold as the dead.

One of my passions is this very place. This magnificent peninsula that we often call "the Baja." Its deserts are beautiful and dangerous and full of mysteries and stories. Its seas are abundant. Over five hundred species of plants and animals are unique to it. Its history is tortured and full of brave hearts and big dreams and mighty failures. This little town of Mulege is the only recurring mark on my calendar. The week from Christmas to New Year's Day usually finds me here, though I come here whenever else I can. Its trans-peninsular highway, twisting for a thousand miles, is the symbol of my other great passion: the road. The great, long road to all the world. It is where I live, in the fuller sense of the word. It is where stories are most alive. It has led me around the planet several times. I've followed it down dank alleyways and up grand boulevards; into mansions and into huts; into the company of the sacred and the profane; and into the innumerable stories that make up my life. Stories of Baja, and stories of far away. For these things my passion never cools; and for this I am always alive. The fire never dies. I always feed it anew.

Guillermo, who owns the Cafe Almeja, where we have observed the passing of the year, has hobbled out on his crutch and his one leg to the fire. One of his girls follows him with a chair. The other with a bottle of Mumm's Cordon Rouge. He throws back his blond hair and says, "Ricardo, you know that my grandfather was French. And so I always keep a bottle of this for a special occasion. I've had this one for six years. Now

I open it not for the new year, but because of the honor you do me in wearing such finery in my humble restaurant." Who could not help but smile? And I have indeed worn it to honor him and the town. This is a country where people still dress up, rather than down. It says something to wear nice clothes. And my black and white has spoken well for me.

Others in our party are bringing chairs to the fire. For this is going to be a night of stories. In this desert there are no theaters or amusement parks, or much else in the way of modern entertainment. But there have always been stories to tell. To be listened to and savored, and told over again, the way one might play a favorite song over again, and once in a while interpreting it differently.

Guillermo pops the cork and pours the mirthful wine. "You start, Ricardo," he says as I sip the bubbly stuff. The taste arouses the Muse. I cannot remember all the wines I have tasted, but I know that the best ones are those that are bound up in stories. The three others at our fire speak some English, but Guillermo speaks none. I speak what I call "kitchen Spanish." I get by, though I take no prize for erudition. But I can describe the sea and the sky. And I know the words for death and hope.

As the cheerful fire crackles here on the beach I recall another kind of fire, one that burned within the clouds, and on the water, and in souls. And the story is a fitting one for this moment of transition, where one epoch ends and another begins.

1   *Defeat*

At the mouth of the Mekong River I stood on the fore deck and watched the sun come up on the last day of the long conflict the Vietnamese have come to call "the American War." It was the most beautiful dawn I have ever seen before, or since. The air hung warm and moist and soft. A thick, creamy quilt of cloud lay along the coast and the rising sun painted it red, orange, and yellow. The colors blazed and constantly changed their patterns: mixing and moving and dancing majestically as though they were heaven's own fire. To the east of the clouds the sea lay quietly glassy and blue. The jungled hills that stood to the west were the greenest of green and they formed a dam that held back the fluid cloak of clouds so that we could watch the sun paint them a while longer. It was gloriously beautiful, and deceptively peaceful.

By degrees the painting vaporized and the last story of the war began. The scene opened when a lone helicopter streaked in at low altitude from the direction of Saigon. Coming over water it circled the command ship USS *Blueridge*, steaming just off shore. Orbiting the ship, the bird climbed and fell several times and its tail wagged back and forth as though the pilot were in a dither. Crossing the ship's bows a second time, it ran out of gas and fell into the sea. It sank quickly, and if its passengers were not drowned they were run over by the *Blueridge's* fat prow.

Soon another helicopter appeared. Then six, then a dozen. Then I couldn't count them all. They were everywhere and their roar filled my ears; out on the weather decks we couldn't even hear alarms or commands and had to communicate with hand signals. All the choppers were low on gas. Those that ran out stopped in midair, wobbled for a moment as though they were wounded birds struggling for flight, then went down. Left and right they fell out of the sky, crashing into the water, their rotors beating it into a froth until the sea swallowed them. They sank astonishingly fast, taking their occupants to the bottom as often as not. We launched boats to rescue those we could. They were precious few and coxswains reported sharks and pink water. Those choppers that stayed aloft were lining up one behind the other to land on any vessel large enough. They began to land on our deck, and to my surprise they were carrying mostly women and children and old people.

During the chaos of the day we went ashore to gather up people. Some were deserters, and by now there were a few "spooks": CIA men wearing dark glasses and clutching briefcases; some people from the CIA's front company Air America; even the families of Vietnamese President Nguyen Van Thieu's bodyguard. But mostly they were civilians, noncombatants: women, children, and old people.

We took the people to ships, any ships: fighting ships, cargo ships, support ships, any kind of ship that had room for them. Some of them were wounded. Some were still bleeding. And a number had died. Many were alone, while some were with families, or pieces of families. They stood at the lifelines, clutching all that they now owned and stared mutely landward as they embarked on lives of exile. Some wept. Some were too tired. Others were too scared.

On that day we gathered up more than one hundred thousand fleeing people. They huddled on the weather decks of every vessel in the fleet; exposed to the sun, the rain, the wind, and their enemies whom they still feared would pursue them. And they were all hungry.

I would have thought that the loss of homeland, family, and future had killed their appetites, but they hungered deeply. Maybe it was a hunger that expressed another kind of emptiness. Maybe their stomachs were in sympathy with their souls. I don't know, but they begged wearily for food.

Navy cooks are trained to expect sudden increases in the number of mouths they must feed. Ships will sink and their crews and passengers need rescue; soldiers and marines might need to be picked up from the beach; natural disasters call for relief efforts. In all such cases people need to be fed. Towards the end of the long day I noticed a smell from the galley of a rich stew. The navy recipe book calls it "El Rancho Beef Stew." It's common for GIs to bitch about the chow they get but the U.S. Navy feeds them fairly well; its beef stew isn't bad. We liked to call it "El Rauncho Beef Stew." When they took their care with it, it reminded me of something my own grandmother would have made. I've heard other men say similar things about it.

Two by two the cooks came up from the mess deck carrying great pots of stew and the thick aroma hung about the ship like a cloud. They ladled it onto trays and passed it to the hungry people. The spooks took theirs quickly and ate with gusto and were restored. They even asked for more. But the Vietnamese merely picked at it, hungry as they were. I watched a pretty lady, tall and slim and fashionably dressed, take her tray and sit down on a bollard next to the lifelines. She took little tiny bites and drew deep sighs in between. Now and then she glanced landward for last looks of home. Then she looked back at the stew and I thought she would weep. Bravely, she always took another tiny bite and repeated her longing glances. All the Vietnamese seemed to catch the same mood. The more they ate the bluer they became.

Somebody, I don't know who, hollered to the cooks, "Hey, these people don't eat beef stew. In fact I bet they don't even eat beef very much. They eat rice. Why don't you give 'em some rice?" In a short time two beefy cooks hauled a stewpot full of steaming white rice up to the weather deck. When the people saw it they quickly lined up for it in good order and reverential silence. The cooks gave them each heaping mounds, and the people smiled with relief and bowed slightly as they received their portions. I saw a man in a torn, dirty flight suit put a fat spoonful into his mouth and just hold it there, as though it were a kind of communion. An old man ate with his hands, running his fingers through the rice like a farmer testing good soil. And the pretty lady sat down on her bollard again and eagerly mixed the stew and the rice together, and she fed well. A very simple meal she had; but it gave her solace and was enough. The cooks served the people rice with every meal during the several days they were in our charge.

On that last day of the war I ate a great deal of El Rancho Beef Stew. If the refugees' stomachs were in sympathy with their souls, so was mine. I felt sharp sympathetic pangs of homesickness for them. Pangs that made me feel the need to reach out for something from home, something elemental, something primal, something that would connect me body and soul with all that I am and have been and come from. I needed the food from home.

I think that for every eater there is a food from home. There is some food, often a few, that are of and from the place we call home, that our bodies have long assimilated and our souls have anchored themselves on, and will always help to restore us when we are far away and feeling lost or alone. To feed on them is to suckle at the breast of one's homeland and be one with her again, if only for a while.

After days or weeks at sea or in the field, soldiers and sailors begin to talk about memorable meals at home, what their wives and mothers cook best, and what they will have as their first meal upon returning. Through countless such conversations, I never heard anybody long for *duck a l'Orange* or *tournedos Rossini*; no tarted-up dishes, elaborate concoctions, or elegant entrees. The food from home is simple, prepared with the easy grace of untold repetitions. At home it is always offered up with love, assurance, promises of continuity, faith, reaffirmation. It makes strong again the bonds with family, history, culture, and the soil from whence they all came. The Indians of the American Southwest attach religious significance to corn, and they believe that to eat it plain is to commune with God. The peoples of Asia have long had similar attitudes toward rice, and the Egyptians have revered their unbuttered loaves of wheat bread for four thousand years. The Jewish Passover feast, the Seder, takes its participants to an ancient spiritual home with simple dishes set around the plain unleavened matzo.

For most of us the food from home is heavy and stays long as a presence in the belly and the mind. I know of no one who can take comfort in lettuces, bean sprouts, or watercress. It has to be substantial and offer something to the teeth, be big in the mouth and warm going down. It is often a carbohydrate; heavy starches have a sedative effect on most people and help promote a sense of well being.

For some people it is something sweet: layer cakes, made by mothers on Sundays or holidays; cookies warm from the oven and heavy with the orchidian scent of real vanilla; dark and chewy brownies, or something else very chocolate. The sweetness helps to chase away the bitterness of the moment. It awakens the child, takes one back to another place and time; takes one home for just a little while. And the magic work of chocolate, whether it works upon your own self or not, is a phenomenon we have all observed. Its Latin name is apt— *Theobroma*: God's food.

For me the food from home can be a simple stew made the way my grandmother would make it, or fried potatoes and the venison chops that speak to me of the Pacific Northwest timberland where I lived as a child. Being from California I take great solace in the deep red wines of my native state and always carry two small bottles when I travel. Their bouquets carry their home address, enabling me to identify the individual counties where they were grown. The distinctive aromas of the California soils billow up from the liquid and I am instantly transported to Sonoma, Napa, Monterey, or my own Mendocino. On the ship or plane that brings me home I plan my first meal after arrival, the same one every time: a cheeseburger, French fries, and a draft beer served in a sawdust bar and grill where the jukebox plays Elvis, Chuck Berry, or Hank Williams Sr.

Mark Twain speaks to us all in *A Tramp Abroad,* longing for the food from home. Throughout Europe he hungered for the taste of America. The grandest cuisines of France and Italy, at first interesting, became ordeals, and every mealtime he thought of yet another dish he might have if he were home.

> Imagine a poor exile...and imagine an angel suddenly sweeping down out of a better land and setting before him a mighty porterhouse steak an inch and a half thick, hot, and sputtering from the griddle; dusted with fragrant pepper; enriched with little melting bits of butter of the most unimpeachable freshness and genuineness; the precious juices of the meat trickling out and joining the gravy, archipelagoed with mushrooms; a township or two of tender yellow fat gracing an outlying district of this ample county of beefsteak; the long white bone which divides the sirloin from the tenderloin still in its place; and imagine that the angel also adds a cup of American homemade coffee, with the cream afroth on top, some real butter, firm and yellow and fresh, some smoking-hot biscuits, a plate of hot buckwheat cakes, with transparent syrup. Could words describe the gratitude of this exile?

I agree, Mr. Clemens. And I know a hundred thousand Vietnamese who agree, too.

2 *Heat*

THE PEOPLE AROUND THE FIRE APPROVE OF my story, and Eduardo the guitarist remarks on the East Asian love for chili peppers. "I'm sure I would like their food if I was there," he says. "I'm sure I would remember it, just like you remember such a thing."

"I believe you would," I said. "The fiery foods of Vietnam are not much like the fiery foods here, yet they still burn their memory into your mouth and mind."

Eduardo absentmindedly strums his guitar, and I think we all take a moment to recall the dinner Guillermo served us that evening. The unique tasting rock scallops of the local Sea of Cortez, a stingingly hot salsa based on the bright red cactus fruits harvested from the desert the previous July, course upon course from Eduardo's guitar, and heaps of Mexican *alegria*. What we might call *joie de vivre*. Eduardo's remark, I realize, is revealing of how perceptive he is. It is ever amazing to me how much memory can be bound up in dinner. Especially a dinner of intensities: of taste and smell, of drama in the setting, and of company.

As the wise woman Margaret Visser has written: "Much depends on dinner." Thackeray says that "next to eating good dinners a healthy man likes reading about them." And Homer, in an oft-repeated refrain, breaks his narrative to tell how the Greek heroes laid down their arms and feasted during their wars and travels. The message for us is that feasting and adventuring are inextricably intertwined; cuisine is an integral part of the landscape, a character in the tale. Too often, I think, we take the subject of food out of its context and treat it as some discreet activity unconnected to real life. Or we insist that it be kept in a realm of gentility, refinement, at a far remove from daily life, adventurous life, or life on the raw side.

But let's not pluck the Muse of Cuisine from the continuum of life in which she resides. And she resides not only at the tables of the refined, the wealthy, and the well scrubbed. Like any other art, like any other thread in the pattern of life, she thrives also in the backstreets, dark alleys, and tables and kitchens of the profane. Wherever people invoke the Kitchen Muse, there she is.

Too often we fail to acknowledge the relationship between the food we eat and the drinks we drink on a given occasion and the people and events that attend the eating and drinking. My travels have taught me that the staff of life is something the soul and the memory lean on as well as the body. Dinners, especially dinners on the road, become a part of us. They become a part of our memories, our cares, our loves, and our stories. They become a part of who we are, of what makes us each unique. As that other wise woman, Gertrude Louise Cheney, has written: "All people are made alike. They are made of bones, flesh, and dinners. Only the dinners are different."

In the heart of the ancient Burmese necropolis of Bagahn a bush bearing small red chili peppers is growing wild in a temple ruin. This lively spice, thriving amid tombs, is a metaphor, one for all of Indochina. This is a vast land of necropolises. Ghost cities both lost and found nestle in the vital living landscape of the present day. Remnants of golden ages and dusty ruin are so common that they go unseen by the people who live among them. But the traveler, the stranger, and the sojourner can feel the ghostly presence at every turn.

Side by side with the ghosts of dead days are the vivacious cuisines of Indochina, mirroring the pulsating life of the present day. And those cuisines are symbolized by the fire spices used by every cook in Burma, Thailand, Cambodia, Laos, and Vietnam. Thoreau said that the difference between the quick and the dead was simply a matter of "animal heat." Whether that heat comes from Promethean fire or spice fire, it's all one to those of us who love the Lively Spice. And Burmese cookery provides it in judicious abundance.

The chili pepper, *Capsicum frutescens*, was introduced to Indochina in the sixteenth century, probably by the Spanish or Portuguese. The most commonly used are local varieties of jalapeño and serrano. As the name indicates, Indochina is a blend of Indian and Chinese cultures. Burmese cookery leans closer to the Indian and so the lively spice plays its role most often in curries. The Burmese cook approaches curry in a way that is constant with the ancient past or the monsoon cycle. Using a grinding stone the cook pulverizes together onion, garlic, ginger, turmeric, and chili, making a thick paste. Many recipes will contain other ingredients as well, but this is the basic mixture for all true Burmese curries.

The process is particular as well. The oil, usually light sesame, is heated to smoking, then the curry paste is stirred in. The cook reduces the heat to low, covers the pan and simmers, stirring often for ten or fifteen minutes. This mellows the ingredients by slow frying and cooks off all their water content. When it is done, the oil appears at the edges or on top of the paste. This stage is what the Burmese call *see-byan*, the return of the oil. Meat or vegetables can be added to simmer, releasing their own liquid to form a smooth curry sauce. The result is somewhat oilier than many cuisines, in the way that salad dressings and many Mediterranean cuisines are oily. It produces a silky smooth, tasty sensation in the mouth that not only satisfies but soothes. The best meal I ever ate in Burma was prepared in this fashion, one starry night in the midst of the ruins of Bagahn.

Today there is a sleepy little village of Bagahn on the outskirts of the ghost city. A lacquerware school operates there, as well as a small Buddhist seminary. But a thousand years ago Bagahn was a young and eager city. She grew up from a level plain on the right bank of the Irawaddy River, about one hundred miles downstream from Mandalay. Her buildings were wood, thatch, and bamboo; her hardy people devout and industrious.

In the year 1057 Anawratha, king of Bagahn, led his army south against the rival city of Thaton. Thaton fell and was sacked. The victors bore the spoils back to Bagahn in processions rivaling Roman triumphs. The booty included whole libraries, scholars, religious texts, and gold. Their sudden abundance sparked an explosion of religious, artistic, and cultural enterprise that brought about a two hundred year golden age in Bagahn. Temples and temple complexes, on a scale unseen in Indochina, greater than Angkor Wat, clogged the twenty square mile plain. Houses and palaces were still made of wood, but the temples were all of heavy masonry.

In 1287 Kublai Khan led his army south against Bagahn and razed the city. All the wooden buildings were burned and the people driven away. But the innumerable temples remained, gravestones to the dead metropolis. In time nature reclaimed the land. Foliage hid the temples and the world passed by. Bagahn would not come to light again for centuries. The whole of Indochina is strewn with such ghost cities; Bagahn is simply one of the grandest.

To reach Bagahn, Bruce Harmon and I traveled from Bangkok by plane, train, and automobile for three days. The last two days were true Third World travel and we felt like death warmed over when we finally arrived.

Visitors to Bagahn can stay at a pleasant thatch and tin-roof guest house for a few dollars, or in a neat bungalow at the government-owned hotel for a few dollars more. Most of the ruins have been relieved of their jungle shroud and are only a short walk away.

Trudging to the guest house, we passed a merchant selling one of the Lively Spice's kin: the melon-like durian fruit. Durian grows wild all over tropical Asia. Wild pigs and orang-utans feed on it voraciously. I call the durian kin to the lively spice not because of heat (it has none), but because of sheer gastronomic power, a lot of it in its smell. Anyone who has ever sniffed a durian will tell you that it smells like pig's manure and turpentine whipped in a blender and garnished with a dirty gym sock. But if you hold your breath, the taste is sweet and delicious and leaves a pleasant tingling on the palate. Durian is high in complex and simple carbohydrates, vitamins, and many other nutrients. It is as nourishing and wholesome as a potato and leaves the belly feeling satisfied—if you hold your breath.

The Bagahn merchant knew how to make the durian hold its breath instead by drying it, which reduced the horrible stink to a sweet and pungent aroma. It was still recognizable as durian, but no longer unpleasant. The man cut the yellow flesh into squares, and sold them on bamboo skewers for about a penny each. I ate several, which not only banished my hunger, but also cleansed some of the orange tea stain from my mouth. Revived, I was ready to visit the ruins.

The sun was near its zenith and dust hung still in the air. There are no guides in Bagahn so we half-dozen foreigners started out in a loose group for the ruins. As we passed a row of trees, huge squat temples with bulbous domes rose up from the ground; large temples and tiny chapels, temples with walled courtyards and a hundred spires, temples sprouting demons and sprites, temples covered with carved stone flames representing the fire of enlightenment. They stretched out across the plain as far as the faraway hills, all of them empty and breathing the breath of echoes, like seashells held to the ears.

As our little group explored the monuments we began to spread out till we were ones and twos and out of each other's sight. Bruce and I stopped to peer into the dark recess of what seemed to be a tomb. We were standing in what must have been a broad avenue, a processional route. A silence so profound it almost moaned lay upon the plane, but in my mind, bells and trumpets of processions sacred and festive rang. Saffron robes and prayer beads, and god-kings on litters glimmered fleetingly in the mind's eye. A hot wind blew up from the south, shaking the palm and the banyan trees, rattling their leaves and fronds.

All afternoon we plodded through the ghost city while the light lasted. Bruce and I returned toward the village as the sun set in a sky of blood. In ones and twos we all regrouped in front of the hotel, in sight of a great cluster of temples. We were two Americans, two New Zealanders, one Australian, one Briton and three Irish, all quite subdued as we greeted each other. Wordlessly, the hotel manager appeared with lawn chairs and we sat in a close circle, saying little. We were served tea. The light waned. Dour silhouettes of the ancient temples stood against the sky in their ranks and brooded, threatening to let slip their ghosts. We huddled more closely, and spoke of home. Night fell. The Milky Way shimmered, casting kaleidoscope shadows that flickered among the ruins. The day's awesome silence returned, as a heavy cloak muffling the scene.

Suddenly, a tinkling little kitchen clatter broke the silence, as though it were crystal, its shards breaking off and fluttering to the earth like leaves. A pungent, pleasantly stinging aroma found its way to our nostrils. The Lively Spice was afloat upon the air. A sputtering, sizzling sound gave it voice: "I'm here, I'm here. Let the ghosts walk if they will." The cook began to hum a tune and chopped and pounded and clattered some more. Sniffing hungrily and smacking lips, we began to speak again. "Wonder what the old sod's got for us," the Aussie pondered. "Chilis," Bruce said with satisfaction.

Scurrying workers set a table with a clean white cloth in full view of the starlit monuments. Upon it they set pots of glutinous rice, plates of tidbits, and bottles of the coldest Mandalay beer. Then they brought curries—eight or nine—of meat, fish, and vegetables, red, green, orange, and yellow, a vibrant chromatic display that glowed alive. Steam billowed from the porcelain bowls, swirling about and caressing us with warm, savory tendrils of vapor. We fell upon the good fare. The spirited firespices awoke our palates, glowed down to our gullets and filled us with Mr. Thoreau's animal heat. As beads of sweat appeared on our foreheads, perhaps the lowering monsters of Bagahn issued forth their legions, and ghosts howled, but vainly; the Lively Spice hummed on our palates and sang in our bellies. We ate, drank, talked, and laughed, and then ate more in the midst of old Bagahn. At dinner's end we sat with pepper-full bellies and slow-burning mouths.

We paid our bill, then ambled off in a warm and friendly gaggle to the guest house, about a mile away. The only light was starlight and we passed many an empty tomb and temple as we blithely wove our way, our Aussie sucking on a chili. The monuments held no spooks for us for we were too much aglow. I could have slept in a tomb that night and called it warm and cozy. I thought of the chili bush I had seen that day growing in the ruin. It sparkled red and alive against the dead gray of the walls. Indeed the quick and the dead are side by side in Indochina; but when we are filled with spice fire and animal heat, there is no room in us for ghosts.

Bruce Harmon, myself, and our fifteen-year-old pedicab driver/guide, Din Tun, lingered in the small amphitheater near the grand market of Mandalay in the heart of Burma. Attendants were snuffing the red and gold paper lanterns one by one, and the women of the classical dance troupe were gathering up bits of costume jewelry and swaths of silk. The audience had melted away into the night, leaving behind a faint scent of the sandalwood paste that all the women wear on their cheeks as sunscreen, makeup, and perfume. All else was open starry sky and stillness.

"Go now?" Din Tun asked. "Time...late."

"Yes," I said. "Time to leave Mandalay. It was a long time journey getting here, Din. But now it's time to go."

"Go," he nodded. "Come back Mandalay? Sometime?"

"Ha. That's what Kipling says in his poem, you know."

"Kipling, yes," he nodded and smiled indulgently, knowing and caring nothing of the imperial poet. But he knew that Kipling held something special for me. Din had taken me to Mandalay Hill, the great temple complex with its "thousand steps" heavenward. We took off our shoes at the bottom of the hill and mounted the steps that go straight up the steep slope like a causeway. Reaching the top of the stairs and the uppermost temple that crowns the hill, I paused to catch my breath and mop my brow. Then while Din watched in bemusement I shinnied up a drainpipe, clambered onto the roof, and mounted the peak of the highest gable. Far below me lay the green and abundant Mandalay Valley, rich with the season's planting. Surrounded by abrupt hills it calls to mind a huge serving vessel, for such it is. Looking down into it and into the town I recited aloud Kipling's poem, "The Road to Mandalay," for it was he as much as Din that had brought me to this high point.

> So ship me somewheres east of Suez
> Where the best is like the worst
> Where there ain't no ten commandments
> And a man can raise a thirst.
> For the temple bells are callin'
> And it's there that I would be
> By the old Moulmein pagoda
> Lookin' lazy at the sea.

Din watched and concluded that I was on a pilgrimage of some kind.

Many of my travels in the East have been inspired by the writers who preceded me. Kipling is high among them. Though he wrote from another century and another land, the experience of the soldier or sailor in the Orient is universal. He speaks to me as clearly and as currently as though he were reporting directly to me about his most recent voyage, patrol, or evening in a tavern. Kipling's poems have always been a compelling call echoing through time and space, through mind and imagination. My sailings would never take me to Burma. As a navy man I would never call at the ports of Rangoon or Moulmein. Yet the power of poetry is such that Kipling made it necessary for me to see the land of Burma, and the city of Mandalay.

But it was not an easy necessity to fulfill, because in the late twentieth century a clique of generals, led by Ne Win, with xenophobic and hermitic leanings and a vaguely leftist vocabulary, took over the gentle land of Burma. They closed the borders, shut out the world, and embarked upon an ill-defined, and very slow, journey down "the Burmese path to socialism." It was a unique enterprise, whose successes have never been tabulated. Had they been, few would have had the interest to read the slim record. Burma became a place where nothing ever happened. No news issued from the capital of Rangoon because no news occurred. The nation's once lively trade dropped off to the barest trickle. Journalists, travelers, and geographers showed no interest. The generals liked it that way.

Burma is now a land of echoes of things past. So many things and places are not what they are, but shadows and provocative suggestions of what they were. The generals have held the land in stasis for so long it seems that time stopped when the British Empire departed. Auto manufacturing is nonexistent and imports so few that the most common motor vehicles on the roads are 1940s vintage Willys jeeps. A native parts industry, scrap metal, and brilliant mechanics keep them going. The mechanics make housecalls, and even road calls. A team of them will travel for two days by boat, train, or bullock cart to reach a broken-down jeep or truck. Arriving on the scene, these consummate masters of their trade can effect a complete overhaul using only the tools they carry and parts they cannibalize or fashion from tin cans and old tires. For such a job they might receive twenty-five dollars.

The trains in Burma are slow. The airplanes rarely fly. The warehouses, offices, and houses of trade the British built are all in a general state of disrepair with peeling paint. Nothing happens to make it better. Nothing seems to happen to make it worse. Nothing happens. The generals like it that way.

But even generals can become desperate for cash. When nothing happens in the economy, nothing comes to the taxman. Tourist dollars are needed to make up the loss. Visas can still be difficult to get, and they might not last long. But we got ours, and I had finally arrived in Mandalay. Bruce and I had landed in Rangoon from Bangkok and immediately departed for the old royal capital on the Irrawaddy. And nearly all that I hoped to find, I found: the beauty, the ease, the history and culture. It is a dusty town of memories. Everywhere are tantalizing hints of what was, and what might be again on that near day when the last general dies. When the last salute is fired. When the last flag is furled and the warless warriors are no more.

I found everything I wanted with one exception: the food. It's almost impossible to find a complete, well-made Burmese meal! The restaurants in the city are all either Chinese or Indian. They might offer the odd Burmese dish, but seemingly only as a nod to the dominant culture. The occasional market food stall offered something vile and unfit for healthy palates, and while they called it Burmese I felt sure it was slander. I had read about Burmese cookery. I had spoken to knowledgeable people about it. But I had been warned: "There aren't many Burmese restaurants in Burma. If you want real Burmese food, it's best to get yourself invited home to dinner."

I believe we cannot know a people, or claim to have truly visited any land without experiencing some of its arts. But painting and sculpture can be confusing; literature needs translating and explicating; most of the other arts need some kind of introduction. But cookery is comprehensible by all. Even the most untutored wanderer, with a willing palate and a passionate curiosity, can acquire at the table an intimate knowledge of any land and its people. "Tell me what you eat, and I will tell you what you are," wrote Brillat-Savarin. Well, it's time.

So, from Mandalay we planned to travel by riverboat, and somewhere along the river, somehow, I would get myself invited home to dinner.

We climbed into Din's pedicab with all our gear and rolled through the night across town to the booking office to pick up our boat tickets. Taking our leave of Din, he asked, "You give me a present?" Everybody we met in Burma wanted a "present." Not anything of value necessarily, but a souvenir, something of that outside world that was forbidden to them by the generals. Anything manufactured, anything of cultural significance, anything personal was a rich gift to the Burmese. In the market we found that our property was more valuable than our Burmese money. We each bought beautiful hand-woven cotton blankets. Bruce paid for his with a Daffy Duck t-shirt; I got mine for a collapsible umbrella. The merchant seemed to be afraid he had cheated us. On departing Mandalay we gave our guide a brass belt buckle. His eyes shone like the metal itself. Din Tun took his treasure, mounted his pedicab, and rode away.

"I still wish his name were Din Gunga," I said to Bruce. "It would have been perfect on government forms."

We turned toward the river. High clouds had rolled in and the resulting darkness was so profound and thick that it seemed to have texture. It swirled and engulfed like a black tar fog. I half expected it to feel gooey. As we approached the docks the road narrowed to a sinuously snaking alley with dark, somber shapes of decrepit buildings squatting on either side. I said to Bruce, "Keep your eyes and ears open. If there's one thing I learned in all my years as a sailor it's that a darkened waterfront is not a very salubrious place."

"Huh?"

"You wouldn't want to take a date there."

"Oh. Dangerous?"

"Could be. Why don't you go first."

Neither of us considered my remark remarkable. Bruce is a good man with his fists. We originally met in the boxing ring when we were both amateur pugilists with a California athletic association. Our first meeting was attended by flurries of lefts and rights, one small shiner (his), two headaches, and one very bloody nose (mine). We became instant friends. Neither of us compete anymore, but Bruce continues to work out, spar regularly, and keep his fighting weight. I think about it a lot.

Bruce's keeping in top form has come in handy. He once bounced a bothersome Iranian fellow from the kickboxing ring in a nightclub in Pattaya Beach, Thailand. The crowd went delirious and started chanting "USA, USA!" The manager was grateful enough for Bruce's excellent service to pay him a fighter's purse and offer him a job. During a trip to China, Bruce coldcocked an armed mugger with a one-two combination worthy of the great champions. The bad guy hit the pavement like a sack of bricks. "Let's boogie," Bruce said. And we did.

And so in Mandalay I told Bruce, "You walk on ahead. I'll see no one comes up on you from behind."

"Thanks. I guess."

We came to a point where we could smell the river and hear it lapping against the pilings of the wharves. A large, dark shape loomed ahead, but I couldn't tell if it was a building or a river boat. I remembered my seaman's training: when you're on lookout duty on a dark night, objects are difficult to see if you look directly at them. If you look at them askance, observe them obliquely, they come into better view. So I shifted my gaze first to port, then to starboard, and the shape revealed itself as a flat-bottomed, two-decked, Mississippi-type riverboat. Screw-driven. "Is it ours?" Bruce asked.

"Dunno," I said, slipping off my pack. You watch the stuff and I'll go see." I felt around gingerly with hands and feet for a gangway. Finding it, I went aboard and ascertained that it was ours. Returning to Bruce I said, "You're going to love this boat."

"Why?"

"Because of the story you'll have when it's all over."

"Is it that bad?"

"Yes. But only trouble is interesting. Come on."

The two open decks of the boat were crisscrossed with painted lines that marked out spaces six feet by four feet. Each space was occupied by a family: parents, children, baggage and all. In that space they would eat, sleep, and while away the time for the next two to four days, depending on their destinations.

We found that there were no spaces left. Both decks were thickly carpeted with humans. Arms, legs, and torsos seemed all tangled together into a single, massive, quivering, unevenly woven blanket of flesh and clothing. Smells of fuel oil, bodies, babies, and onions drifted about the deck in currents. Snores, murmurs, grunts, and mumbling floated up from the flesh blanket. There was no place for us even to set foot, let alone lie down.

Out of the gloom on the far side of the deck a piercing female voice rang out with a shocking Irish brogue, "Piss off or I'll chuck ye into the Irrawaddy!" A thumping sound and a masculine groan followed. At almost the same moment a harried-looking Burmese man in a formerly white shirt and a tattered seaman's cap appeared out of the blackness. He gestured impatiently for us to follow him. We complied and he led us up a spiral ladder to the upper deck where another fold of the human carpet lay wriggling and yawning. Just forward of the ladder head was a cabin door. Our conductor opened it and gestured us in, grumbling something about *farangs*. Apparently the boat's captain, or the generals, didn't want us pressing the flesh too closely with a discontented populace. Forbidden thoughts might be exchanged, untoward criticisms offered. The door closed behind us and we were in complete and fathomless darkness. Somewhere in the inky space we heard a shuffle, followed by the click of a cigarette lighter. Behind its cheery flame grinned the man we came to know as "Mad Max the Aussie."

"Hello, mates," he said. "Yanks?"

"Yeah. How'd you know?"

"It's a gift."

Other voices spoke up, though their faces were still obscured. "Hello; Allo; Good evening. Accents from New Zealand, France, and England. But no native tongue sounded. We had been billeted in a foreign ghetto. We were in the only passenger cabin on board.

"Pull up a bit of deck, mates," Max said as he let the light go out. "There's only two bunks, and the sick girls have 'em."

We felt around among the other Western bodies for open deck space and let down our packs. Then the door opened again and two Irish women and a man joined our exile. Max repeated his welcome ceremony and we all chimed in.

"Seems we've all been shunned," the Irishman said with something combining relief and bewilderment. He told us that the three of them had ensconced themselves among a pile of rice bags on the stern of the lower deck, and had been looking forward to a night of relative comfort. "But it seems we were situated directly below the spot on the upper deck where the Burmese gentlemen relieve themselves. Why I thought at first it was raining a wee bit. But no, not at all!" I could hear sniffing sounds in the dark as he inspected his clothes and bag.

"That ain't the worst of it all!" I recognized the female voice of several moments ago. "One o' those Burman lads was lyin' right beside me and 'e kept tryin' to touch me tits! An' 'e kept grinnin' at me an' sayin' 'Boom Boom! Boom Boom' 'e wants now is it? I gave 'im Boom Boom with me right foot. 'Piss off,' I told 'im. Boom Boom indeed!"

We all went resolutely to sleep; and before dawn the boatmen cast off their lines and quietly headed the craft down stream. We awoke sometime after daybreak, with Mandalay miles behind us.

The Irrawady was in flood, and the river's vast expanse stretched out in all directions. The green and distant shoreline, roiling with tropic growth, lay flat throughout the morning. In the afternoon it rose into wavy hills. From time to time we saw little army posts, keeping an eye open on behalf of the generals. The two sick girls whom the wildly bearded Max had mentioned the night before were sisters from New Zealand. They were slim and pretty, dressed in Burmese sarongs and blouses. They were unfailingly polite and proper and suffered their traveler's ailments with Victorian stoicism and propriety. Fortunately, our cabin had a private toilet, such as it was (a closet with a hole cut in the floor overhanging the water). When the bellyache flared they were able to reach "the lavat'ry" without unladylike haste or display. In their times of gastrointestinal calm they sat up with correct posture and wrote demurely in their journals bound with creamy white paper. Any of us who spoke to them, even in the worst of their suffering, received a genuinely friendly and courteous reply. I wanted to tell them that if ever I had to spend days and nights huddled in a bomb shelter and suffering illness, danger, and deprivation, I hoped they would be there with me. But somehow that just didn't sound like what I meant to convey, so I didn't say it.

The rest of our cabin mates were a quiet lot. The Frenchwoman kept to herself and a novel. The young Englishwoman, who looked like a basketball player, would chat as long as anyone spoke to her but never said anything first. Max contemplated the river with a special intensity. A cigarette always hung from his mouth, but he tended to forget about it and the ash would drop onto his beard. Periodically he brushed it away, like a bothersome fly. The Irish played cards.

Around midday, as the sick girls politely voided their guts yet again, I realized that mine was empty. A breeze from astern told me someone was cooking. Bruce stepped out the door to reconnoiter. In a few minutes he returned to say, "There's a galley on the stern and they're serving food."

"Can we get across the populated deck?" I asked.

"No. But I think I know a way. Follow me."

Bruce led me through a dim passageway along the cabin wall to the starboardside railing. Directly below, the brown Irrawaddy frothed in the boat's wake. Stretching aft from where we stood, the dense human tapestry that carpeted the deck had come to life and was even more impenetrable, if such a thing could be.

"Are you ready?" Bruce asked.

"For what?"

He swung first one leg and then the other over the rail. With his feet on the deck's outer edge and his hands gripping the rail he began crabbing his way aft. When the tapestry people saw him they began to laugh and wave and cheer him on. He grinned hugely and waved back, once even letting go and saying "Look, no hands! Ha ha!" I wiped my sweaty palms on my trousers and followed. We reached the little open-air galley to general applause.

The cook was dressed in a frayed and faded loincloth and a tattered undershirt that was a lot less of its original self than more. He had dark stains on his teeth, thick black dirt under his nails (all ten of them), and his galley matched him in all the important details. We sat at his greasy plywood counter and he greeted us in passable English: "Good afternoon! You want food? You want drink?"

"Do you have tea?"

"Oh, yes yes yes. Tea." He picked up a pot from the stove and reached for two cups on the counter. Seeing that they had not been emptied by his previous patrons, he casually dumped their contents over the side and refilled them.

"Do you have soda?"

"Soda, yes yes yes." He opened two bottles of greenish froth and set them before us. They smelled of wet cow pasture. The bottle mouths were surrounded by a brown encrustation.

"Do you have straws?"

"Yes yes yes." He stuck a straw into each bottle. They had teeth marks on them.

"Do you have beer?"

"Beer no. No no no. Nowhere on boat. Captain say. Too bad, eh?"

The coming days stretched out very long and dim. Deciding to make the best of it we asked the man what he had in the way of food. He removed the covers from a pot of rice and three pots of things we could not recognize. One of them looked like curried dirt, but I could not be sure. The others were anyone's guess. I pride myself on being able to eat anything. I might even eat dirt. But it has got to be clean dirt.

"I'll have rice," I said.

"I'll try the green one," Bruce said pointing to one of the pots. "And rice, too."

The rice was clean and smelled wholesome. The cook served it with his stained smile and a small dish of condiment. "In Burma we eat rice every time," he explained. "Sometimes only rice. It's O.K. when you have something for taste. This one is good."

His offering was simply peanut oil infused with garlic and sesame. But drizzling small amounts of it over the rice, or forming the rice into balls and dipping them into the oil, made it as good as pasta with a simple sauce of olive oil and Parmesan. As we ate, I told Bruce, "Somewhere between here and Rangoon we've got to get invited home to dinner. It's the only way I'm going to see enough of Burmese cooking."

"So what have you learned about it so far?"

"I know that their hospitality is extravagant. I've heard that they'll even get up from the table to fan guests who are overheated. And they like to have dinner together at sunset. They have a saying that, 'Eating together is a buttress against night's approach.' And of course they eat curries, and a lot of different salads and greens. Like the Chinese, they connect food and pharmacology and rather than use medicine for an ailment they might prescribe a change of diet. Although, unlike the Chinese, who have the concept of the Five Flavors, the Burmese have thirteen! One of the most interesting things I've learned is that they are connoisseurs of water. H_2O is never simply agua. They divide it into numerous categories: rainwater, hail water, pond water, water from a creek, water from a ravine, water from a well; it goes on and on."

Sipping through his chewed-up straw and sniffing at the bottle, Bruce said, "You think they do the same for soda? You know, soda from a swamp, soda from a ditch, soda from a puddle?"

We finished our meal and returned to the cabin the way we had come, amusing the deck passengers yet again. We told the others what we had done and the Irish followed our example. After they reached the galley the woman with the shocking brogue leaned over the stern and located Mr. Boom Boom on the lower deck. When she caught his eye she gave him the finger. She returned to the cabin exhilarated, though somewhat put off by the bill of fare. All the other cabin mates, except the sick girls, eventually crab-walked to the galley and got something to eat.

Except for our brief trips to the galley, the day was long, uneventful, and quiet. And with the heat in the river valley we all became lethargic and sleepy. The sun was just touching the horizon when the boat slowed and her pilot guided her to a sandspit where a huge banyan tree had overturned. Crewmen leapt ashore and wrapped two hawsers around the tree, securing the boat for the night. The deck passengers began arranging themselves for sleep, gathering up their children, rolling out their cotton blankets. The two sick girls were relieved that the vibrations from the boat's engines had ceased and they lay peacefully with no angry rumblings from their tired tummies. The others in our exile lay down too. Even the river seemed to still itself. In the gathering dusk, through jungle foliage, I saw lights winking on a short distance downstream. "Bruce," I said, "there are people down there. And I'll bet they're about to have dinner. Do you think they'd like to invite us?"

We headed for the door and the English basketball woman spoke first at last. "May I go with you? I'm frightfully hungry. Couldn't eat a thing at the galley."

"Of course. Glad to have you."

"If you see soldiers after dark," Max warned, "give 'em a wide berth. They won't take any cheek."

No gangway had been laid out when the boat was tied up, so to get to shore we had to climb over the rail and shinny down one of the poles that supported the upper deck. From there we swung down the hawser to the banyan tree and jumped down to the beach. We followed the shoreline downstream in the last of the light, and by the time dark had fallen we were able to follow the happy sounds of feasting.

We arrived at a thatch and bamboo village of about a dozen families who were just sitting down to a communal dinner. At their first sight of us a shout went up as though both the circus and the Wells Fargo wagon had just come to town. The children instantly ran to us and took us by the hands, laughing and squealing. At the lantern-lit tables set up in the village quad, the fattest and most prosperous looking man present looked up in happy amazement and immediately set aside his dinner, knocked back a swallow of an unknown beverage, and came waddling up to greet us. He pressed his hands together in a prayerful attitude and made what must have been a speech of welcome, to which all the villagers chimed in approval. Somebody said something funny and the whole populace broke into waves of laughter, the kids jumping up and down in a kind of ecstatic dance. Nobody spoke a word of English.

I began to wonder if we had been expected and that I had slept for many days and forgotten about it. Had Din Tun told us to look up his people downriver? Had he sent word ahead to treat us like heroes? Did one of us resemble somebody's prodigal son? Or were we being mistaken for someone else who would soon arrive? Or fail to arrive? Would we end up hogging someone else's glory? Were we, in reality, in a Hope and Crosby road movie, and was the Englishwoman really Dorothy Lamour? One of the men approached us with a red two-and-a-half-gallon gasoline can, all the people making way for him. As he got near he began to screw on the nozzle. Was the movie turning into a nightmare? Were we about to become a roaring sacrifice that would guarantee this year's crops? Had we trespassed? "Maybe they'll just kill the girl," I thought. "Maybe they need somebody for a *suttee*, and being a head taller than us, she'll make a better blaze." Reaching into a shoulder bag the man produced three small glasses and filled them with the clear contents of the gasoline can. It was rice wine. And powerful rice wine, too.

My companions sipped theirs, but I knocked mine back neat and the people cheered. I came to wish they hadn't done that, as it inspired me to further acts of alcoholic bravado, which culminated in a big headache.

The village children seemed to lay particular claims to us and soon we each had our own retinue, if not rival faction. They clung to us, led us around the village, never took their eyes off us, even petted us. I began to feel like a show horse they had just purchased. But then they took us to the tables and I felt like a king. The portly speechmaker spoke again. He seemed to be offering a toast or a grace, some prologue to dinner to which everyone nodded agreement. Then it was time to feast.

The women laid out a great variety of meats, vegetables, rice, and condiments. And the variety of salads was amazing. Anything that grew in the ground was likely to be chopped up raw or cooked and tossed with oil and herbs. Different kinds of greens arrived, each cooked with a different spice bouquet or aromatic oil. A flurry of cutlery sounded from the nearby open communal kitchen as still more food was prepared and sent to the table. The gas-can bearer stood by, never allowing an empty glass. The kids all schooled around their chosen ones and the men all beamed with pride and amusement. It struck me that we three were the only ones eating, but the people didn't seem to mind a bit. We were nightclub entertainment and they weren't going to miss a thing.

The jewel in the crown of this night's table was braised pork. Its color was like a burnished copper. It swam in a decadent, thick sauce of ginger, garlic, soy sauce, and light sesame oil, and undercurrents of chili and black pepper swirled through it. It was cloaked with rings of translucent golden onions and sat enthroned in a silver server, as all the lesser dishes paid it humble homage. One of the girls in my troop of young followers dished it up for me. She kept speaking to me and seemed to be saying, "This is my mother's dish. It's the best you'll ever taste." It had been cooked long and slow and the meat fell apart on my tongue, resolving itself into a saucy, rich and heavy dew that coated the mouth with tasty pleasure. The rice wine was its perfect foil as it cleansed the palate of the not-quite cloying richness and made it ready for more.

We ate our fill. And after dinner we were led around the village again, presumably to shake it down. We returned to the tables and more rice wine flowed. We tried to converse with our hosts in sign language but it proved a poor second to the language of the table with its unambiguous messages of welcome and cheer. And then some of the kids began to sing. At first it was two girls and a boy. And it was clear they were singing to us. Soon all the village children were singing, their parents clapping time, a few even swaying to the music. At the end of their song we all applauded. Then two men took the stage. They sang what I thought must have been a working song because of the lifting and hauling gestures. They were followed by more applause and more wine.

Then Bruce said, "Richard, do Gunga Din for 'em!"

"But they won't know what I'm saying."

"It won't matter. Just be dramatic and rhythmic."

So I stood up, and lifted up my hands to ask for their attention. "You may talk of gin and beer, when you're quartered safe out here," I began, stressing rhythm and rhyme. "And you're sent to penny fights and Aldershot it." They were immediately rapt. They had no idea what I was about to do, but they were going to savor every bit of it. I acted out the story. I hammed it up. Kipling would have been aghast. They loved it. With very little coaxing I got the kids to join in at the refrains with "Din, Din, Din!" They might have had no idea what the poem was about. They might have thought it was "Little Red Riding Hoo" or the *Ramayana*. But they loved it. I ended with a dramatic flourish: I portrayed Gunga Din dying. They went bananas. Another song followed.

By this time I could see that Bruce was up to something he loves: arm wrestling. He is very good at it and often wrestles for beers in taverns. He taught me the trick of leveraging yourself

from the foot up in order to gain maximum advantage of an opponent. If the other guy doesn't know how to do that just right,
a smaller man can often take a bigger one.

Bruce was gesturing to a man whose arms suggested he
lived behind a plow and had some good-natured pride in his
strength. Everybody else saw it at the same time and a cheer
went up: the entertainment program included not only arts,
but sports as well! Amid shouting and wagers on the con-
querer the two men were led to where the whole village could
see: the terrace of a thatch and bamboo house raised on stilts
that put the floor at eye level. A perfect stage.

I mounted the steps with Bruce to act as his second. A
friend of the plowman did the same and we were accompanied
by the portly greeter whose house it turned out to be. He addressed the people like a Las Vegas ringside announcer and the
whole population whooped and hollered. The two contestants
nodded to each other, then lay down on the floor and took
each other's measure. I looked carefully at the Burmese's body
language and could see that he didn't know how to play this
game. "He doesn't know the trick, Bruce. Play it out. Give the
folks a good show." I knelt down and put their hands together.
Out in the crowd I saw the Englishwoman, who looked worried. I gave her a wink, counted loudly to three, and hollered,
"Go!"

Bruce gave the man a couple of inches to start, then played
him like a fish on a line for a good two minutes. The crowd
went delirious. Then, pretending it was a huge effort, Bruce
brought his foe to an honorable defeat. All cheered, and
Bruce's child groupies gloated. Money changed hands.

As Bruce congratulated his opponent for fighting the good
fight, I noticed a line of strong men form at the bottom of the
terrace steps, happily awaiting their chance to wrestle. Bruce
took on two of them, not drawing it out this time, so as not to
lose his strength too soon. For his fourth combat he had to
switch to his left arm, which necessitated finding southpaws
among the challengers. He dispatched two more.

By now he was beginning to tire, though the crowd was lustily yelling for more. I was massaging his arms while his child pages brought him drinks when I felt someone tap me on the shoulder. I turned to see a walking collection of cord-like muscles topped by a shaggy head with a gap-toothed grin. One of his tree-trunk arms was making wrestling motions, the other was pointing at me and the whole population of the village was screaming its approval. I began massaging Bruce's arms more quickly. "Come on, Brooster. Let's get those arms ready!"

But he insisted I take the challenge. "Go ahead," he said. "You can do it."

"What if he falls on me? I'll be crushed!"

"You can take him. Remember, it's like boxing, where the jab begins at the foot and works its way up through the body like a whip. It's just like that."

I looked at my would-be opponent. At least he didn't seem hostile. I looked at the Englishwoman who was now enjoying the show. And the village folk who had feasted us were chanting. Then I looked at my child faction, the kids who had fed me, sang to me, and Gunga Dinned with me. They were hopping up and down in transports of ecstasy at the thought that their knight was about to do battle. If I were to turn such a tide of enthusiasm by refusing the challenge, I would regret it forever. Better I should suffer whatever injuries might befall me. I dropped down to the floor and held up my hand to be crushed, twisted, or deformed in whatever way fate might feel disposed. The tree-trunk man lowered himself in sections, settling his mass onto the floor one joint at a time. My arms felt like matchsticks. I wanted to ask the crowd to pray for me, but I didn't know how. The portly householder, Bruce, three other guys, and a couple of kids now occupied the terrace with the man mountain and me.

A relative calm came over the crowd as Bruce knelt down and placed my hand into the other's. "You're in perfect position," he said. "And he's got both feet together. He'll have no leverage. All you need to do is work against his weight."

"Well there's enough of that, I'll tell you!"

"Go!"

I felt a sudden twisting in my shoulder joint accompanied by electric-like shocks, and an enormous pressure running laterally through my forearm as though the guy were trying to drive my elbow through the floor like a knife. It hurt, too. But Bruce was right. The man didn't know how to direct his strength in this kind of contest. If I could hold out, and throw him off balance by feints, I might beat the big SOB. At the least, I'd make him work for it.

Sweat streamed down our faces. Our bodies shook with effort. The crowd screamed. It seemed to go on forever. The people on the terrace with us were jumping up and down, causing the thin floor to undulate and making it difficult to stay positioned. And then with a loud snapping sound two of the bamboo poles that held up one side of the terrace broke, the floor came out from under us and fell to an angle of thirty degrees before hitting the ground. Of the jumpers-up-and-down, some slid down the incline as though on a waterslide, some tumbled end over end, and the owner fell off completely and went straight to the ground with a splat. My opponent and I rolled like a drum, hands still locked in the struggle, all the way down. I didn't even realize what had happened till we were halfway to the ground. We were still wrestling when we hit bottom. The entire village, even the ones who had been on the terrace, the owner included, were beside themselves with laughter. The tree-trunk man suddenly became confused. I took advantage of his momentary distraction and with the mightiest heave of my life put his arm to the ground. I stood up the victor.

I offered congratulations to the defeated, who was a good sport about it, and calm was returning to the crowd. The excitement had peaked with the breaking of the terrace and we all needed to catch our breath. But the night was still young. Or so we thought.

"What are you doing?!" a voice at the rim of the crowd demanded in broken English. "What are you doing?!" Before we could even realize what was happening the crowd had melted away just as quickly as breath into the wind, leaving behind only the scent of sandalwood paste. All else was open starry sky and stillness. We three *farangs* stood alone facing one of the generals' watchers. A soldier, in army-issue underwear, stood there panting, an old submachine gun leveled at us. We had apparently disturbed his rest.

"What are you doing?" he shouted again. It must have been the only English he knew. We began backing off slowly.

"Well...uh," the Englishwoman said.

"Yeah...uh," I followed.

"We're getting the hell out of here!" Bruce said. And we all turned and ran like Frenzy back up river. I remembered to weave as I went, just in case he tried to draw a bead on me. As we approached the boat, still running like bats out of hell, I could hear him, though faintly, still repeating his demand. Then he fired a burst into the air for good measure. When we reached the boat we leapt up onto the banyan, hauled ourselves up the hawser, and shinnied up the deck support. We found the passageway blocked by cargo, so we crabbed along the railing forward to a cabin window. Our cabin mates were waiting for us as we crawled through breathless.

"What happened?" they all asked.

"Cross a soldier?" Max wanted to know.

"Are you all right?"

"Are any of you hurt? We heard shouting and shooting. Was it a riot of some kind? A revolt? What ever happened?"

I braced myself against the cabin wall and slid down to sit on the deck. "Nothing at all to be upset about," I said between gasps. "Nothing to worry about. We just got invited home to dinner. That's all."

4 *L i g h t*

How the desire for a good dinner can lead me into impossible situations! Sometimes in good company, and sometimes without. This time I was alone in the club car on the night train from Singapore. I was heading north for Ipoh where I would stay at the Station Hotel and meet my friend Stan the next day when he came up from Malacca. From there we would travel to Penang, and then on up through the Isthmus of Kra to Sattahip, Thailand where we would meet the rest of our trekking party. I was hungry, and in the mood for some lively Malayan chilifare, but the dining car was closed. I would have to wait until I reached my destination where, once again, I would have to sup in the old imperial dining room.

I was not really keen on going to the Ipoh Station Hotel again. I had a Malaysian Railway pass and could have stayed on the train in a cozy compartment all the way to Penang. Stan, however, was eager to see this bit of British Imperial history and wanted me to show it to him. He wanted to have kippers in the dining room, or gin and tonic in the bar, and pretend that we were British empire builders in white linen suits and pith helmets. "O.K.," I said. "If it means that much to you. I guess everybody should visit the Hotel of the Living Dead at least once."

The Ipoh Station Hotel had been a place of some renown. But though it still stood and still operated, it was a ruin. It had been one of the furthest outposts of the British Raj, where empire builders and hangers on met on the road to riches or rags. When it was occupied, though, by the soldiers of General Yamashita, the Tiger of Malaya, during the Pacific War, it went into the same irreversible decline as the British Empire. The adventurers no longer came to stay. The imperial administrators no longer came; the mercenaries, the planters and miners, the hustlers and the whores had all gone elsewhere. As the Empire receded like the tide, the hotel was left high and dry. The staff remained. The service (more or less) remained. Everything was as the Empire left it, but in a slumping, twilight world of decay.

The train arrived well after dark and the hotel stood big, white, imperial, and incongruous at the edge of the moonlit Malayan jungle. When I stepped off the train I noticed that I was the only one on the platform. Nobody else had got off. As the train fled into the night I asked myself, only half jokingly, if the other passengers knew something I didn't.

I walked into the lobby. The old electric lights produced a dim, yellow, hazy glow. The wallpaper had turned a tasteless gray and the place felt airless. I could see into the dining room, which was large and gloomy, yet somehow claustrophobic. The tables were all set with the old empireware and heavy, starched napery. One cadaverous old waiter stared blankly in my direction.

That dining room had been full of people once. It had hosted sultans, colonial governors, mysterious ladies, tin magnates, mining engineers, and fortune hunters. A lot of big deals had been consummated in there. Now it seemed to yawn wide and tired, exhaling the reluctant shadows of those I imagined.

I went to the registration desk and signed my name in the book. Every full registration book in the hotel's history was on a dusty shelf behind the desk. The earlier volumes bore many illustrious names; the volume I was signing carried only the names of occasional wayfarers, like myself, and the pen names of local adulterers. It seemed the vultures were feeding on the corpse. I noticed that there were only two other people registered for that night. They were a Mr. and Mrs. Patel. (Mr. and Mrs. Patel would be the local equivalent of Mr. and Mrs. John Smith.) I wondered if they had already trysted and gone.

After checking in, I went to the lounge to have a drink. I needed fortitude if I was going to go into the dining room for any length of time. Like the rest of the hotel the lounge was dim and close. A fat Malay barman in shirtsleeves was behind the bar. He was conversing very softly with a waiter in a red jacket. All Malays converse softly. When they saw me come in they broke off their talk and stood looking at me with mildly glazed eyes. I moved toward the bar but the waiter gestured me to a table and kept nodding his head saying "Please, please." I thought maybe he wanted something to do, so I sat where he directed. I ordered gin and tonic and it came—true to British style—with just tonic and gin, no ice, no lime. I finished the drink quickly and moved on.

In the sepulchral dining room I took a seat near the entry. As I waited in the thick, dim gloom, I wondered what ghosts might look like. I could almost hear the echoes of tinkling crystal, the clatter of china, the hum and buzz of conversation as deals were struck, information was exchanged, and successes and failures recounted. I suddenly became aware of the old waiter standing beside me. The menu he brought me was English to the bone: meat, fish, boiled potatoes. At the waiter's suggestion I ordered steamed sole.

As I waited to be served I realized that there were others in the room. On the far side were an Indian man and a Chinese woman. (Mr. and Mrs. Patel?) I couldn't figure how they got there without my noticing. I had sat near the entry so I would be aware of anyone coming or going. They were sitting shoulder to shoulder and were in a whispered and animated, but deliberately subdued argument.

When the sole arrived I found it bland, insipid, uninspired; fit food for ghosts. "This is like eating death," I thought, "I need food for the living!" I caught the waiter's attention and the old bag of bones shuffled over my way. "This is...very nice," I said, referring to the meal. "But isn't there anything on the menu with a little bit of...spice?"

"Pickled eggs, sir?" he suggested.

"I was thinking of something spicy hot."

He excused himself and disappeared into the kitchen. He soon returned to say, rather apologetically, that "Cook is fixing himself and staff a bit of Malay curry if..."

"I'll take it!"

He returned with a blue Chinese porcelain bowl filled with cubes of snowy white potato and toasty brown peanuts swimming in a thick, red-flecked yellow sauce. A sheen of red chili-scented oil floated on top and a sprig of green cilantro graced it at the edge. He set it in front of me, ceremoniously turned the bowl 90 degrees, then shuffled quietly away.

The vapors rose up and stung my nostrils. The smells of chili, garlic, and ginger were sharp and powerful. The buttery smell of peanut and the mellowness of turmeric combined with them as they formed an almost visible wreath around my head. I ignored the spoon and picked up the bowl with both hands. I sucked at the creamy sauce. Savory spicefire rushed through my mouth, tiny beads of sweat popped from my brow, and my pallet sang "Alive!" I had sucked in a small piece of chili so I bit into it and it burst into an explosion of flavorheat. I swallowed and the glow went down to my gut and it screamed "Alive, Alive, Alive!" I took up the spoon and scooped curry into my mouth and chewed. The capsicum struck my taste buds and they resonated like tiny tuning forks, each one a different tone, all together in harmony, a resounding air that kept the ghosts at bay.

As I reached the bottom of the bowl I tipped it up and let the last tasty, searing bits slide into my mouth. Had the bowl been shallower I'd have licked it. The curry was so hot my mouth throbbed with a burning, life affirming pleasure-pain. I felt like the only man of flesh in a cold charnel house.

I sat back for a few moments to bank the fires. Savoring the now slow burn, I thought I might sustain it with a glass of whiskey. I signed the check, rose from the table and ambled over to the bar. When I got there the lights were out and it was deserted. I turned back toward the dining room and found that it was now darkened and deserted too. Outside, even the platform lights were off. I could find nobody anywhere.

The only light still burning was the single bulb leading upstairs to the rooms. I creaked up the steps to the narrow hallway and found it dark too. Not finding any light switches I felt the numbers on the doors till I found mine. I felt for the keyhole beneath the porcelain doorknob and guided in the antique steel key. Entering, I found the old light switch and turned it, breathing a sigh of relief when a small bulb glowed faintly in the corner.

The room had a nightstand, a bureau with a pitcher and basin on it, a lumpy looking bed, and shadows. It had the same gray wallpaper as the lobby. I wished the bar were open or that I had some valium or a bottle of gin so I could knock myself out and wake up when the witching hour was over.

I turned down the bed and was glad, at least, to see that it had a heavy comforter; the jungle gets cold as a tomb at night. As I lay down the bed creaked, the mattress sagged, and the musty smelling pillow wrapped itself around my head. The entire hotel was fast bound in silence. A shaft of moonlight pierced the room and illuminated a small rectangle on the floor. All else was darkness. With the tip of my tongue I probed my lips for any remants of hot oil that might still cling to them. I found a lively, stinging deposit at each corner. I licked them off slowly, clinging to that fiery essence like a child at unwelcome nap time, eyelids heavy, clinging to wakefulness. "If I could see taste," I thought, "this would be pure light."

5 *Victory*

THIRTY MILES SOUTH OF MULEGE, IN THE BAY of Conception, lies the tiny islet of Requeson. At low tide it is connected to the mainland by a narrow sand-spit. At high tide the spit is awash and the only way off the island is to swim. This is where I make my camp at Christmas-time. Santa can't find me here, there's no Muzak, and no shopping frenzy. I've come here in the company of as few as one and as many as nine. I set up an eighteen-inch artificial tree that Charlie Brown might have rejected. I throw some desert wood onto the fire as a Yule log, and that is my nod to the Nativity.

Though the desert wood produces a lot of smoke, I can spend rich, fat hours by its fire. My clothes become permeated with the smoke. Others tend to move aside when it comes their way. I bask in it, knowing that its pungent aroma will stay in my jacket for months. When I am home and longing for this place I can bring the jacket from the drawer in which I keep it, bring it up to my face and inhale deeply. The sense of smell is a powerful reminder. One Christmas night as I sat next to the smoky memory maker one of my companions said, "For one who doesn't smoke, you sure do like smoke."

"You don't know the half of it," said I. My mind drifted back, like the smoke of fire, like the smoke of memory...

AT SEA, TUESDAY, 20:00 HOURS: Before turning in I called the Messenger of the Watch on the bridge. "This is Petty Officer Sterling," I said, "in compartment Bravo-37-87. I need a wake-up call at 03:30 tomorrow morning."

"Why so early?" the messenger asked. "You got some early lookout?"

"Yes," I lied.

Then I called Corporal Durum[1] of the ship's Marine Corps detachment. "I need the usual guard at the Special Weapons Office at 04:00 tomorrow."

"Till when?"

"About 04:30."

"And who'll be with you?"

"Seaman Henderson."

"Very well."

The marines never ask why, they just do. I had made these arrangements because I had to take the Dragon's temperature. Periodically, we in the missile battery had to measure the temperature and humidity of the nuclear warhead magazine, and it was my turn. We usually did it in the wee hours because the Dragon's presence on board was top secret. I was taking Ricky Henderson with me because a nuke magazine is a No Lone Zone, the Two-Man Rule is in effect. No one is supposed to be left alone with the Dragon.

WEDNESDAY, 04:00 HOURS: We arrived at the office door and found the two marines already posted; their boots, buckles, and weapons gleaming. We showed them our access passes, pinned on our film badges, and signed the log. They

---

[1] Because of ongoing security considerations, the name of the ship, a cruiser on which this story takes place, cannot be revealed, and the names of crew members have been changed.

passed us through the portal, and the door closed behind us. No one else would enter.

"You really need me to go down with you?" Ricky asked.

"Nah. Stay here and read your skin mag. Just don't answer the phone if it rings. And don't make any noise."

We moved the office desk and exposed the scuttle—a small, circular hatch just wide enough to allow a man to pass through. Pausing to remember, I dialed the combination on the lock, opened the scuttle, and looked down the shaft that sank three decks to another locked scuttle. Beneath that lay the magazine, three fathoms below the waterline, at the very bottom of the ship.

I slipped down the hole, and Ricky closed the scuttle after me. Descending, the hard soles of my safety shoes rang on the flat steel rungs of the ladder, echoing in the shaft. Only a dim shaft of light from an electric lantern shone from above. By the time I reached the next scuttle, I was in a half-darkness. I noticed that the roll of the ship was reversed now, indicating that I was below its fulcrum, the waterline. The scuttle had been battened down tightly and I had to use a dogging wrench, a lever, to break the closures. Straining, I lifted the heavy portal and eye-squinting light shot through the hole, driving a column of it up the shaft like a fountain. I held my face over the streaming light for a moment to adjust my eyes, and then dropped down inside.

Everything was white: the deck, the bulkheads, the overhead, the lights, the fixtures...and the warheads. All were white, white, white; pure white, cold white, death white. Melville would have known this shade of white. Twenty-four nuclear warheads rested in two rows of six on the port side and two rows of six on the starboard with a four-foot-wide aisle between them. Each one was lying on its side in a steel cradle frame, strapped in with a steel belt. They looked like eggs—three-foot-long eggs—Embryos of the Apocalypse. A few of them had thick, black electrical monitoring cables snaking out of their aft ends, giving them the look of huge spermatozoa, perhaps the gametes of Mr. Melville's leviathan.

I stood at one end of the aisle and regarded them for a moment. Then I listened to the silence. A warship is usually a noisy place. Engines thrum, chains clank, men shout, machines whir, and wind and wave sing their song or roar in anger. But the magazine was a quiet place. The only sound was the soft whisper of the water slipping past the hull a fraction of an inch below my feet. And although Death slumbered here, it was not the quiet of the grave. This was a womb. This was a holy place. The End of the World slept here. This was Destruction's chapel, and we were his altar boys. At the other end of the aisle, a shelf jutted out from the wall. On it lay the open, black-bound logbook. Above the shelf, like two candles mounted on the wall, were the thermometer and the humidity gauge: a pulpit for this worshipful cure of nukes.

Walking down the aisle to take my readings, I stopped at warhead number W-18. It was a tactical device, small by nuclear standards, its power in the kiloton range. In it were half, maybe three-quarters of a million kills. A Nagasaki. I ran my hand over its perfect, seamless skin. It was smooth like pearl and perfectly symmetrical. The thing was superbly designed to slice through the atmosphere at two and a half times the speed of sound at the tip of a surface-launched guided missile, one that even I might be called upon to fire. I admired the magnificent craftsmanship, the skill, the talent, the care—yes, even the love that had gone into the making of so perfect an artifact. "Who are the gnomes," I wondered, "who hammer away in the secret smithies of Bendix and the nuclear agencies? And what should they be called? Armorers? No, too archaic and not powerful enough. Nuclear Device Technicians? No, too clinical. Death Smiths? Yes, that's what they are, Death Smiths."

I took my readings, and as I was writing them in the log I noticed a bit of ash at my feet. I picked it up and smelled. Correli and Morgan had been smoking dope in here again. I checked the electronics aperture in the rear of a few warheads to see if they had stashed their supply in one. It was, after all, the safest place on board. The only people besides us Missile

Men that even knew this place existed were the captain and a few of his officers, none of whom ever came here.

My search yielded a pack of Salem cigarettes (had to be Arnie's; he was the only one who smoked them), a lighter, and a deck of cards. Some of the guys liked to play cards here. They would place a board across two of the warheads, then sit on the adjacent ones. Arnie always made it a point to fart on the one he sat on. He said it was how he showed his "contempt for war." A. K. Douglas and Ricky Henderson would rub their groins against a couple of Doomsday's Children and then pretend that they "glowed at the gonads." They'd say things like, "Look out wimmen! Nuclear love!" or "Ooh! A 120-kiloton orgasm, comin' at ya. Yahoo! Measure my virility on the Geiger counter."

I pocketed the goods, took one last look at my charges, and ascended, out of the light, through the darkness, and up to the light again. Ricky and I closed and locked the scuttle and replaced the desk that covered it. We secured the office and notified the corporal of the guard that he could dismiss his two marines. On Friday we would return. In obedience to the faraway councils of naval command, our ship would rendezvous under cover of darkness with an ammunition ship at some secret point on the map of the South China Sea. There we would haul Death's Cocoons out of their chamber, pack them in individual drums, and send them by the highline across the water to the other ship. A very delicate operation. What a time for me to quit smoking.

WEDNESDAY, 10:00 HOURS: After breakfast we met in the Missile House to confer on the warhead movement. We assigned stations and duties to every man: magazine, ammunition lift, topside, and so on. We would prepare the goods for shipment, then turn them over, one at a time, to the chief bosun's mate and his deck crew for highlining.

During a highline operation, two ships, displacing, say, fifteen thousand tons each, steam alongside each other, close enough for the crews to yell out to each other when they see old buddies on the opposite deck. When the ships are in position, a bosun on one vessel fires a shotline to the other. The shotline gun is like a shoulder-held flare gun. It fires a tennis-ball-sized wad of compressed nylon cord trailing a slender, white line. It looks like a big, white tadpole. The men on the other ship dodge the speeding head and grab for its tail. When both crews have a hold on the line, one crew ties a heavy line and a smaller line to it. The other then pulls the two lines back across. The heavy line is wrapped around a pulley on each ship, and ten to twenty men grasp it at each end, as though in a giant tug of war. As the ships roll and pitch, straining or slackening the highline, the men pay it out or haul it in, keeping a constant tension on it. A hook and pulley are hung from the highline, the smaller line is tied to that, and both crews can pull it back and forth like clothes on a line. You can hang anything from the hook: pallets, drums, bags, people, even a flexible pipeline to carry fuel or water; or as the navy saying goes: "Beans, bullets, and black oil."

Highlining is a complex and delicate dance in which every man and machine has to perform without error. Even the elements have to cooperate. Crosscurrents, rogue waves, or sudden gusts of wind can carry as much disaster as faulty mechanisms, inattention on deck, or a twitch in the helmsman's arm. Ships that carry bands usually muster them on deck and have them play during highlining. It's a tradition, and it calms nerves.

On one memorable occasion we were alongside a thirty-thousand-ton replenishment ship. She suddenly lost command of her rudder, and it jammed left. The movement ripped apart the highline tackle and threw its handlers to the deck. She bore down on our starboard side like a moving mountain of gray-painted steel. Many of our men ran like hell for the port side. On the flying bridge, the Captain and his seventeen-year-old phone-talker stood fast as the runaway monster loomed. Relaying orders to helm and engine room through the cherub-faced phone-talker, the Captain masterfully conned the ship out of danger. Everyone on deck cheered. It was a very close call, as the two ships nearly kissed. We liked to say that the plucky young phone-talker's beard grew out the next day.

WEDNESDAY, 21:00 HOURS: That evening I lay out on the main deck near the anchor chains, smoking. The month was July, and we were in tropic seas. The wind was abaft, about the same speed we were making, so the relative air drifted slowly. The moonless sky was clear but dazzling with stars that swung back and forth with the slow rolls of the ship. They glistened and twinkled as if alive, inviting me to linger. The ship yawed, and the stars spun on the axis of the zenith, as though changing partners in a cosmic dance. I heard the splash of flying fish as they leaped out of the water and raced ahead of the prow. The warm and fecund smell of the sea bespoke its countless living things. And the ship, as all good ships, felt alive with the low thrum of her engines and her quickening shivers as she met the sea swells. The bitter smoke of my cigarette smelled of ashes and death.

I had been smoking since my early teens, and I was thoroughly addicted to tobacco. I smoked two packs of cigarettes a day while aboard ship and up to three ashore where I had plenty of beer to cool my burning throat. In the mornings, I lit up before heaving out of my rack, and it was the last thing I did at night before getting into it. I smoked between courses in restaurants, and I smoked before and after sex. I smoked in my dreams.

For the last year my health had been deteriorating. I couldn't walk far without wheezing badly. I often had a cold. Lately my heart had been "fibrillating," as the doctor said. To me, it felt like an engine freezing up for lack of oil, trying to continue but stripping bearings in the effort. I was always tired. I took up cigars and a pipe to wean myself away from cigarettes, but I ended up smoking those *and* cigarettes. I would smoke a satisfying eight-inch Manila cigar and as soon as it was out I would light up a butt. Like most smokers, I had already quit many times—but only long enough to know what nicotine withdrawal was like. Ricky Henderson would laugh and say, "Anybody can quit smoking, but it takes a real man to face up to cancer." I feared I wouldn't live long enough to face cancer.

I knew, I had known, and on this starry night I accepted, that I would die of tobacco if I did not forswear it. I held my cigarette close to my face and gazed at the blushing ember. I did not want to quit smoking. I loved tobacco. My body demanded it. I loved the mellow tar and honey smell of cured pipe tobacco and cigars. A cigarette in my hand, fiddling with it, rolling it between my fingers, had the same effect on me as worry beads in the hand of an Arab. I loved to take a great lungful from a Marlboro and then let the smoke curl slowly out of my nostrils and form a wispy, gray wreath around my head. After smoking, I often smelled my hands, and they smelled good to me.

Tobacco soothed, like a friend. It was sharp and pungent and masculine and familiar, a constant companion. And sucking on the instrument, whether pipe or cigar or cigarette, was as good as nursing at a breast. A good cigar was better than a kiss. "A woman is only a woman," Kipling wrote, "but a good cigar is a smoke." With the effusive and aromatic stem of a pipe, I could tease the nerve endings of my mouth as well any lover's tongue. And it would never say no. Tobacco was another kind of Dragon, and we had each other by the throat.

But this Lover/Dragon would kill me. It would consume me even as I consumed it. And all the fine nights of dancing stars would be darkened and made void. I reached for the metal navy-issue ash receptacle, the kind that looks like a funnel set into the top of a beer can. I looked at my glowing Marlboro one more time. Without taking another puff, I crushed it out against the side of the funnel, smashing its cherry head into tiny sparkles that sifted down into the hole and disappeared. The crinkled butt followed. "That's the last one," I said lowly. I did not feel very good.

I told no one I was quitting. If I did there would always be some asshole who would blow smoke at me and say, "Sure you won't have one?" I went to the berthing compartment, let down my rack, and crawled in. I was hoping I might sleep through the worst of the withdrawal. Since I had already been up since 03:30, I managed to force myself to sleep, but not without my head beginning to buzz for want of nicotine.

THURSDAY, 20:00 HOURS: All day I fought off thoughts of smoking. Every time my hunger for tobacco gnawed, I found something to do, something to read, someone to talk to, something to eat, something to think about. Repeatedly throughout the day I automatically reached into my empty shirt pocket for a cigarette. Several people offered me one, and I made excuses. By evening all my mental energies were occupied with keeping my thoughts away from smoking. My eyes began to blink spasmodically. I had vague, unpleasant contrary feelings, like the cold chills that accompany a high fever. I felt at once drowsy, as though from barbiturates, and wired awake with amphetamines. I felt no single discernible physical sensation and yet I felt profound discomfort. I went wearily to bed, hoping for and dreading my smoky dreams.

FRIDAY, 02:00 HOURS: Typhoon Sally had been running a course parallel to ours. By midnight she had shifted our way and soon engulfed us. I awoke with the sea change. I assumed the highline operation would be rescheduled due to the rough weather. Just sending a pallet load of groceries over a calm sea is risky enough business. But to sling a thousand pounds of Doomsday under a single line in the midst of a gale would be folly, I thought. I went back to my feverish sleep, and dreamed of tobacco.

FRIDAY, 04:00 HOURS: A messenger woke me up. I was in a sweat, both from the weather and from withdrawal. The brass had decided to go ahead with the operation. We were keeping to the edge of the storm where the winds and the seas were lower. The weather would give us the cover the brass wanted for what was, after all, a secret operation. The deck crew boasted some of the finest practical seamen in the navy. They wouldn't know what they were transferring, and they wouldn't ask, but they were confident they could do the job. They respected Howling Sally, but they did not fear her.

FRIDAY, SUNRISE: The winds and seas were high, the temperature a steamy eighty degrees when the ammo ship hove into view. She was coming up from behind us, her fat prow plowing through white water and rain. The eye of her blinker fluttered on the signal bridge, telling us to keep steady, and she would come alongside. She moved gradually through the froth, giving us a coy, wide berth at first. Our ship drove its prow into a wave, shipped eleven tons of water and hurled it skyward in a tower of spume.

We, and the opposite crew, stood on deck and watched each other through the twilight and flying foam. We watched to gauge the roll and yaw of the two ships to see how closely they would swing toward each other in the sea's churning. The ammo ship yawed and swung her stern teasingly away and then dangerously toward us. We adjusted our courses to put the oncoming sea more closely behind us to even out our keels. Gingerly rolling, yawing and pitching, the two big ships eased closer together, narrowing the froth between them.

When the two shipmasters judged that they were as close as they dared, they gave the signal. Our bosun stood on the rolling deck and aimed his shotline gun through the spray. The gun recoiled and barked, its report bouncing off the steel flanks of the ammo ship. The shotline sang out. It streaked across the abyss and draped itself over the deck. A perfect shot—the bosun had laid his line right between her stacks. The two ships were coupled. If all went well, they would remain in their tenuous, thrashing embrace until the one had emptied its terrible seed into the other. The deck crew sprang to their tasks. The marine guards took up their posts. We, the Missile Men, struck below.

We prized open the warhead magazine. We opened up the ammunition lift shaft that ran from topside all the way down to the magazine. A squad of our men took the lift topside and rolled out the specially designed, nondescript-looking drums that would each hold one nuke. Three men handled the lift. Others stood by as runners and relief. Gunner Cassidy, Ricky Henderson, and I manned the magazine.

The end of a seesaw travels much farther than that part closer to its fulcrum. A rolling, pitching ship is like two see-saws, one across the other, with its fulcrum in the middle at the waterline. The farther from the middle, and the farther from the waterline, the more travel when the ship rolls or pitches. The magazine was as far down from the waterline as it could be. And it wasn't very close to the middle. That day the magazine traveled like some nightmarish amusement park ride. It could have been mocked up as a huge box of dice being shaken and tumbled by a gambling titan: "Come ride the Giant Nuclear Crapshoot!"

Our first task was to attach the warheads' nose cones. Each warhead comes equipped with two, and while in storage, they are bolted to the rear of the cradle. For launch or transit, one is removed and attached to the leading end of the head. In transit the spare is packed along in the drum. The nose cones are extremely sharp and smooth, as they are designed for supersonic flight. If a man were to fall on one, it would pierce like a spear. The task of attaching them was simple, but I had a hard time concentrating. My nicotine withdrawal was fast approaching its worst stage.

After the nose cone attachment, we began the warhead movement. To facilitate this, the ceiling of the magazine was crisscrossed with slotted tracks. The central track ran fore and aft down the center of the room. Branching out from the central track ran shorter ones. They each hung over warhead locations. Into the slotted track we fitted a hoist that we could slide to a position over any single warhead. Once the hoist was in position, we could unbolt the steel strap that held the nuke down, lower the hoist, pick up the monster, and slide it over to the lift shaft. There we could transfer it to the lift, send it topside and the men there would secure it in its drum. The drum would be rolled out past a cordon of marines and high-lined to the ammo ship, which was named after a volcano—I won't say which one.

Ricky and I took ratchets and began to unbolt the strap of the first warhead. Gunner handled the hoist. A buzzing sound penetrated my ears. It circled counterclockwise around my brain and made me dizzy. The dizziness moved like a slow current down to my stomach and nausea flickered; the nicotine withdrawal was taking my sea legs.

"How embarrassing," I thought. "They'll razz me for sure." A seasick sailor is like a cowboy afraid of horses. A slow fire burned in my lungs and they demanded nicotine to quench it. I took huge breaths and held them, hoping to fool my lungs into feeling that they were full of smoke. My right hand, of its own accord, rose up to my face and covered my nose. I sniffed hungrily for the aroma of tobacco, but smelled only soap.

We loosened the bolts, and through the buzzing sound in my head the ratchets sent their raspy clicking. The hoist whined when Gunner lowered it. The hooks clattered as we attached them to the warhead. The hoist whined again, and the chain rattled as the little behemoth arose from its resting place. It cleared the cradle, and Gunner stopped the hoist. The inchoate thing hung three feet off the moving deck, smooth and white—its nose cone glistening. Its nose bobbed up and down slightly, like a hound picking up a scent. It began to swing, straining at its chain leash, a dog of war eager to be let slip. But we were taking this one to kennel.

We drew it out to the middle track. In my distraction and dizziness, I failed to note the arc of the warhead's swing. The ship gave a roll. The heavy weapon swung my way. The tip of the nose cone hit me in the right thigh, just below the hip, all one thousand pounds of its terrible weight concentrated behind that one, tiny point. It pierced the skin to an eighth of an inch, and withdrew. Blood seeped from the wound and made a purple stain on blue cotton trouser cloth.

We regained control of the weapon and slid it to the forward bulkhead. We slipped it onto the lift and secured it, then sent it topside. The process took about ten minutes. Twenty-three warheads to go.

"Is that a 'Broken Arrow'?" Ricky joked. That was one of the code words we were to use in the event of an accident. "Broken Arrow," if we dropped a warhead and cracked it open; "Bent Spear," if we just dropped it. Who in blazes thinks up these code words, anyway?

Ricky and Gunner walked easily by me on fluid sea legs, their bodies never deviating from the vertical, as though they were hung from gimbals. I steadied myself by grasping onto protruding nose cones and followed. We worked mechanically for a long time, one weapon following another and another and another. In the process I got stabbed again, this time in the left leg. It was a glancing blow, leaving more bruise than wound, but it tore my trouser leg. I didn't think about it. I couldn't think about anything except standing up straight on a heaving deck and the maddening craving for a smoke. A smoker's longing for tobacco is like thirst—insistent, unceasing, and steadily worse. I swallowed repeatedly, hoping to satisfy the clutching in my throat. I clenched my teeth and bit down hard. I pinched myself. I sweated. My eyes ran. I sucked in air like a man who could get none. I suffered, goddamn it.

As we were setting another warhead into the ammo lift, I heard a loud sophomoric giggle from above. I looked up the shaft to the next deck and saw A. K. Douglas, Ricky Henderson's "nuclear love" mate from Arkansas with a silly grin on his face. He had just opened his fly and was shaking his "glowing gonads" at us. "You want some of this?" he asked with a "Yuck, yuck, yuck." He was inordinately proud of his tool, and I have to admit it could take your breath away seeing it for the first time. It hung in elephantine fatness halfway to his knees, and the bulbous crimson head resembled nothing so much as a big meaty strawberry, ready for plucking.

A. K. never referred to his unit as his penis or his tool or any of the many Anglo-Saxon appellations for the male equipment.

He called it "The Ol' Arkansas Strawberry." And he never said that he made love to a woman, or fucked a woman, or enjoyed female embraces. He always said, "I took her to bed, you know, and then I give her the Ol' Arkansas Strawberry. And she liked it real good, too. Yuck, yuck." He always made a sharp jabbing motion with his arm when he said, "I give her the Ol' Arkansas Strawberry," and he ejaculated the words rather than spoke them.

As I stood there looking up the shaft in my misery he repeated, "You want some of the Ol' Arkansas Strawberry there, Petty Officer Dick? It's nukified. Yuck, yuck." Ordinarily I would have made some pat remark, like "Don't point that thing at me when you don't know how to use it." Then he would have proudly holstered his gun having once again demonstrated its mighty caliber and that would have been that. But I had no sense of humor at the moment. And A. K. saw I had no sense of humor. He wagged the Ol' Arkansas Strawberry at me every time I brought a nuke to the shaft. I knew if I told him to zip up and shut up it would just encourage him.

So I began to think about strawberries. I thought about my grandmother cutting them up to make jam. I thought about the robins and other birds that used to peck at the strawberries we grew at home in Mendocino, California. Their sharp little beaks left deep wounds in the flesh, which turned an unappetizing brown. My frustration with A. K. began to subside. Finally, I thought about piña coladas and margaritas I had seen bartenders make with strawberries—how they whipped and beat them in a blender till they were reduced to a blood-red puree. In my mind, I concocted such a cocktail, and called it an Ol' Arkansas Strawberry. My agitation with A. K. disappeared and he noticed and finally repackaged himself. I was free to go back to being merely miserable.

Halfway through the operation, word came down from topside to hold up for a while. Packing a warhead is not simply a matter of sticking it in a drum and putting a lid on it. Everything has to be done by the book, and it takes time. We were stacking them up, and they didn't want them rolling around on deck.

"Jesus Christ, let's put some hustle on it and get this thing over with," Ricky bitched. Gunner calmly sat down on an empty cradle. I, wobbly at the knees, made my way over to W-18, the small tactical device, sank to the deck next to it, and lay my head against its smooth side. I held on to the cradle to steady myself and curled my knees up to my chest.

"You seasick, Dickie?" Gunner asked with some surprise. Still, no one knew.

"Uh huh," I moaned.

"Ha!" Ricky hooted. "What a nonhacker. Ho ho."

I didn't care. I was, indeed, a little queasy, though I wouldn't call it *mal de mer*. I was just plain miserable. A taut string ran inside my skull from the top to the bottom. At one end a screw turned and with each passing minute tightened that strainful cord. It was now so tight it began to sing in a piercing, painful note. The ship kept rolling. The deck rose and fell. I pressed my head against the bulbous Death of a City and hung on.

We had had no breakfast that morning. Because it was so early, we hadn't bothered. Somebody sent down a couple boxes of C rations to snack on. They were the kind where all the food comes in a can: canned meat, canned vegetables, canned fruit, canned pound cake, canned bread, canned peanut butter and jelly, and canned crackers. Also a pack of instant coffee and sugar, six matches, one stick of gum, a little P-38 can opener, a wad of toilet paper, and a pack of three cigarettes, all packaged in olive drab. "You want anything, Dick?" Gunner asked, as he and Ricky went through the contents.

"Nah, I'm not hungry," I said through a now-snotty nose. I sniffed and thought about those three cigarettes. The string in my head strained to perilously near the breaking point.

"Well, here. Take these then," Gunner said. From one of the boxes he handed me two thick, round soda crackers—the kind you'd see in a cracker barrel.

"Ha!" Ricky yelped again. "Nonhacker!" Nibbling on a

soda cracker is a remedy for ordinary seasickness. Gunner was doing me a kindness in giving them to me, but still it was embarrassing.

Determined to put my best face forward, I said, "Well, gimme the goddamn peanut butter then, too!" Gunner handed me the flat can of peanut butter, three inches in diameter and three-quarters of an inch high.

With shaky hands I unfolded the can opener and removed the lid. The roasted peanut smell rushed into my nose. The roasted, slightly burned, almost smoky smell filled my nostrils and half-clogged nasal passages with a swirling cloud of relief. To my smoke-starved senses the rich, mellow, sometimes sweet aroma was almost like pipe tobacco. I sucked it in like snuff. I snorted it like cocaine. Like a diver who breaks the surface after staying too long under water, I gulped in the smell as though it were life-giving air.

With a forefinger, I dug into the peanut butter and scooped out a gob. I scraped it off onto my lower teeth. With my tongue, I maneuvered it to the middle of my mouth and pressed it against my palate, gluing my mouth closed. A buzzing, tingling feeling spread through my lips, as though sensation were returning after a long absence. As I breathed, the air in my windpipe moved past the back of my tongue and picked up the roasty, toasty aroma and channeled it back and forth through my nose. With my tongue, I smeared the peanut butter in circles against the roof of my mouth, melting it, dissolving it, driving it into my taste buds, and intensifying the flavor and making my salivary glands gush. The whining string in my head eased ever so slightly.

I used one of the crackers as a knife to scoop out the peanut butter and spread it on the other cracker. I put the two crackers together and made a thick sandwich. I took a crunchy, creamy bite. I held it in my mouth and sucked on it like the end of a good cigar. In time it dissolved into a starchy, sticky paste, which I tucked into my cheek like a great pinch of Copenhagen snuff. That one bite lasted several minutes. It didn't satisfy any of my body's craving for nicotine. It didn't quench the fire in my lungs, nor still the buzzing in my ears. But it gave me just enough of a tobacco-like sensory fix to keep the brain string from snapping. It was no substitute for a Marlboro, but I would make it suffice. It would be my Marlboro sandwich; my Nuclear Marlboro sandwich.

I sat there holding the cradle with one hand and my pacifier with the other. I heard Gunner and Ricky start to work again. They let me sit it out for a while. Finally, they came over my way. Standing over W-18, Gunner said, "It's time for this thing to go." I took another chaw of my plug and stuck the remainder into my shirt pocket. I chomped down hard and pulled myself up. I took a moment to steady myself, then held out an open hand to Ricky who handed me a ratchet. I took a strain on one of the strap bolts and broke it free. We uncradled W-18, hoisted it out, and sent it topside. We continued working, and I kept a piece of my Nuclear Marlboro sandwich in my mouth at all times, making sure to pass the aroma through my nasal passages often. Sometime during the remaining hour or so of the operation, I got nipped again by the Great White Beast, in the right knee. It hurt and it bled, but I ignored it as best I could.

When we had sent the last of the Dragon's children topside, we unhooked the hoist and put it in the lift to send it to its storage place above. I was about to activate the lift when Gunner said, "Dick, you look like death warmed over. Go ahead and ride up with the hoist. Get those punctures on your legs bandaged. Me and Ricky'll secure."

"Thanks, Gunner," I said, and climbed into the lift and sat down next to the hoist. As I reached for the "Up" button, Ricky got in one last jibe.

"Just a nonhacker," he said grinning. "Just a nonhacker. Ha!"

"Oh yeah?" I challenged him, indicating the three bloody spots on my trousers. "How many guys do you know who have been wounded three times by nuclear weapons and lived to brag about it?" I punched the button and rose up. And I never smoked again.

6 *E x c e s s*

LIFE CHANGED WHEN I SHOOK OFF THE BURDEN of tobacco. I became stronger, physically and mentally. I became hungrier. I was more alive, and my life was enlarged. And the larger life had room for new things, and time and energy for more interests and more adventures. I could not only better pursue a burning passion, I could have more burning passions. The fire began to roar.

In an Iban tribal village in the heart of Borneo, Entili, the chief, sat cross-legged and bare-chested, his big tattoos animated by rippling muscles. Through our interpreter he commanded me to stand up and give account. He demanded to know who we were and why we had come to his domain. "Good question," I thought, as I stood before the assembled tribespeople. "Why in the Sam Hill have we brought ourselves into an uncharted jungle peopled with headhunters? We don't even know if we're in Malaysia or Indonesia; we've gone clean off the map!"

One of many reasons for this mad quest was my interest in spices, an abiding passion I acquired during my naval service in the Far East. This time I was pursuing black pepper, that ubiquitous, taken-for-granted necessity of virtually every kitchen on Earth and every ship's galley at sea. I had come to find its source, where it grows wild in profusion; where it is used in food, magic, love potions, and healing; where it expresses itself in ten genera and over a thousand species.

Of its many varieties, the best known is *Piper nigrum*, the dried berry (a peppercorn) of a woody perennial vine native to tropical Asia. Over one hundred thousand tons are shipped annually from Asia and Brazil, almost a third of it to the United States. It accounts for 50 percent of the world's spice trade. It finds its way to the table, into processed foods, perfumes, and medicines.

Pepper's curative powers are reflected in virtually all the ancient pharmacopoeia. Hippocrates prescribed it for feminine disorders and Theophrastus as an antidote to hemlock. (Socrates should have consulted Theophrastus.) My experience in Borneo would become further testimony to its medicinal value.

Its most dramatic impact on human affairs has been in its trade. Until modern times it was so precious that it was sold not by weight but corn by corn. Pliny complained that Romans spent more than fifty million sesterces on it. In A.D. 412, Rome was ransomed to Alaric and his Visigoths for gold, silk, and 3,000 pounds of pepper. Columbus and others were in search of a route to the Indies where Marco Polo had told them they would find the source of pepper. It was used as a medium of exchange in medieval Europe. A pound of it could set a serf free in France or buy a slave in the Levantine bazaar. In the Spice Islands, pepper fiefs sprung up like Columbian drug baronies, and nations went to war for it. Except for gold, no other commodity has been so prized, so fought and died for, or has brought so much satisfaction to so many people.

And so we went off to find it in Borneo, largest of the Spice Islands. My friend Mack and I followed the spice route to the Land of Pepper. We arrived at the town of Sibu at the mouth of the muddy Rajang River in Sarawak, Malaysia. From there we traveled upriver by scheduled passenger boat, then by motor launch, then dugout canoe and, finally, by foot. Along the way we stopped at the little settlement of Kapit. This was the farthest reach of the old spice traders. Here they were met by the jungle dwellers who brought them pepper, game, and tree resins. This was the jumping-off point into the unknown, into the immemorial pepper forests.

Our luck was good in Kapit, for we met David. Half Chinese and half Malay, he was working at some fetch-and-carry job, and not only could he speak a pidgin-style British English, but also Iban, the local dialect.

In the voice of strong young men on a mission we told him, "You come with us, pal. We're on an adventure." (We were even wearing pith helmets. I swear.) David didn't think twice. He threw a toothbrush and a shirt into a bag and said, "We bloody go!" That was his favorite word, "bloody," and it rhymed with "body."

David advised us to bring some presents for the native people we would meet in the interior. He suggested a case of whiskey, five pounds of tobacco, printed t-shirts, and a few cans of food and an opener. He said the people might not care for the food but would appreciate the "bloody" cans.

With all our supplies we set out for "Indian country." As we traveled Mack and I often sang. Our favorite was the theme from *Rawhide*. We tried to teach it to David, but he just giggled and looked extremely amused. After strenuous jungle travel, somewhere upriver, we met up with one of the jungle dwellers. He wore a loincloth and gorgeous tattoos all over his body. Some were floral designs, others geometric, others resembling an intricate paisley print. Each one represented an enemy slain, a child fathered, successful hunts, and rites of passage. He carried a blowpipe with poison darts. We told him that we were friendly and that we came bearing gifts. He told us his name, which sounded a bit like Jerry, so that's how we addressed him. He took us to his slim and pretty wife, whose name was Eetwat. She wore a sarong and also had tattoos, like all the other men and women of their tribe, and she looked at us with large-eyed delight. The look on her face was like that of a young girl who has just been given a new Barbie doll or a kitten, and she adopted us on the spot.

They led us into their village, where the people dwelt in a longhouse by the river. It stood on stilts to accommodate the river's flood, and was divided into apartments of roughly equal size, with a large common room in the center. A veranda ran the length of the structure. Jutting out from the common room was a deck of bamboo poles laid about an inch apart. Beneath that lay an enclosure containing some two dozen very large pigs. The pigs were fed when somebody simply walked out onto the deck and dumped refuse through the bamboo poles.

A great commotion erupted when we arrived. Most of the adults seemed to be aware that there were palefaces in the world, and a few had even seen them, but the children had never even heard of such critters, and they fled at the sight of us. We were introduced to the chief, Entili, and a few of the elders. Entili was taller than most of his fellows, about five foot seven. He had the body of an iron pumper, hard and sinewy. His eyes gazed coolly from a face that bore a look of calm satisfaction. The face seemed to say, without boasting, "I can lick any man in the world." We hauled out our presents, which the chief gave a cursory examination. He declared them to be good and us to be welcome, for the time being. He told us to stay with Eetwat and Jerry, which seemed to please them.

As all this was in progress Eetwat began to prepare food according to the Iban custom of hospitality. We were invited to sit on the ground and wait and I watched as she cooked a fish over an open fire. She was obviously taking great care with it as she turned it and sprinkled it with some kind of seasoning that she took from a section of bamboo, crumbling it in her palm and letting it sift through her fingers. The spice was red warrior ants.

Eetwat presented her offering to us with smiles and cooed some sort of happy incantation. The people crowded around to watch, sure in the knowledge that the pale strangers had never before tasted a dish so fine. The tattooed men clutched their blowpipies and rested their hands on their knives. The tattooed women watched us wide eyed, their bare bosoms heaving with the excitement of the event. The ants were only barely crumbled, just enough to break up the major body parts. I hesitated.

"Mack," I said under my breath. "It's ants, they're feeding us ants!"

"I was trying to pretend they were paprika. Do you think they'd mind if we scraped them off?"

I looked at the tattooed multitude. I looked at the expectation on Eetwat's face. I looked at Entili who seemed to calmly say, "Eat it or I'll kill you." I looked at the post in the village quad where they hung up the heads of their vanquished enemies. "I think we better eat 'em," I said. "And I think we'd better smile, too. They're starting to look unhappy."

"I'm smiling, I'm smiling!"

I took a large piece with lots of ant parts on it. Hoping none were in a condition to bite back, I put it in my mouth and chewed, smilingly. "Mmmm," I said, nodding to our hosts.

"Yum!" said Mack, patting his tummy.

The heads and jaws crunched audibly between my teeth. I saw David chewing calmly, glancing at us with a sardonic twinkle in his eye. I had expected the bitterness of gall, but to my surprise the ants tasted good. The formic acid that coats their bodies tastes like a mixture of lemon and tarragon, giving them a sort of Bernaise flavor. Once I got past the idea of the wriggly little critters in my mouth, Eetwat's fish made a pretty good meal. The only thing I didn't quite get used to was the crunch. I made a mental note to suggest to Eetwat that she mash the ants in a mortar and use them like pesto.

The day after our arrival, Mack went hunting with Jerry and some of the other braves. As an avid hunter he was pretty excited at the thought of a primitive chase. "I'm gonna get a wild boar!" he announced. "I'll borrow somebody's blowpipe and some poison darts and get a wild boar! Maybe they'll teach me how to make my own poison. Or do you think that might be some witch doctor's secret?"

I went with Eetwat and some others to help gather wild pepper, which they harvest for their own use as well as for trade. On a hillside not far from the longhouse the vines rioted, creeping and climbing everywhere we looked. They sported large, philodendron-like leaves and they climbed up trees and curled around rocks higher than a tall man's head. The berries grew in slender clusters that hung from the vines like jewelry, each bearing fifty or sixty gems. The immature ones were green and the ripe ones red.

As we gathered berries, Eetwat introduced me to the pleasures of betel nut, the fruit of an Asian palm tree. Crumbling about a teaspoon of the soft nut meat, she wrapped it in a leaf of the pepper vine's cousin, Piper betel, and smeared it with lime paste. Then she handed it to me and cooed something in Iban. As I chewed the prepared wad, the three ingredients mixed and turned the bright red that stains the mouths of millions of Asians. Soon my salivary glands gushed, and I had to swallow repeatedly or the juice would overflow my mouth and stain my chin. The taste was pleasant, sour, and a little fruity, like an acidic wine or a tart berry. Some people spit the juice but I swallowed it. It's mildly intoxicating due to the alkaloid arecoline. In exchange for this initiation I taught her how to play tic-tac-toe, which she thought wonderful and later taught the whole village to play.

With several baskets full of both ripe and unripe berries, we returned to the village where the women processed them. To produce black pepper, they spread immature berries on mats to dry. As they dry, their skins wrinkle and turn black. They are then ready to use whole or ground.

White pepper is a more involved process. Ripe berries are soaked to soften the skins and then threshed, like grain, in order to extract the white core. They are then left in the sun to dry. To thresh the berries the Iban put them in a wooden trough and pound and knead them with the ends of heavy staves. White pepper is less aromatic and more biting than black because the nonvolatile piperine (the hot stuff in pepper), is concentrated in the core. The volatile oils that are the aroma constituents are more plentiful in the skin.

The Iban can produce another kind of white pepper by rubbing the skins off dried berries using a wooden mill that resembles a hand-operated millstone. The result is "decorticated" pepper. It's the same color as white, but tastes more like black.

Toward the end of the day I sat on the longhouse veranda relaxing and Eetwat brought me a handful of betel all prepared for chewing. She smiled and cooed in her winning way and we played tic-tac-toe, scratching our marks on the wood of the veranda. She seemed to think that Mack and I were a pretty agreeable sort of stranger. Sometimes she would reach over and pinch me on what to her was my big nose and then she'd giggle and chatter about who knows what. I'd tell her things like "If you ever get divorced I'm going to come back here and marry you, and we'll have two point seven children and a Ford station wagon, ha ha." Of course she didn't know what I was saying, but I think she got the gist of how I felt.

When Mack returned from the hunt he had a long face.

"What's the matter, mighty Nimrod, no luck?"

"Worse! You know those bamboo sections they carry, the ones we thought were for water?"

"Yes," I said through the betel nut buzz.

"Well they're not for water! As they go through the jungle they catch bugs. Then they pull off their wings and their legs, and they put them in the bamboo. Then when they get hungry they have a nice, fresh snack!"

"No!"

"Yes!"

"Did they?..."

"Yes!"

"Did you?..."

"Yes, I had to. I'm not gonna refuse anything from a head-hunter on his own turf."

"How did they taste?"

"I don't know. I didn't want to chew them, so I took only small ones and swallowed them whole."

"You mean they died in your stomach?"

"Yes. And they gave me heartburn. And gas. And now every time I burp it's like one of their spirits gets caught in my throat."

Poor Mack. I gave him the biggest chaw of betel I had. "Here you go, buddy," I said, "cop a buzz. No telling what we'll have for dinner tonight."

On another day Mack and I went for a walk in the jungle. David was nowhere to be found. The Iban have some interesting sexual mores and he was taking full advantage. We learned that they refer to the amorous pursuit as "hunting." David was proving a very mighty hunter, and not disposed to hunting in a pack of, say, three. We bitterly regretted our inability to speak the language.

As David hunted that day, we went on a gathering expedition. We were seeking a local fruit that I have never seen anywhere else in the world. It's the color and size of a lime, and shaped like an egg. It has a rind the thickness of an orange but it breaks easily. If you hold the fruit in your hands and give it a twist, the rind will break in a clean line around the circumference. Then you lift off one hemisphere and see, shimmering inside, what looks like a golf ball-sized Thomson Seedless grape with the skin removed. ("Beulah, peel me a grape.") It even tastes like the grape, and might have made a monster raisin. We had no idea what the thing was called, so we called it "grapeyfruit." We ate gobs of them but the Iban use them for making wine.

We were out in back of the village and had gathered up a lot of grapeyfruit. I was sitting under a tree relaxing and Mack was throwing stones into a leafy, bushy hillside. Suddenly we heard a crashing sound and then the gurgle of running water. One of Mack's stones had hit a precarious little clay pipe that the villagers had rigged up to bring clean water from a spring into the village. They had it pouring into the pigpen beneath the deck, next to the chief's apartment.

"Uh oh," we both said.

"Mack, you've destroyed the people's water supply."

"Do you think they'll take it hard?"

"They won't take it easy. Their lives are in peril now." Mack knew I was kidding him, but didn't know how much.

"Maybe we could fix it," he said hopefully.

I told Mack that in cases like this they strip the offender naked and give him an hour's head start into the jungle. If they catch him they hog tie him to a pole and lug him back to the village like so much meat. There they lash him to a stake. All the kids get to throw stuff at him while the men beat drums and chant. When they get to a fever pitch they bring out the women who torture the unfortunate sod with hot firebrands, taking care not to neglect the family jewels.

"Jungle justice ain't pretty, Mack. But it's effective."

Like I said, Mack knew I was teasing him. But he was starting to sweat. We were, after all, in Indian country. And the cavalry was very far away. Mack kept touching his crotch, just to reassure himself, I suppose.

We started trudging back to the longhouse with our harvest of grapeyfruit. "Hey," Mack said brightly, "we don't have to tell them. We could just play dumb. Maybe they won't even notice."

"I dunno, Mackie. Seems to me the men will be pretty thirsty when they come back from the hunt. And if they haven't had any luck, they won't be in a very good mood."

We were getting pretty close to the longhouse and Mack said, "Maybe I'll just confess. Be up front, you know? I'll bet they'd cut me some slack."

"Or cut your throat. You never know with headhunters."

Mack laid low all that afternoon and chewed an awful lot

of betel nut. I saw two guys notice the dry pipe. They went up the hill, the water started flowing again, they came down the hill. And that was the end of it. But I didn't tell Mack. I was having too much fun. I kept making up and telling him of newer and better tortures that the natives might perpetrate on offenders. Like the one where they chop off a piece of your living body every day, then cook and eat it in front of you. After a month you're nothing but a blind and tongueless basket case stinking of gangrene. You wish they would just make a roast of you and have done with it. But instead they let the kids use you as a football. Boy, did I have fun. And boy, did I get mine that evening

That evening Eetwat and Jerry decided to give us a feast in their apartment. They killed a chicken (I think it was a chicken), picked some strange looking vegetables, and got out a great quantity of rice, which they grew in a small field nearby. They also invited four or five youths and maidens of the tribe. David told us that this was "big bloody honor." We hadn't seen David for some time, but he was joining us now to rest up from so much "hunting" and to fuel up for further pursuits. The way he eyed the girls in the apartment made it clear who his next quarry would be. (And he would stalk them alone, the bastard.)

Eetwat put all of her ingredients into a black iron pot with some ants and herbs and made a stew. Nothing much of it was recognizable but it tasted good and Eetwat seemed to love playing hostess. Jerry looked on proudly. I told Eetwat that her husband was the luckiest guy in town. I think she understood me, too, even before David translated.

After we had all eaten our fill Mack and I sang "Rawhide" and they all liked that, though David giggled all the way through. I then took out my camera and snapped a flash picture. The Iban froze for a second when it went off, then laughed till their faces hurt. They thought it was the funniest thing they ever saw. They made me take several more just so they could have some more laughs.

We were all having a high old time when one of the men of the tribe came through the door in great excitement. He announced that we were summoned to the presence of Entili. "Chief say you come," David translated. "You have dinner with him."

"Great. When?"

"Right now."

"Tell the chief thanks, but we're stuffed."

David looked at us as if we were joking or stupid and he couldn't tell which. I think the survival instinct returned to Mack and me simultaneously when we both blurted, "But we'll go, we'll go! Oh yeah!"

David looked relieved and Eetwat and Jerry looked like they derived some kind of honor from having their guests invited to the chief's table. (Actually, they sit on the floor and eat with their hands.) The youths and maidens looked excited.

The messenger conducted us to the chief's apartment where an old woman met us at the door. She took over from there, ushered us in and seated us next to the chief on the floor. A gray-haired elder and the chief's dad sat with us. Chief Entili addressed both of us as "Tuan." David said, "That mean bloody good chap."

We were all sitting cross-legged in a circle and the old woman set a big dish of rice in the middle. Then Entili brought out two cans of the food we had brought and opened them, using the new opener, with a satisfying expertise. We tried to eat sparingly but he kept pushing food at us and calling us Tuan and smiling a lot.

When we had forced down all the food we were finally able to call it quits. I tell you, my head was spinning, I was so full. With a certain gravity, the chief presented the empty tin cans to the elder. He seemed to offer him advice or instructions on their use, and they turned them over and examined them carefully. That done, the chief held up one finger and made some kind of announcement. He called to the attending woman and she brought us a bottle of something. It wasn't the whiskey that Mack and I had brought; we could tell from the old reused bottle. It was grapeyfruit wine.

The woman brought a couple of glasses, two coconut shells, and a clean empty can. With great ceremony the chief poured us each a measure. I could smell a strong odor of grapeyfruit, almost overpowering, spicy sweet and alcoholic, like grapeyfruit perfume. The tribesmen knocked theirs back neat, rinsing their mouths with it before swallowing, so I did too.

I want to tell you that stuff tasted like piss! And searing hot piss too! And those savages sat there smacking their lips and called for another round. Jesus, Joseph, and Mary, I don't know how I got the next draft down. And on my full stomach too. It's a wonder I didn't just puke on the spot. Maybe the first round just knocked my tastebuds down for a count of eight, and that's how I survived the next shot.

I looked over at Mack and he seemed a bit shaken too. Then the chief made another announcement and David and the tribesmen heartily approved. David said, "Hey, big news. Entili say we have big party, all for you blokes. Bloody good news, eh?"

"Now?" Mack wheezed.

"Right now."

"Oh, God."

We were taken to the common room where the people were gathering. Some old women rolled out a big ceremonial mat in the center of the room. The thing was woven from several different grasses and had the most intricate designs reminiscent of the peoples' tattoos. David said it belonged to the chief and was used only on special occasions. In a corner another woman attended a small cast-iron brazier that smoldered with a heady incense. She replenished it from time to time from a bag of leaves, twigs, and pepper berries.

When all the tribal members had arrived, they sat around the walls in ranks three deep, leaving the center space empty. The chief made a big announcement and all the tribe nodded agreement. David translated: "Entili say you tell your story."

"Eh?"

"Chief want for you to stand up and say who you are, why you come, what you want." You may find it curious that we had been in the village for some days and no one had asked us our story before. The answer is simple: people who are still happily living in the Stone Age are just not in a hurry for much of anything. At least that's my theory.

I looked at the people of the tribe. They were all very quiet and expectant, eager to hear whatever we might have to say. I wondered what they would do if they weren't pleased by what they heard. I looked at Entili and I couldn't tell if his eyes were cool or smoldering. I looked to Mack, "Maybe you ought to make a speech, Mack," I said as casually as I could.

"No."

"C'mon."

"No."

"You're bigger than I am, maybe they'll be scared of you."

"You're older, and it was your idea to come here in the first place."

I was stuck. Mack was adamant and the folks were starting to stir. I stood up, hoping for the best. Drawing a deep breath I began: "My friends, and I hope you are my friends." I waited as David translated. The people nodded. "We come from America," I continued, "a land far away. We come in peace."

Mack choked on a giggle.

"And we come because we heard that you are all nice folks, that you have the best pepper in the land and we wanted very much to visit you." I smiled hopefully all around. Mack waved. The people seemed to approve and I warmed to my subject. Nodding to David to continue translating, I proudly said, "We are two men who travel far. We are men of the United States Navy." I waited for the translation and the good impression that would surely follow.

"Hey, what you think?" David chided. "I can't say that."

"Why not? It's true."

"I can't say navy. They got no word to say navy. You look. You see ship? Ha ha ha."

"Oh, yeah, O.K., tell them we're military men."

That wouldn't do either. They'd never seen an army. The chief and a gray-haired elder had an idea of the word army. The chief had seen British Colonial troops during a trip down-river in his youth. And David said the old guy had taken the heads of five Japanese soldiers who had gotten lost in the jungle during the Pacific War. "But nobody know military. Ha ha ha. They don't even know bloody ocean!"

"Well," I said, taking a little linguistic license, "say we're warriors."

"O.K.," he said with that sardonic smile. "They know that word."

"And do the best you can with ocean."

And so it was. To the people of the village we were warriors who went about in a big canoe, on the big water, way downstream. And our tribal name was "Merica." The chief was satisfied, and so were his people. Entili announced that a party should commence, that wine should flow, that drummers drum, musicians play, and the people dance and sing as much as they desired.

The first thing they did was bring out more of that grapeyfruit paint thinner and start pouring liberal drafts for men, women, and children alike. As full as I was I didn't want to drink anymore, but this was a party in our honor. The stuff had started to go down a little easier, though. Partly due to previous exposure and partly due to pride. I couldn't let those women and children outdrink a Warrior of the Big Canoe. They were knocking that stuff back like Gatorade between puffs on their home-rolled cigars. They make them from some kind of wild tobacco that I'm sure would make a strong man weak. I was just glad I had quit smoking and didn't have to match them stogie for stogie.

A couple of the braves came over to us and asked to see our tattoos. Obviously, to them, we would have some since we were warriors. After all, they had them. Now I have never had a tattoo and have never wanted one. But how does a Warrior of the Big Canoe explain that to a guy who wears his bravery all over his body? This, my friends, this is where I got mine. Mack, the son of a bitch, does have a tattoo.

Although his is not even a worthy tattoo. Compared to the swelling scenes on the chests of mariners, the Louisville Slugger labels on their penises, and the grinning faces on their buttocks, his is miniscule. He has a little tiny chain around his left ankle. B.F.D! But he has one more than I do.

He told everybody that each link in the chain represented an enemy killed in battle. He said that when you got your chain to link up like his then you become an official Great Warrior. I was sick. I was sick, I tell you. Everybody made a fuss over Mack, the official Great Warrior. They poured him more grapeyfruit wine, which was starting to taste O.K. by now. And the women all wanted to wear his pith helmet. I showed them the scar on the bottom of my left foot where I stepped on glass and had to have stitches when I was six years old. I told them an enemy soldier had bayonetted me there when I tried to kick him. But nothing was as good as a tattoo. Yeah, I got mine all right. Yessiree. (And Mack, if you're reading this, up yours!) I had some more grapeyfruit to soothe my injured ego and I was starting to feel better when two of the tribal maidens were brought over to us by a delegation of young men. David said that they were going to honor us now with a song. And as it was a ceremonial song it had to be done in proper form. We were to sit on our heels with hands on knees. One of the girls would sit in front of each of us and look shyly at the floor. She would then tap us lightly on the hands to indicate to whom she was singing. Everyone had hushed and was listening to hear the song the maidens would sing to the Warriors of the Big Canoe.

Mack got his song sung to him first because he was the god-damn official Great Warrior sonofabitch! Damn! And I was his senior in rank. Was I in a snit. David said the song was about a Great Warrior and I listened carefully for any word that might sound like "official." When the one girl finished, the other girl sang the same song to me, so if Mack was official in their eyes so was I, and I told him so.

Everybody liked the singing and wanted more. So the chief said that Mack and I should sing a song. I was ready for this. I sang "Moon River," because they lived on the riverbank. I sounded pretty good too, I don't mind telling you. I put lots of feeling into it. And I didn't forget any of the words even though the grapeyfruit wine was starting to go to my head.

"Top that," I told Mack. "Mr. official-ass Great Warrior."

Ha! He couldn't think of anything to sing. He asked me for a suggestion. "How about the official-ass Great Warrior song, there must be one." But then I relented. I figured we were even. "Do you know the national anthem?" I asked him.

"I can't sing that very well."

"How about 'America the Beautiful?'"

"Oh yeah. I can sing that." And so he sang it with gusto and it was well received.

The best was yet to come, including more grapeyfruit, which was going down like water by now. Two guys brought out these one-stringed instruments, one of them plucked, one played with a bow, and a third fellow had a drum. Everybody settled into their seats around the wall, three ranks deep, and the guys started playing.

They played a haunting melody, rhythmic and simple but lovely. It was a graceful tune, that's what it was. And it bespoke something very, very ancient. It calmed the people like a narcotic mist. They made little sounds that emanated from the backs of their throats and they swayed at the shoulders and hips. Then one of the maidens of the tribe got up, almost in a trance. She moved to the center of the room and began dancing. Her dance had only a few steps but like the tune it was simple and graceful and haunting. She looked like a piece of silk, hanging in space and undulating in a drifting air. She spoke with her hands, a little like a hula, and turned slow pirouettes. She was a flower, blossoming to the time of the music.

Three of the maidens took turns dancing as the people murmured quiet approval, and also poured more grapeyfruit.
Suddenly the music changed to a banging, drumming sound
and the girls ran back to their seats. The tallest man in the village (about 5' 8") leaped into the center. He was waving an
ancient looking sword that they call a *parang* and he was
wearing a robe made from the skin of a Malaysian bear stuck
with eagle feathers. The drummer drummed and the banger
banged and the dancer whirled around with his *parang*, doing
battle with unseen foes. Everybody made ooh and ahh sounds
and drank more wine.

After winning his battle the dancer and the tune changed
and he started doing a masculine version of the maiden's
dance. He had the same kind of simple steps and grace and it
actually looked pretty easy. I said, "Hey, Mack. I bet I can do
that."

"Why don't you go cut in?"

So I did. I knocked back another noggin of grapeyfruit nectar, then got up, walked over to the guy, and pantomimed that
I wanted to try his dance. Everybody loved the idea and the
band played on. The dancer gave me his bearskin but he kept
the *parang*.

I found that I could imitate the dance perfectly but I threw
in another step of my own just to amaze them. They were fas-
cinated! They bent forward for a better look, taking careful
note of my intricate footwork. They exchanged many remarks. They were obviously pleased to learn that people of
the Merica tribe could do a proper dance. I said, "Mack!
Quick! Take my picture. I'm dancing among the headhunters." He got out my camera and took a good shot of me
in that bearskin.

Then they made Mack get up and dance. He kind of
jumped around the floor for a while and they couldn't decide
if that was art or not. Then I did an Irish jig, thinking to
broaden their experience. I don't think they understood it. So
Mack then tried out a square dance on them. He doe-see-doed

with an imaginary partner and tried to dance a square with only one corner. The people seemed to think it looked kind of dumb, and since I still have a picture of it I can tell you they weren't far off the mark.

By this time a dozen or so of the people had got up and were dancing variations of the maidens' dance. Mack and I each had another pull of the grapeyfruit, this time right from the bottle, and Mack said, "I know. Do your fish face for them." I sucked in my cheeks and brought my lips together vertically, then moved them up and down like a perch. I was getting sort of blind by this time so I don't know how the people took it, but I was having a great time. I borrowed somebody's blowpipe and pretended that I was hunting for wild boar or the neighboring tribe or who knows what. I shook it at some imaginary enemies and issued a few dire threats to them.

Since the pipe was about the length of a rifle with a bayonet on it I started going through the manual of arms. But I kept bogging down at position number six. I couldn't remember if it was parade rest or port arms or what. So I just held it up at right shoulder arms and went marching around the room singing, "Hut two three four." I thought I could give the tribesfolk the flavor of the military life that I had been unable to express by means of vocabulary. Mack started singing "Oh we oh, we ohhum," like the witch's guards do in *The Wizard of Oz*, so I marched around to that for a while too, weaving in and out among the dancers. Then I thought I would use the blowpipe to demonstrate the art of pole vaulting but Mack warned me I might break it and the owner would get sore.

I decided to show them backward somersaulting instead. Now I have to take Mack's word for what happened next because I sort of checked out. He says that I was doing a pretty good, though wobbly, backward somersault when I reached the position where you're standing on your hands, ready to curl up for another roll back. I was right near the chief, fairly vertical and head down when I sort of tipped over sideways and twisted forward and fell on my face and belly in an attitude of genuflection or kow tow in front of Chief Entili. It must have looked pretty good, like I'd done it on purpose. And I'm sure the chief thought the Warriors of the Big Canoe were putting on a good show. But when I didn't move afterward it was pretty obvious that the grapeyfruit had got me.

Mack says that's when I began to vomit. He says that I began to push up a mole hill of undigested rice, red flecked with ant bodies, right there in front of Entili. Worse, I was doing it on his swell ceremonial mat. Now remember that I hadn't told Mack that the water-pipe situation was O.K. He was afraid that might still be a hot issue and here I was desecrating something that might even be sacred.

Mack will tell you himself that he was pretty scared. He started scooping up my vomit in his hands and running to the windows to throw it out. He kept saying, "I'm sorry! I'm sorry, chief! I'll clean it up!" Then he'd run back for more, all the while saying, "I'm sorry, please don't be sore." For all I know he broke down and confessed to wrecking the water pipe, too, and threw himself on the mercy of Entili. But the chief wouldn't have understood and David had long since disappeared for a liason with one of the dancing girls.

Mack got up as much puke as he could, using only his hands. Then he picked me up by the collar and dragged me out of the building to clean me up. He is a real pal. I know he took me down to the river, because I woke up floating face down in it. But only briefly. After that I remember the sound of voices and feeling many hands carry me. That is the end of my personal record of that evening.

I woke up the next day on the floor of Eetwat and Jerry's apartment. A herd of water buffalo was stampeding somewhere between my ears. The world was spinning and I can honestly say that I've never felt worse in my whole life.

My bladder was about to burst and, excuse my language, but I had to piss like a racehorse. Nobody was around and I was afraid to stand up so I struggled, slowly, up to my hands and knees and crawled out of the apartment. On the way out I smelled some of the grapeyfruit vino from somewhere and went into the dry heaves. Shaking and weak, I dragged myself, half blindly, down the walkway and stopped when I found myself on the big terrace that overhangs the pigpen. I collapsed face down on the bamboo poles and lay there gasping for breath. And it didn't smell too good either, above those pigs.

I really had to go something terrible but I just could not move. It is a tribute to the human mind that I was able to devise a plan, even under these stressful conditions. I reached down, with only one hand, and unzipped my pants and pulled out Mr. Happy. I then stuffed him between two of the bamboo poles then relaxed and let go. I don't know how the pigs took this because I passed out again, in midstream. When I came to I was in a position of coitus, as you might say, with the bamboo. Mr. Happy was dangling like a piece of bait above the swine who were only about two feet below. I was glad that pigs are not generally taught to sit up and beg. I pulled myself together, as it were, feeling very sick but proud of my achievement.

I crawled into the common room then and propped myself up against a post. I sat there in a daze until Eetwat came and found me, having discovered that I was gone from the apartment. She said, "Oh, tsk tsk tsk," and patted me on the shoulder. It's curious how "Oh, tsk tsk tsk" sounds the same in almost any language. She ran and got me some water to drink and a pile of betel nut. She wrapped up several chews for me, then she straightened my hair and wiped my sleep-sodden eyes out with her bare fingers. She made signs that said Mack and David had gone for a hike or a hunt and would be back later. I couldn't hold back a belch, and it became obvious to Eetwat that I had a bellyache, lots of gas, and heartburn. She went and got two dried peppercorns, which she crushed between two small stones then wrapped in a betel leaf to make a fat pill that she gave me with some water and soon my stomach felt much better. The rest of the day I did nothing but sit against that post, chew betel, and swallow pepper pills. Sometimes I found enough strength to moan but I had to husband my resources. Later in the afternoon, when the sunlight was slanting and highlighting the dust particles in the air, the men of the tribe came back from forest and field and they all trooped into the common room where they saw me. The chief pointed down at me and said something and they all laughed. Somebody else said something and they laughed again. They went chuckling off to their apartments, two of them marching and singing "Oh we oh, we ohhum."

"Ya lousey savages," I thought miserably. "I'd like to get you in a Hong Kong cocktail lounge and see how you stand up to a dozen frozen margaritas. Ya goddamn cannibals." I swear, I felt like I wanted to cry. But soon Eetwat returned and she said, "Oh, tsk tsk tsk," and she patted my shoulder, and she cooed a little Iban coo and I soon felt better. She nursed me all day and into the night. Sometimes she even put the pepper pills into my mouth with her own fingers and let me spit the spent, dry betel pulps into her hand. That woman is the soul of human kindness. And I ever after called her "Doctor Pepper."

7   *Through the Looking Glass*

 THERE ARE FEW PLACES ON EARTH WHERE ONE can step in an instant from one world into another. The United States/Mexico border is one. The formerly divided Berlin was another. And from the snowtop of California's Mount Whitney you can at least see the great dry expanse of Death Valley. But nowhere is the juxtaposition of two worlds more suddenly dramatic than where the Baja California desert meets the Sea of Cortez. Down the east coast of the peninsula, from Gonzaga to La Paz, lies some of the world's harshest, most threatening, and oddly beautiful landscape. Along the shoreline the sun-blasted desert glowers. Here the land is hostile to most life, monochromatic, glaring in the midday sun, and frightening in its beauty. Here the land-bound tourist may know only the desert. But, stepping through the looking-glass surface of the sea, the scuba diver enters a lush tropical world of color and life.

My friends Claudia and Miguel are divers. Claudia is a tall, good-looking American woman who used to be a registered nurse. Miguel is from Mexico City and is well known among divers for his competence and his wry sense of humor. The couple met in Mexico City when Claudia was on her way to a South American vacation. The fates had other things in mind. The result of that chance encounter on the road to elsewhere was a marriage and a move to Baja. They live about a two minute's walk from the Cafe Almeja where, over lunch, we made plans for a day of diving. The following morning I met them at the harbor and we boarded their launch and set out upon a quiet sea. Even at that calm early morning hour the desert was blowing its hot breath upon us. But as the arid shore receded, the abundant sea beckoned. Less than a mile offshore we passed the shallow reef that Miguel calls "the su-permarket" for its plentiful fish and shellfish. The only shopper at the supermarket that moment happened to be an orca, so we kept on going. As we sped along into the rising morning sun the water all around us suddenly erupted like geysers, and we found ourselves being escorted by an enor-mous pod of dolphins. Miguel throttled up and tried to race the beautiful creatures. But the twin outboards of the launch were no match for them, and they left us behind.

After about thirty minutes we reached Punta Concepcion just outside the mouth of Bahía Concepcion. Here we would have our first, and deepest, dive. The Sea of Cortez experi-ences wild temperature swings over the seasons. In winter and spring it drops to around sixty degrees. Over the summer it steadily rises until, in the early fall, it reaches temperatures as high as eighty-nine degrees in the shallows. When it's that warm it's important to move slowly. Even though you're un-der water, you still perspire, and you can actually dehydrate or suffer heat exhaustion. On this occasion the water was about seventy degrees, and we wore only Neoprene vests and about ten pounds of weight.

It was still only about nine o'clock, but the sun was intense. The brooding promontories of Punta Concepcion shimmered in the heat as they glared down at us. We leapt into the look-ing glass. For forty feet we descended slowly through a murky middle world. Then the water below us exploded with color and light and a thousand living species. Descending to sixty feet, we gently touched bottom and were immediately surrounded by curious fish. A giant tuna swam by so close I could have touched it. Spiny lobsters peered at us from behind the rocks. Delicate little shrimp and other small creatures scattered before us as we swam. Magnificently colored parrotfish fed among the nooks and crannies of the reef. I had been here many times before, but as before, it always seems new. We followed the reef down to about eighty feet. There I looked into a small cave and saw a familiar character: a moray eel that I like to call "Claudia's dog" because she knows these waters and its creatures so well that she can feed this animal by hand. "He likes Vienna sausages best," she tells me.

Down where the eel lives a diver's air burns up fast. So we began our ascent through this living kaleidoscope, all too soon for me. Breaking the surface, my first sight was of the massive rocks of Punta Concepcion, barely a quarter mile away, reminding me of the portal I had just passed through.

We spent the next hour or so at a rocky beach full of tidepools, snorkeling, rock picking, and venting off the nitrogen. Then we turned the launch northward to a collection of small islands known as the Santa Inez Islands.

Upon reaching the rocks we dispensed with wetsuits altogether. The water temperature here was in the high seventies. We decided to keep our depth above twenty-five feet and enjoy a good long, warm dive. Beneath the islands are numerous rock shelves, and within them are scores of species in countless numbers. Golden grouper, cabrilla, redjacks, pipefish, trumpetfish, barracuda, all swimming in great schools through and among the rocks. Clinging to the rocks are large sea urchins, even larger rock scallops and, careful where you put your hand, poisonous stonefish. They look just like the rocks, until you get close. A lazy blowfish swam by, uninflated. I decided it was time to play. I grabbed him and shook him by the tail till he puffed up like a spiky basketball. Then I "swished" him through the basketball hoop of Claudia's arms. Sometimes it's hard not to laugh underwater. Then once again, we rose and passed through the looking glass, out of the aquatic wonderland and back into the fierceness of the desert. Then we returned to shore, changed, and readied our gear for the next day.

There's nothing like a cold one after having been in the salt water for a while, so I went to the beach and took a seat at Cafe Almeja, only a few feet from the surf. The first one went fast. But as I nursed the second I noticed for the thousandth time, yet always anew, how the harsh face of the desert softens in the slanting light of the late afternoon. And how the face of the sea darkens and seems to close itself off to humans. In a curious exchange of roles the sea becomes forbidding, and the desert, in its turn, is welcoming. As though even they, too, can pass through the looking glass.

On the light cruiser USS *Oklahoma City*, we were crossing the Java Sea. We were bound south for Jakarta that morning. The equatorial waters were so warm and still that we seemed to be on some quiet pond rather than the furthest reaches of the Pacific. Only our ship disturbed the glassy water. In the distance, clouds rose and formed, and metamorphosed and puffed and spread with startling rapidity. They were mottled with pink and the color fell shining on the sea. The blue of the water, in turn, reached up to the clouds where the colors mixed and mingled and unraveled the horizon, confusing the distinction between sea and sky, making the world a billowy sphere of pink and blue and white for us to glide through.

The sphere was composed of two perfectly matched opposing hemispheres, each reflecting into the other. The sky and clouds shone from the sea, and the sea was visible in the sky. The ship's ripply counterpart shimmered upside down, an undulating alter ego. The ship's eye hung forward and above the prow, where the water was yet undisturbed. To stand there and look down was to see the sky in the sea and the sea in the sky, and yet both still in their proper places, too. One's own face stared up at one looking down and yet still looking up, each into the other, into the other, into the other, "stretching out to the crack of doom," as Macbeth said. To fall in at that place might be to fall into infinity, or the looking glass, or one's self. We sailed in a cosmic house of mirrors, where, after a time, the real and the shade are indistinguishable. The perfect calm had made this dizzy, delirious thing possible. Only a sudden gale, or other rough weather, could have spun this tangled scene apart, and torn the real from the tendrils of illusion.

Joseph Conrad called this the "Shallow Sea" because of its submarine mountains and plateaus, rising up within an anchor chain of the surface. Our captain had said that if we found a shallow enough spot we would drop anchor for a few hours and have a swim in the sea and a barbecue on the fantail. And that would be fine. The ship's cooks would bring out their best. The band would play jazz and show tunes. We'd sun ourselves and swim and eat and talk about all the beer we'd drink in Jakarta. And the whores. Beautiful Java whores lolling beneath their big umbrellas or beside their little shepherd's tents, scattered along the beaches like starfish. "Venus's little starfish," we called them.

"I'm gonna fuck a ton o' whores!" bantam Sammy Seacrest crowed.

"How many whores in a ton?" I demanded, as ritual prescribed.

"Two thousand, unless they're small, ha ha!"

"Then I'm gonna fuck two tons of whores, yo ho!"

"Yo ho!" a chorus answered.

The ship's sonar fathometer was in working order, but still a bosun's mate stood on the fo'c'sle taking soundings with a plumb line. Standing above the prow, like David about to slay Goliath, his watery reflection mimicking him, he swung the weighted end of his line into a blur, then sent it flying from his hand. The little stone arced through the air and raced ahead of the ship, trailing its slender line. Then, like a fisher bird, it dove to the surface and sought the bottom. As the ship made way the bosun hauled in the line till it hung vertical and called out to the navigator, "By the mark...five!" Five fathoms, thirty feet, from the keel to the bottom. Should we have two fathoms he would call, "By the mark...twain!"

Sam "Malibu" Robinson and I were standing at the lifeline, drinking mugs of the bad and ubiquitous navy "joe." Coffee to a landsman. Black as night, bitter as death, and hot as hell, despite its deservedly rotten reputation it seems at times that the U.S. Navy is fueled on this terrible, biting brew. Anyone can tell you that aboard ship no man is ever more than sixty seconds away from an urn full of it. I have heard people joke that it's made from what the coffee dealers sweep up off the floor. Joke or not, I believe it happens sometimes. It really is bad stuff, but American sailors drink gallons of it.

Sam and I were drinking our mugs of mud, making our obligatory complaints about it, and trying to look through the sea for the bottom when we heard Seaman Simms holler from aloft, "Go fuck yourself! Eat shit, you motherfucker, eat shit and die! Eat a mile of shit and die!" He bounded down to the main deck and continued his argument with another seaman. I couldn't tell what the argument was about, but it didn't matter, Simms argued about anything. He was always arguing. He was always right and the whole goddamn world was wrong and it could all eat shit and die.

"You know, I hate that sonofabitch," I said to Sam. "I really hate his fuckin' guts."

"You and me and a hundred other guys. If he was in our division we'd have to give him a little 'extra military instruction.'"

"I wish something bad would happen to him," I said, still hearing him bitching at his shipmate. "I hope he gets injured. No, no, I hope he fuckin' drowns today. I hope the bastard goes swimming and drowns!" And I meant it.

Simms finished his tirade and stomped past us. He was twenty years old with blond beach-boy good looks and a muscular frame. His face was red and had a look of angry disgust. His eyes bore an injured expression, as if to say, "What's the matter with these assholes? Why don't they shut up and get off my case?"

He stopped near the lifeline and quivered a little. Simms didn't enjoy being angry; he just *was* angry. And he always wanted to do things his own way. Whatever he did he would do a good enough job and he didn't want anybody telling him how to do it, when to do it, or who to do it with. Simms was uncooperative. And that's a maritime and military sin. On shore, individualism is often valued. On a ship, you need co-operation. A ship's company is a family business.

Simms went back aloft to the cable winch he'd been working on and glared at it. That's how he always started a job; he got mad at it. A slow, sustained, internal rage, that was his style. "Bitter as navy joe" is how a bunkmate described it. He stripped off his shirt with determined speed, picked up his tools, and began again on the offending winch. His lower lip pouted and the muscles of his arms bulged as he forced the machine to submit to his will. He stripped off its protective plates and ripped at its insides. When he found the guilty piece he was looking for he tore it out and flung it on the deck. Then, still bare-chested, snorting, he paced deliberately back and forth in front of his quarry. He nudged it with his toe. Satisfied that he was alive and it was dead, he picked up the corpse and tossed it overboard.

About midday the bottom came to the mark three. The engines reversed, sending a shudder through the cruiser, and then stopped and the ship glided to a slow halt. Chief Bosun's Mate Smith directed the anchor crew as they dropped the massive hook and the chain thundered through the chute.

I changed into swimwear and met Sam and three others on the main deck. Sam was dressed in his Malibu jams, Sammy Seacrest was buck naked, and the rest of us were in government issue. As cooks set up barbecue grills on the fantail and the ship's band prepared to play, about twenty-five men gathered on deck in a holiday mood and were waiting for the lifeboat to be lowered before we went into the water. Hearty, beer-bellied chief petty officers made jokes and slapped each other on the back. A couple of shy junior officers on their first cruise wondered if they should act decorously in front of "the men" or let their hair down and enjoy themselves. Seamen and apprentices were skylarking and playing grab-ass. And we petty officers admired the scene and told ourselves that it was "us who operate this goddamn ship, ain't it?"

A gunner's mate, sitting on one of the ten-foot gun barrels of the forward turret hollered up to the flying bridge, "Captain, captain, fly the Jolly Roger!" Captain Butcher leaned over the rail and beamed and gave the high sign. He liked playing pirate, too. He gestured to his yeoman. Seconds later the skull and crossbones flew up the signal mast and caught an upper level breeze.

"Hurray!" we all shouted. "Shiver me timbers! Hurray!"

Another flag ran up alongside the Roger and snapped open. It was Captain Butcher's personal standard: Popeye with cutlass in hand and an eye patch, and the motto, "Press On Regardless."

"Yahoo!" we cheered and applauded.

"Press on, press on regardless! Yeah!"

"Haze gray and under weigh, this motherfucker is A-OK!" we chanted.

"She's the Gray Ghost of the Nam coast!"

"Fuckin-ay right!"

Senior Chief Howard, oldest man on board, veteran of the battles of Iwo Jima, Okinawa, Inchon, and a score of duels on the Tonkin Gulf's Yankee Station spilled over with delight and danced a hornpipe. Others jumped up and down, laughing, cheering, exulting.

The lifeboat was in the water now. It was manned by a cox'n in the stern and a swimmer amidships. And in the bow, armed with an M-14 rifle and watching for sharks, was Bosun's Mate Al Trevino, who had a Purple Heart, and whose

uncle is Lee Trevino the golfer. Waving his rifle and shouting he
signaled all safe and secure. Several men leaped in and made a
great splashing.

"Let's play abandon ship!" Sam yelled.

"Yeah!" the five of us shouted in unison. We raced to the
prow to stand above the ship's eye and ran through the navy
drill.

"All hands stand by to abandon ship!"

"Ship's position is…"

"Nearest land is…"

"Your mother's name is…"

"Steady men. Go in feet first in case you hit some flotsam."

"Cross your legs to protect the family jewels."

"Arms crossed in front and elbows up to protect your
handsome face."

"Eyes on the horizon to keep you vertical all the way
down."

"Now, leap through the flaming oil and swim under it to
safety, just like it says in the book. Away!"

The sea rushed up and swallowed us with a gulp. Breaking
the surface in a froth, we swam aft to the stern. Treading water there, we could see through the ocean's perfect clarity to
the ship's huge screws. Sammy took a great breath and dove
down to the ship's keel where he "tickled her belly." We went
forward again to investigate the anchor chain.

Equatorial seas are delicate and changeable. The reflecting
half-domes of the Java are as fragile as the mirrors they imitate.
They can shatter and take new form suddenly, from placid calm
to churning torment without warning. I felt the sea change before I was consciously aware of it. Then I saw the ship swing on
her anchor as she would do in harbor when the tide shifts. A
swell of water, from nowhere, rose up under me, lifting me with
it, then dropped me back down into a trough. The next swell
rolled heavily over my head, forcing brine into my mouth. I
heard some shouts of the other men but I could see no one
among the sudden hillocks of water. The current was carrying

me toward the starboard quarter of the ship so I went with it, rising and falling with the sea, till I was alongside the hull. There I found I had to swim hard against the growing mountains of water just to stay put. "Hey," I hollered to the main deck, trying to sound calm. "Somebody throw me a line."

"Hey, hey someone on deck. Somebody, help!" A swell came from behind. It lifted me up. With the sound of the surf it rushed toward the ship and bashed my body against the steel hull. The flowing water pressed me against the ship, forcing air out of my lungs until the wave was spent. As it receded it took me back with it. Salt burned my eyes. I tried to lift my head to breathe but the next wave fell on me, tumbling me over and throwing me against the ship again. As the steel hull came at me I held my arms out to cushion the blow but several tons of rushing water bent them like sticks. My lip split against the shock of steel. I drank blood and brine and vomited underwater. A throbbing, spinning buzz filled my head. I clawed the air to rise to it. I could hear the shouting of others as the ocean swirled around them too, but I could now see only shapes and swirls of light and dark.

The ship continued to swing on her anchor till she was nose into the sea. Then the swells dragged me along the side of the hull. They rolled me, scraped me against sharp little barnacles that lacerated my body and cut to the knee bone. I tried to swim against it. I swear I tried with all my might. But I just couldn't swim up those hills of water.

They took me beyond the ship. My body ached from blows and fatigue and blood seeped out of my scraped arms and legs. The swells wouldn't let me have any air. When I tried to breathe they forced brine down my throat and I vomited and my mouth and nose burned. They hurled their monstrous weight on me and beat me down into the troughs. I couldn't move. My strength was gone. I was sleepy. I always thought that in a matter of life or death I could huff and puff and gather the strength to do whatever was needed. But I couldn't even open my eyes.

To me the world became quiet. The thunder of the sea was muffled and distant. I heard no more shouts. The hammering of the waves became a gentle undulation. I became aware that I could see the depths. I saw where the clear blue water near the surface began to darken and then turn black and become void. "I'm dying," I thought with bemused disappointment. "I'm only twenty-two, and I've never even loved a woman, and I'm dying. I've never loved a woman and I'm dying...I've never loved..." In my soul's eye I looked down upon a white sand beach. It was perfectly clean. No driftwood washed up on it. No fire rings dotted it. No sculpted sandcastles, and no footprints betold my passing. I slid sadly, gently, painlessly down toward death. The sea rolled easily over me now.

I began to feel cold. It started at my feet and moved slowly up. But it was an easy cold. It didn't make me shiver.

Suddenly, I heard a splashing sound, like a hooked fish fighting for life at the end of a line. Someone pulled my head up out of the water and I began to hear the sea again. "O.K.?... O.K.?" I heard him say above the roar. My body wouldn't move, it still belonged to death, but my eyes half opened of their own accord. I recognized Seaman Simms. He had me about the waist in a bear hug. My head leaned against his and we rose and fell with the waves. "We're gonna swim together back to the ship. O.K.?" he shouted.

"No," I murmured. To murmur "no" was all I had the strength to do. If he would cheat Death of me, he would do it alone. He hesitated. Maybe he thought of leaving me. He looked past me, through the hostile sea to the ship. A hue of melancholy softened the ever-present anger in his eyes as he judged the task ahead of him. I can't tell you exactly how a man reaches down to the bottom of his soul for strength. But I can tell you that at that moment Simms did. The muscles of his face set and I know, I can swear to it, that he had prepared himself to keep me afloat even if it had to be for the rest of his life. He hugged me very tight and began to swim against the murderous swells. He swam with conviction for 350 yards.

He swam without the use of his hands, pushing my dead weight before him. He was wearing fins, but they were speed fins, giving him little advantage. He swam mainly on faith and commitment.

I slipped back into darkness on the way home but I came to as we reached the starboard quarter. Crewmen had hung a cargo net over the side for men to climb up, but I still had no strength. Simms grabbed a line that somebody had thrown down and tied it around me. Then he slipped, exhausted, under the water. Trevino came by in his boat and caught him by the hair and pulled him aboard. A man on deck began to pull me up out of the water. I don't know who he was. All I could see were his arms, big, muscular, tattooed black arms. I decided that's what angels look like.

I rose from the water by those arms' lengths and they laid me on the old-fashioned, teakwood-covered deck. I lay there motionless until two men picked me up and carried me below to sick bay. They put me in a bunk in a dark, quiet corner, covered me, and left. I lay there between sleep and waking, between death and life, hearing, feeling, thinking nothing. No sound, no smell, no sensation penetrated my senses; no time elapsed. I floated in oblivion or infinity. After a long time an old, familiar sensation ran through me. I heard and felt the comforting, caressing thrum of the ship's engines as they came back to life. Then the grinding windlasses lifted the anchor from the bottom and pulled it snug into its socket. The vessel shivered slightly as she gathered way and pitched easily, shaping her course southward, away from the maelstrom. Then I slept.

When I awoke I smelled coffee. Not the coffee you smell in the morning at home, or in restaurants. It was the heavy smell of navy coffee, sharp and burned and bitter. The U.S. Navy's favorite saying is that "There's the right way, the wrong way, and the navy way" to do anything. That goes for coffee as well as anything else. I opened my eyes to see a hospital corpsman departing, having just given Seaman Simms a mug of joe. Simms was in the bunk across from me.

I wriggled my toes and it hurt. I wriggled my fingers and it hurt. Anything I moved hurt. Every muscle in my body ached, and the now bandaged barnacle cuts burned. I felt empty, as if the sea had torn the kernel out of me and thrown back the useless chaff. I gave a little groan and Simms looked over at me. His usual suspicious, hostile expression was back on his face. I took a little comfort in that, thinking that at least I'd be dealing with the devil I knew. He looked away and took a slurp of his coffee. He rolled it around in his mouth and swallowed, smacked his lips and sniffed. He looked back at me.

He didn't say anything, but he got up and came over to me like he had something to say. He stood there for a moment, suddenly confused or unresolved. He looked like a man standing naked and not knowing what to do with his hands. He sat down on the edge of my bunk, then stared into his coffee for a moment. He looked up at me and, still saying nothing, offered me the big, navy standard, blue-trimmed, white china mug.

I struggled to sit up and took the mug from him. I could see and smell that the coffee was made to the usual strength: strong enough to wake the dead and scare the living. Some people would call it cowboy coffee because it's said that you could float a horseshoe in it. The aroma was powerful, almost stingingly bitter and burnt. This was not coffee a man would offer to his wife. But I could feel that the smell alone was bringing my senses back to life. I took a cautious sip. It was hot and thick and strong and it warmed my gut, sending out life-giving rays of heat. Its bitterness almost made me shiver and I caught my breath. I heaved in a huge gulp of air. The burned-black coffee taste clung to my tongue and my taste-buds resonated, sang like vibrating harp strings with the old familiar flavor. The powerful potency of the brew was softened ever so slightly by the traditional navy cook's method of preparation. He had added a tablespoon of clean seawater to the five-gallon urn. There is some debate as to whether the seawater should be added before or after brewing, but either approach will take some of the snarl out of the coffee. It's not enough seawater to taste salt, only enough to alter the flavor.

I continued to sip the coffee and with each swallow the empty feeling inside me filled up a little more. I marveled that something so bad could be so good. I drained the cup and finally Simms spoke. "You want some more?" he asked. I nodded. He took the mug and returned with it filled. "I put a little sugar in it," he reported. "Cook said it would give you strength." With that Simms left. I wrapped my hands around the hot mug and hugged it to me. I breathed in the good, bittersweet vapors. "Not a bad guy, that Simms," I thought. "Not a bad guy."

8   *The Feast of Fatima*

I SIT OUTSIDE AT THE CAFE ALMEJA, WATCHING THE looking-glass sea as it changes its state in the twilight. And observing this process often leads me to think of how it seems that I, too, so often pass through the looking glass and the world is turned askew when I encounter women on the road. I ponder this and sip my beer. The darkness falls. Someone kindles a fire here on the beach. Guillermo is in the kitchen working. A pair of itinerant musicians are tuning up their guitars. I contemplate the fire. Since my earliest memory fire has been a comfort, a symbol of life and passion, renewal and hope. The fire gives heat, the fire gives light, the fire gives protection and assurance. But the fire also produces ashes. And the god of travelers, perhaps in league with the god of love, often conspires to make me taste them.

We had sailed the cruiser USS *Oklahoma City* to the island of Penang, down near the equator. It belongs to Malaysia these days and it used to be a part of British Imperial Malaya, until about 1950. It sits at the western mouth of the straits of Malacca, right where the Pacific and Indian Oceans meet. It's about ten miles across.

Now my story takes place in the days before they built that long causeway to the mainland and started selling those noisy, smoky, two-stroke motorbikes that rip the air and turn it blue and stinky. Until that time the principal means of getting around were foot and pedicab. Autos were few, and many of those that existed were vintage '40s or '50s models. The pedicabs were sometimes called trishaws because they had three wheels. Two passengers, three if they were small, sat on a love seat mounted on two of the wheels, one at each end. Behind that was attached a half a bicycle contraption on which the driver sat above and behind his passengers and pedaled. They all had those ringy-chingy little bicycle bells and were painted in bright colors.

It was a magical place. An Island of the Gods, where all the world's great religions and civilizations meet and live in harmony under the law willed to them by the Empire and the enlightened rule of the Sultan. About a third of the people are Malays, a third Chinese, and the remainder Tamils, Sikhs, Thais, and Europeans—mostly Brits and Aussies. Most of the people lived in the principal community of Georgetown.

We were coming in for R&R, rest and rehabilitation; although we called it rape and riot. We came into port that day as ready to invade as to visit.

But the instant we rushed ashore, we could sense a difference and we slowed like a sea wave coming up the beach. There were no neon signs. Didn't need them either; the place was colorful enough with all of God's houses. There were none of the usual waterfront people waiting on the docks to sell us worthless junk, do our laundry, or pick our pockets. Life in Penang went on as usual. The air was slow and silky. And there were sounds, like the music of *gamalans* and the chants of muezzins, but there were no harsh sounds, no grating sounds, no clanging-banging sounds. No one seemed to be in a hurry.

I heard the "ring ring" of three little bicycle bells as pedicabs rolled up. Their drivers had fixed umbrellas over the love seats, for it was hot that day. Two of them smiled; the other was stoic. Six of us got in and had an easy rolling trip into town. My five mates were: burly, Castro-bearded Sam Robinson; curly blond Ricky Young; Al, the preacher's son; Jack "Tarkus" Wells, who was a misfit seaman although his dad was a U.S. Navy captain; and Tiny Rowan, the yeoman.

We rolled past money changers and jade dealers sitting cross-legged on the ground, their goods spread out on lengths of cloth. The walls of Indian temples, simple of design, extruded gods in sculpture, and their portals spilled them forth in deluge.

I think the essence of the magic of Penang is in the uniqueness of its air. Like a drug in its ability to dissipate tension, it's thick, it's moist, it's warm: a tactile sensation. It has a viscosity like some unknown element between air and water. You can glide slowly through it like a boat on a still pond.

As we sailed in our little three-wheeled vessels through the viscous and scented air, someone said, not altogether sarcastically, "Well, this is all very nice, but I, for one, have had a long voyage, and I'm thirsty."

"Beer." Sam growled.

"Yeah!" We affirmed. "Beer!"

"Well I, for two, have had a long voyage, and I am hornier than a three-peckered billy goat in the spring!" Ricky yelled.

"Yeah!"

"Naked skin!"

"There is nothing like a dame," we sang.

We wanted to swim through a sea of beer to a soft woman for an island. We yearned to leave behind the hazy gray and steel, the bark of commands, the uniforms and guns, the great machines, and the smells of men.

Our three drivers pedaled us to several different places where we were able to sample the drink, to eye and be eyed by the women, and unwind after a long and stormy crossing. The drivers always knew of yet another establishment where the beer was colder and the women were prettier. At one point we paid them extra to race. And they raced us to the Chung King

Hotel & Bar on Chulia Street. A short hallway led into a parlor with rattan and stuffed furniture. On the right was a counter, behind which a middle-aged-looking Malay, lean and wrinkled but not gray, and kind of dour, bent over a ledger. At the far side, a door led out to an atrium or courtyard, and some narrow stairs went up to the rooms on the next floor. About a half-dozen girls looked up eagerly as we came in. A well-fed, but otherwise nondescript Chinese man introduced himself as Tang, and said he was the owner. The Malay at the ledger was his "clerk," Ohsman.

Tang must have encouraged a competitive environment, because the girls rushed us. One was a Tamil in a sari, the darkest person I'd ever seen. Two were Chinese, one tall and thin, one short and not so thin.

There was one who didn't get up and rush us with the others. She was sitting on a couch wearing a long red velvet dress. She wore no makeup; it would have been superfluous, as her lips were full and well-shaped and her brows were naturally dark and framed her large eyes that seemed to reach out and touch me. She held a book on her lap. She was Malay, very dark. And red was the perfect color for her to wear.

As the other men were appreciating the ladies, laying their claims and ordering beer, I walked over to the quiet one. She watched as I approached. When I stood over her, and she was looking up at me, I thought I would say something, but all I did was look at her, hard.

"Hello," she said. And she smiled. A real smile. Not a whore's smile; not a stewardess's smile or a beauty queen's smile, but a real smile with lots of very white teeth.

"What's your name?" I asked.

"Fatima."

She pronounced it FAHtima, not FaTIma.

"What's your full name?"

"Fatima Binti Abdulla."

"That's beautiful. My name's Richard. Sometimes my buddies call me Dick."

"Do you want to sit with me for a little?"

"Yeah, yeah, that would be nice," and I sat down with about a foot of space between us and put my arm on the back of the couch. Her hair smelled of coconut oil, and her skin gave off the faintest suggestion of burnt clove.

"What are you reading?" I asked her.

"Oh, just a book," she said, closing it and smiling self-consciously. Book didn't rhyme with "look," it rhymed with "duke." And the word started at the back of her throat and traveled the length of her tongue to arrive at her parting lips. "Just a book," she repeated, stroking its worn cover. "Do you like reading books?" she asked, her R trilling.

"Yes, yes I do. I read novels. And poetry too. I like Kipling, maybe you've heard of him. And I read *Playboy* and all those other magazines with naked women," I grinned.

She blushed. It surprised me to see a hooker blush, but she did, her cheeks turning from mahogany to rosewood. She brought her book up to her face, just beneath the eye, like a fan, and smiled and blushed at me over its pages. A real smile! Again. The smile melted, the blush cooled, and her large eyes danced as they took me in. The book came down slowly.

"You are in the American ship?" she asked.

"Yes." The boisterous voices of the other men and women had grown infinitely smaller. A thread had spun between her and me. A thin, tenuous thread, tied one end to her and one end to me, taut. It vibrated, ever so slightly. I believe it was red, like her dress. I could have touched it, but I'm sure it would have broken if I had because it was so delicate, like spider's silk.

"We just got into port this morning," I told her. "We're only staying a few days this time, but we'll be coming back."

We talked a little about nothing and something. She asked me about my voyages and travels and if I were a war hero or something.

"We're all heroes. Just ask us," I joked. I was watching her lips purse as they formed words like "book" that rhymed with "duke." She hadn't fondled me or anything, and yet she had touched me.

"Well, are ya?" I heard someone say from the distant periphery. I looked up to see Ricky Young standing over us, repeating his question. "You gonna stay here all day making goo-goo eyes or come with us?"

"You're leaving?"

"We been here a fuckin' hour, man. Where you been?" He took Fatima's hand and shook it saying, "By the way, my name's Ricky B. Young and people call me the Youngster. Maybe you and me will do some business later on, but right now I've got to take Dickie away."

I had to go. You don't separate from your mates when you're on the beach together. Not till the end of the day. It's the buddy system; you take care of your buddies, they take care of you. Nobody comes between you.

I didn't want Ricky or anyone else getting his hands on Fatima. So I paid for her, giving the money to Ohsman, and made arrangements to stay in her room on the upper floor that night. I paid a little extra, too, to keep her from having to work while I was gone. "I'll come back later tonight," I told her. "In the meantime, you've got the day off." She smiled that real smile, with lots of teeth and crinkles at the eyes. I left her with the scent of coconut and clove lingering in my senses.

At eleven o'clock the temperature was still near eighty degrees, and I wore a fine, light sweat as I walked the narrow street that led back to Fatima's place. The palm trees lining the street hung their fronds limply in the moist, windless air.

When I reached the Chung King, it had the only light on Chulia Street still burning. Fatima was sitting on the couch again, the only person in the room. She had changed into a white cotton sarong and was still reading *The Drifters*, slowly, using her dictionary. When she saw me, she marked her place with a ribbon, got up, and smiled. She smiled just as real as before, but this time it was a little smile. Not the broad smile of meeting, but the little kind that says "I know you." In her flat sandals, Fatima reached my collarbone. She had a rich black profusion of hair that hung down her back and over her shoulders. Her most remarkable feature was her skin. It was dark, warm, and lustrous, as though she had been burnished or rubbed with oil.

"Ohsman said you're not going to come but I told to him no. I said he's going to come. Richard will come, I'm sure. Or do you like to be Dick?"

I told her, "For you, I'm Richard," because of her luscious trill of the R.

"Got any more beer here?" I was thirsty after the hot walk. She got a bottle of Anchor out of the cooler, from the bottom, nice and cold. When she turned away to get it, I noticed that her sarong was backless, exposing a vast amount of that beautiful shining skin, the muscles and spine working beneath it.

"I'm putting it on your bill," she said as she wrote it down in the ledger on Ohsman's countertop. "I have something else for you," she told me. "Maybe you were too busy to take your dinner tonight, so I brought you these." From a paper bag, she took out four little pleasantly brown half-moon pastries, each a little larger than an egg. "Curry puffs," she said. "Very popular in my country."

So I sat on the couch where we first met, and I took the little meal that Fatima had saved for me. For such a simple dish, the curry puffs were a remarkably sophisticated marriage of textures, flavors, and aromas: a chewy, crunchy pastry smelling of good oil with shrimp, bean sprouts, and chives bringing together the sea, the shore, and the earth, all knit together in an Indian spice bouquet.

"I didn't know Malayans were fond of curry," I said. "I thought it was an Indian dish."

"My country is many places."

She brought me another beer, a large one. Marking it on the ledger, she asked, "Are you ready to go?"

Her room was neat and spare. A plain wooden floor, two wooden chairs, a wooden table, a dresser, and two double beds that sagged a little. The sheets were clean but had been through many launderings and were wood-ash gray. The whitewashed walls were bare except for a small hanging of some local design. The room itself was large and airy. Double windows opened out onto the courtyard, and I could smell the pungent, musky-sweet flowers outside. As I pulled up a chair, Fatima handed me a bottle opener and a single glass.

"None for you?" I asked.

"No, thank you. Do you want to relax a little?"

"Yeah, yeah, I will," and I took off my shoes and put my feet on the bed. As she took off her earrings and sandals I asked, "Where did you learn English?"

"Convent school. At home, in Malacca."

"You're Catholic?"

"No, Moslem, mother sent me anyway."

"How long?"

"Three years. I'm going to close the light now?"

"Sure." And when she had and it was dark, very dark in that room, I could see the white sarong come off and lie across the other chair as though under its own will. Her dark shape then moved toward the bed and got in, pulling the sheet up to her waist. She was a silhouette, reclining on large pillows and outlined with perfect clarity against the wall. In the darkness of the room, I couldn't tell where her skin and hair met, but her outline looked drawn with ink and a fine pen. Her breasts pointed upward. Her belly rose and fell with her breathing. Her lips moved. I listened. No sound. Yet I could see them move.

I sipped the beer for a few moments as she lay still. Then, looking up from my glass, I saw that she was facing me, her head propped up on one hand.

"Tell me about your family, Fatima," I asked.

Fatima was tracing circles on the mattress with her palm. "I have my mother, in Malacca. Sometimes I visit her, or send her some money."

"What about the others?"

"No others." A pause, then she said, "Will you come to bed to me now?"

I hesitated. I was suddenly afraid. I didn't know of what. Of Fatima? How could that be? I had paid the fare, she was mine, I could do what I liked. What's to be nervous about? It was that smile that said, "I know you." I heard it in her voice. It was black in that room, but she could see me. I felt a little like I wanted to hide.

At length I brought my hand up to her face. With it, I began to trace the line of her jaw, just with my fingertips. With the back of my index finger, I felt her lips. They were full and bow-shaped. I crooked my finger. The knuckle pressed against her lips, and they parted. My curved finger slid into her mouth, her teeth scraping against it, and she bit down, almost hard. The pressure shot through my whole body. Finger and groin throbbed. Gut shivered.

I uncrooked the finger, and she let it go, sliding out wet. I crooked my middle finger and returned, into her mouth. She bit. Harder. Hard enough that I pulled, and she didn't release. I pulled harder, and her head came off the pillow, my body came off the sheet, and I pulled myself atop her as her legs parted. Her body took mine, I uncrooked my finger, and she released it. And I was one with her.

Her hands were on my shoulders, and I could feel her long nails against my skin. Her knees were bent, the soles of her feet against my legs; my face in her billow of coconut-scented hair. Then, before I began to move, the muscles of her vagina twitched, then flexed and gripped. It felt like five warm fingers, each gripping after the other. And that was a way of speaking. She didn't need to make that effort. She might have lain there, quite still, her mind in some cool, other place. It was her prerogative. But she didn't.

Again her body spoke, and almost imperceptibly her hips began to rock. It spoke again. She was saying, "Enjoy. You paid."

About the axis of our bodies, the universe slowly rolled and brought the pillow softly to my head. Fatima's body released mine and gave it back to me. My breath, for a while, came in deep, even drafts. Her fingers twined and untwined through my hair, and they said, "There. There, mariner. There. And now sleep, for that too comes with the price. It's all in our bargain. And there's a bargain for you." Though I had no sea to rock me, I didn't wake till morning.

Before leaving Fatima for the ship I gave her the price of her time for the coming day and night. "Here," I said. "Check yourself out and pay Ohsman when he comes in. I'll be back as soon as I can."

Things were slow on board, and I finished at ten o'clock. I had worn civvies the day before, but I thought that Fatima might like to see me in uniform. She had asked about my military career. So I put on my best dress whites with new ribbons. The suit itself was custom-tailored in Hong Kong and I had one of those belt buckles with the shop's logo on it.

She did like it. She grinned hugely when she saw me come into the Chung King. She took my arm and turned me around for a good look-see. She was in black jeans and the usual sandals. She wore a magenta blouse made from wrinkly cotton from India.

The day before, I had had a tour of all the bars on the island. This day she was going to show me its less-sordid side. We saw a pedicab whose driver, an old, short, wiry Malay, was lounging outside the house. Fatima negotiated the fare, in Malayan, telling where she wanted him to take us. We got in, and the wizened little man began laboring down the road.

We went to a curio stall where I was looking at some odds and ends when I noticed her buying something. She took out her wallet and found two old, nicked and dull coins, one copper, one aluminum I think, and paid the seller for two iron-on patches in the shape of a Levi's hip pocket. They each bore the logo of Camel cigarettes. She was vastly pleased with them and insisted on paying for them herself; I tried to buy them for her, but she said no, thank you.

Back in her room that evening, I sat in the same chair sipping beer while Fatima was in the shower. I could hear the muffled voices of the people downstairs as they partied. She came into the room wrapped in a thin cotton towel that clung moistly to her body. At the top, her nipples protruded against it, and at the bottom it conformed closely to her mons. I could see the impression of the thin, dark hairs there. Her glossy skin shone with moisture. She hadn't wet the hair of her head, but it was disheveled and so thick, so long and wild that it looked like a lion's mane. She was so beautiful it made me ache. I knew that if I spoke just then that my voice would crack. I felt seasick, but without the nausea.

As she knelt to put away her shower kit in a lower drawer, she noticed my attention on her. She stopped what she was doing and exchanged gazes with me. Then she came over to me and stood next to the chair. With the long nail of her forefinger, she began to comb through one of my ear-length sideburns. She moved to the hair on my arm, and stroked it, tugged lightly on it, combed her nails through it.

At that moment I felt honored by Fatima, the port girl. I swear I couldn't move for fear I would disintegrate. That's when she kissed me. She put her arms around my shoulders and pressed her face against the side of mine, then kissed and inhaled through her nose sharply to take in my scent. I had read about that way of kissing in Malaya, but I had never seen it. She did it again. And again.

Prostitutes don't kiss their clientele. It's just not done. It's an unwritten code of conduct. They may perform any act, natural or unnatural, but they don't kiss. One reason is that many of the clients don't want a whore to kiss them. But even more than that, kissing is reserved for affection. It's the one thing she doesn't sell. She has to have something to give, after all. Everybody has to have something to give. What good are you without it?

But maybe Fatima didn't see it that way. Her eyes were dancing at me just like that first time we met such a long day and night ago. She sat on the bed as she retucked her towel, keeping her modesty. She laid her hands on my outstretched legs, unthinkingly gripping and ungripping them. She kneaded them, all the while her eyes dancing at me, dancing. The muscles in her jaw clenched and relaxed, clenched and relaxed. Her liquid eyes came to a tense stop, locking on mine, and her hands held tightly. She was a wound-up spring. Then her face began to soften and her grip to weaken. Suddenly she exhaled a smile and let go of me. She laughed. I smiled. And we embraced. And I kissed her.

The world was exceedingly, quietly alive when I awoke. Outside the first raven squawked. A pedicab driver chimed his little bell and another answered him from farther off. A pushcart clattered its way to the open market. And Fatima, her face hidden beneath her hair, was just beginning to draw deeper, waking breaths.

As I was dressing she sat up, covering herself only partially now, and looked at me through sleep-narrowed eyes above a subtle, satisfied smile. A cat with a mouthful of canaries. I smiled. My shoes had gotten kicked under the bed, so I sat on the floor next to it to reach them and put them on. Fatima suddenly loomed over me on hands and knees and barked a sharp, triumphant animal sound. A beast of prey saying "Gotcha!" She grinned, exposing all of her white canines.

It was the first time I had seen her naked in the light. Her lion's mane fell around her face and neck and shoulders and down her back. Her limbs were spread out, her hind section cocked slightly back, ready to spring. "Yes, you are a lion," I thought. "A bronze lion. Not a lioness but a lion woman. You're a griffin, you're a sphinx. You're a mythical creature."

Getting to my feet, I suddenly realized that in forty-eight hours I would be leaving. I began to miss her already. "Fatima, listen," I said, rubbing my ear as she got out of bed and wrapped the sheet around herself, togalike. "How would you like it if we go somewhere else tonight, to stay? Someplace nice, someplace very nice."

"To stay for all night? In a very good room?" she trilled.

"The best!"

"With air conditioner?"

"Yes! The best place in all Penang. What is it?"

"No, that's E & O." That was only for fine folks.

"Then it's E & O." She looked a little pensive, and I figured it was concern that she'd be seen and thrown out or otherwise embarrassed. "Don't worry," I said. "Here's what we'll do. I'll go get the room and pretend that I'm alone. I'll come tell you what number it is, and you come later, on the sly."

I pulled out my wallet and started counting out the cost of Fatima's time for the rest of my stay.

"Here, take it," and I held it out. She reached out and lightly tapped the back of my hand and withdrew. It was the old Malayan way of polite refusal.

"You go to the hotel," she spoke in a low voice. "Get the room and you can wait me. Ask to somebody to tell me its number. When the house is closed I'm going to come to you."

I looked stupidly at her and at the money, thinking only in practical terms. "But you'll have to work."

"I'm going to tell to Ohsman that I have a woman sickness."

"Ah. Yeah, sure. I should have thought of it myself," I said with a wink, dropping the money into her purse. She reached in and gave it back to me. She wrapped my hand around it, held that in her two hands and said, "I'm going to come to you."

I had a lot of things to do on board that day, so I wasn't able to get away till the afternoon. As soon as possible, Ricky Young and I went to the E & O and I got a room fronting the beach. It ran about $100 Malaysian (roughly US$20 at that time). Ricky agreed to tell Fatima which one.

After dinner at the E & O, I walked along the beach to my room. The moon was rising and glittering over the sea to the west. The ocean seemed to sigh contentedly. The moist, warm equatorial breeze ran ahead of me as if to lead the way.

In temperate zones the wind always seems cold and violent. It's something that strikes you, stings your ears and fingers, and makes your nose red and runny. It's out to blow away your newspaper, deposit leaves on your lawn or dust in your eyes.

But in the tropics, the wind is a woman. A sensuous, lascivious woman who titillates your nerve endings and whispers in your ear. It is Aphrodite.

I entered my room and called room service for coffee. After it was served, I sat down to sip and to wait. Just as she said she would, a little after midnight, Fatima tapped on the sliding glass door that opened onto the beach. I slipped the door open and the breeze billowed in, carrying her coconut and clove scent. Wisps of her black hair reached up and touched my face. She looked up at me and smiled a little nervously. I kissed her lightly on the lips, and she pressed her face against my neck and smell-kissed me, in the Malayan way.

"Did anyone see you come?" I asked as she entered the room.

"No. I came around the back."

She wore a red batik sarong *kebaya*.

"You have been swimming?" she asked, pointing to the swimsuit I had changed into.

"No, but I thought you and I might go. It's such a warm night."

"But I have nothing to wear."

Raising my brows and smiling, I asked, "Have you ever heard of skinny-dipping?"

"Skin dipping?"

"No. Skinny-dipping."

"Mmmmm, no," she said cautiously. "This is something from America?"

"It's going swimming with nothing on," I grinned conspiratorially.

"Oh. Well, anyway, I don't swim."

"Well, you don't have to swim. You can just play in the water. That's why we don't call it skinny-swimming."

"You do this?" she asked, looking at me askance.

"Of course. Everybody does," I said, turning out the light.

"Women too?"

I climbed out of my suit and picked up a towel.

She looked out to the beach to see if anyone was there, then quietly slipped out of her sarong. I looked up and down the beach. Satisfied that we were still alone, I took her hand, and we walked past the palms, where the breeze whispered in the fronds, toward the gentle Indian Ocean surf. In the light of the full moon, her darkness stood out against the white, sandy beach. The luster of her skin caught the moonlight and reflected it so that she looked like a luminous shadow. We stood there for a while and felt the sensuous breeze caress our bare bodies with its humid fingers.

We waded into the dark, silky sea and played and splashed and spoke in laughing whispers. The water glistened as it ran down her face and hair in rivulets. It made a sheen on her breasts, and I tasted the salt on her nipples. The moon was so bright I could see into her eyes, and I looked into them, holding her shoulders, for a long moment. She gave a little laugh, and the breeze echoed it high up in the palms. We walked arm in arm to a place under a palm and lay down. I nuzzled my head against hers and smelled the sea in her wet hair, long, thick, and black, clinging in arabesques to her brown face and shoulders. She bit my arm gently. The sand gave way like pillows beneath our bodies. Warm flesh melded. The moon peered mischievously through the palm fronds and the breeze; Aphrodite, flowed warmly over us.

When it was very late, we went back to the room to sleep a little.

The sun was up, and Fatima woke with a start. Her motion woke me and I heard her give a little cry. I opened my eyes to see her dressing hurriedly.

"What's the matter?"

"I have to go," she said tersely. Then under her breath, "Already I will get five slaps."

"Huh? What?"

"Nothing."

"No, wait a minute. You said five slaps. What do you mean five slaps?"

"Five slaps of the face," she said, looking in the mirror.

"Why are you going to get 'five slaps of the face'? And who the hell is going to give them to you?"

"Ohsman, of course," she replied, quickly brushing her hair.

"Ohsman? Tang's errand boy?"

"Ohsman is Mr. Tang's manager of the house." She seemed surprised at me.

"So why is Ohsman going to slap you?" I demanded as I got out of bed.

"Because I left the house without permission."

I stood staring at her, not wanting to comprehend.

"We're not supposed to leave without getting permission," she explained. "Especially for visiting a man. I have to go now."

She turned to the door but I caught her by the arm, pulled her back to me, and said, "Now wait a minute! Just wait a minute. You mean to tell me that he's just going to go ahead and hit you, slap you, five times?"

Seeing that I was getting upset, she tried to calm me. "Oh, don't worry. He's not going to hit me hard. If he does, then I will be ugly, and nobody will want me. He's only going to do it for the noise."

"I don't believe I'm hearing this! Listen, I don't care what that bastard's intentions are. I'm going there with you, and if he feels like slapping somebody, he can try it on me. Then we'll see what he gets for his trouble!"

"No! If you go to see Ohsman it's only going to be worse for me. Please...no...you stay here, Richard. It's our rule. I broke the rule. It's all right. I wanted to see you for a while, so I came here. I know the rule. So, all right, please, stay here."

"No! I won't. A guy who slaps women around needs to get some of it himself. Listen now, don't you worry. He's not going to touch you as long as I'm there."

"But you're not going to be there always! You're going to leave with your ship. And you don't have to worry. And maybe you don't come back." Her eyes were misty and she said, "And maybe you come back and you want another girl. Then I'm alone with Ohsman. And he tells Mr. Tang, and he will make me leave the house. Then they're going to tell everybody that I make trouble, and I won't get another job, so stay here. You have to stay!"

She picked up her bag and went out into the hot morning, down the beach, without turning back, her five-foot, red-clad frame moving slowly home to Ohsman. I stood there, naked, looking after her.

Slowly, realization sank in. "Oh my God. Oh no, no. Fatima, I'm sorry. I didn't realize. I didn't think."

At four in the afternoon, I opened the Chung King's door loudly. Ohsman was at his counter. Fatima was standing near the other girls. They all looked my way as I came in. I looked aside at Ohsman, and he glowered at me, his sour mouth puckered up like a prune. Yeah, he was pissed; we had cheated him out of a few bucks. I locked eyes with Fatima and slowly walked toward her. She stood rock still. She was wearing her white sarong, the backless one, and was ready for work. I could feel Ohsman's eyes on me as I passed him. I refused to acknowledge him, but his glare was boring a hole in my head anyway. Nearing Fatima, I looked for signs of violence against her and so far saw none. "He couldn't have hit her. He wouldn't. No way." Then it occurred to me that he could have hit her on the back of the head, or somewhere on her body.

In her left eye, the little weblike blood vessels were broken. The eye was bloodshot. I looked closely for marks on her face and there were none, but the texture of the skin on her left cheek was different. It had no luster. It was dull, about a hand's width, and it wasn't smooth. She saw that I had seen and looked at the floor.

He had hit her. The son of a bitch had hit her. My mind cried out. Anger pumped up my chest. My hands made fists without my bidding them to. Arm muscles throbbed, bicep, tricep, and forearm. Power trembled in them. I would break something in him. "I'll break his face! I'll hit him in the gut, and I'll open up his face. And if I can't do it alone, I'll get some guys, and we'll all stomp the shit out of him."

I jerked my head his way. He looked at me, his gaze unwavering. The wrinkles of his mouth shifted over to one side, and it curled itself into a tiny, scornful smile. My chest heaving, I realized that if I made a move on Ohsman, he'd just call the cops. He'd probably dealt with guys like me before. Maybe he even had a weapon. And even if I did slug him and get away with it, he would simply take it out on Fatima.

I turned back to Fatima, realizing that I was causing a scene and embarrassing her. But I was still angry, and yet unable to take action on it because it would just come back on her. I thought, "I'll give her some money," but I couldn't do that either. That pig Ohsman would just take it away from her, saying she owed it to him. "Damn!" My ears started to ring. "I'll have Sam bring her the money in an envelope," I thought. "With a note, a letter."

What the hell else could I do? Take her on board as a stowaway? Send her a monthly allowance for life? Float her a big loan or send her home to my mother? I couldn't help her. I couldn't do one stinking, infinitesimal fucking thing! It was her life, and she was stuck in it.

There was a groan or a cry in me wanting to get out, when Fatima reached out toward me and said shyly, "I want to see you again." Her long-nailed fingers reached my abdomen and traced five lines down my shirt. My insides screamed at her touch, "What the hell's the matter with you?" I thought. "Don't you have any buddy system? Don't you have any rights? Don't you have anything?"

Tears were rising up from the bottom. They would soon be at my eyes. I couldn't let that happen in front of Ohsman. Or in front of Fatima, for they were coming to her also.

I took a step back and croaked, "Well, we're leaving in the morning, you know."

"Wait," she said, and grabbed her purse and dug through it. It didn't take long, there wasn't much in it. She drew out those two Camel patches that she had fancied so much. "Here." She handed them to me, sniffling and trying to smile. "For a little remembrance," she said, rolling the R.

I swallowed and took them, forcing my hand not to shake. I took another step backward. Holding the patches in one hand, I waved a few fingers at her with the other, then turned, kind of half-saluted, and left while I had time. On the way out, I heard human sounds through the buzzing in my ears, but I don't know what they were.

I walked out onto the street. The sun was dropping, and I walked toward it. The esplanade lay in that direction; there was privacy in a large space. All the colors of Penang swirled around me: people in their batiks, gaudy pedicabs, pushcarts, dogs, ravens, jade dealers, money changers, all coming, going, doing, being—a maelstrom of people, colors, sounds and smells. I was nearing the esplanade, and the tears were making a movie on my remembering eyes. In it was Fatima, dressed in her white sarong, the backless one, ready for work, and the next man; a bruised eye; and Ohsman.

N EW DELHI IS UGLIER THAN BANGKOK; DIRTIER than Mexico City; duller than Detroit; smokier than L.A.; more crowded than Tokyo; possessed of merchants, beggars, and touts more exasperating than Saigon; and drier than Salt Lake City on Election Day—and I don't mean for lack of rain.

The night I arrived I couldn't find a bottle of beer in this Hindu and Muslim town to save my Christian soul. I knew the sons of the Prophet looked down on suds, but I didn't know the followers of Krishna were teetotalers. I came to learn that the Hindus regard alcohol, narcotics, tobacco, and a host of more innocuous things as pollution of the body. Spiritual advancement requires them to keep pure.

Well, fine. All very nice. I can respect their point of view (I don't have to like it to respect it). But it became very painful for me to bear when, day after day, I watched them breathe the Delhi air, drink water that would fell a moose, eat fly-be-speckled sugar candy by the pound, and walk blithely barefoot through acres of excrement—and then pronounce from lofty moral heights that the brewer's art is pollution.

I finally managed to locate a couple of restaurants that serve beer. But patrons who imbibe are seated in a separate room, a sort of beer opium den, so that women and children will not see their wickedness and be offended. You have to be twenty-five to buy alcohol. Other than in the few restaurants, it's sold in special nondescript stores called "Wine & Beer Shops," though I've never seen wine for sale in them, and beer seems to move slowly. The chief article of commerce here is "Indian-Made Foreign Liquor." Faux Scotch, fake gin, and wannabe brandy are sold by surly, middle-aged louts who slam the bottle on the counter, take your money, and wave you off like a pesky fly. Believe me, I know. The miscreants don't even give you a bag. You are expected to walk out onto the street displaying your depraved desire to pollute your body for all to see and to shun you for a reprobate or a foreigner. I am sure the storekeepers are agents of the government. I took to carrying my own bag. I got a very nice (and big) one, bearing the logo of a well-known silk merchant. I hope his family will not be defamed.

And the liquor sellers are not the worst of the lot! If I were an ax murderer, I'd come to New Delhi and kill shopkeepers and touts. They are a plague. Walk through a bazaar or shopping arcade and they will literally block your path. Using one arm to gather you in and one to point the way, they all say, "Yes, sir. Yes, sir. Please take a look in my shop." An entire row of shopkeepers can witness you dodging their grasp, protesting that you don't want anything, then each one in succession will waylay you hoping that by the time you reach his turf your will to resist will be broken.

I found that if you simply keep walking, as though they aren't there, they get out of your way just before the moment of physical contact. For a while I found that gratifying, walking through squads of merchants, parting them like water. I later discovered that if you speed up just before the moment they part it takes them quite by surprise, and they do a very funny dance in order to stay on their feet. Sometimes they just go down with a splat. I find this excellent sport, and have dubbed it Indian Tag: "Boom, you're it."

Yet for all this, the most beautiful woman, or woman to be, I've ever seen lives in this the ugliest city in all the world. I first saw her while sitting in an open motorcycle rickshaw stuck in the New Delhi traffic. In the corner of my eye I saw a small form dash up to the vehicle from the curb. She pushed an open palm up to me and uttered a request for alms. I had already given that morning, and though I would fain give more, I limit myself to one beggar a day, lest I become one, too. So I tried to ignore her, but she persisted, constantly repeating her plea like a mantra and never lowering her outstretched hand. I was finally moved to annoyance, and looked down to tell her to bug off.

She was only about eight years old, and thoroughly begrimed from head to foot. She wore a dress of tatters and rags, and no shoes. Her unkempt, unwashed hair clung to the sides of her face. She was so beautiful I nearly gasped, and sat transfixed as I comprehended such an incongruous visage. I don't know if she was beautiful in spite of, or because of, her condition. Perhaps if she had been washed and combed and dressed like a schoolgirl she would have been merely pretty.

Her features were flawless and symmetrical, and she had the bodily grace of a dancer as she moved back and forth across the filthy pavement, and her upturned palm with its long, expressive fingers could have been the model for a Hindu sculpture. A raw wildness emanated from her, and despite all the dirt, she possessed a purity of substance. Her large eyes met mine in a way that made me know she was unafraid, and my equal.

A few feet away, on the emission-choked sidewalks, her people lived in a permanent camp, their open hearths and belongings squeezed into any space available. Women nursed their too many babies, and cooked over smoldering fires of dung provided by the innumerable sacred cows. Men sorted through usable trash gleaned from nearby heaps. Everywhere was excrement, filth, squalor; a palpable ugliness covered with flies. "Karma," they call it.

The traffic light turned green. Engines began to rev, yet still I had not responded to the shockingly beautiful girl. My driver released his brake, shifted into first gear, and still I stared. Just as the vehicle began to move, the girl's eyes, those big, luminous, arresting eyes, flashed with fire and anger. Her face contorted with indignation, almost imperious. And at the last possible moment, just before we sped away, her low mantra voice rose in pitch as she spat out a curse, and she doubled up her little fist and slugged me smack on the thigh! For two seconds I was stunned by her audacity. But as I watched her recede into the distance, glaring at me as I rode away, I had to smile. "Good for you, sweetheart," I thought. "Good for you."

As we rounded a corner and she was lost to view forever I felt the presence of Fatima. And that was a comfort. For I know that no matter how big the world and how small her fire Fatima will never let it die. Though she have but one Promethean spark she will nurture it. And so will the New Delhi girl. I saw it in her eyes. I felt it in her fist.

10 *My Holy Grail*

 Halfway down the Pacific coast of Baja
California, accessible only by four-wheel drive or
high clearance truck, lies the beach of Malarrimo.
It's the northwest side of a cape that juts out, sickle-shaped,
into the Humboldt current, harvesting the flotsam and jetsam
of all the wide Pacific Ocean. Junk from as far away as Japan
washes up on this shore. Beautiful blown-glass fishing floats
and styrofoam packing crates; cedarwood boxes and the remnants of plastic gill nets; and once in a while a message in a
bottle thrown into the sea by some romantic soul cruising the
South Sea Isles.

It used to be that the stuff would pile up knee-deep on the
beach. But ever since locals learned that gringos have an interest in it, gleaners have been working the beach and selling
their harvest to those who make the off-road trip. What is astonishing to me is that here in this faraway and isolated place
is testimony to the vastness of the world. The detritus of half
the planet can be found here, and I can wander this beach
reading its messages just as an archeologist reads the messages
in the ash heaps of history.

We call this a global village. We speak of this orb as a speck of dust spinning around a minor star at the edge of a rather ordinary galaxy. Such inverse hubris. Malarrimo shouts out the largeness of the globe. The infinite variety of its peoples. The astonishing distances measured in human terms. Malarrimo says to me that no matter how deep I dig, I will only scratch the surface. And I say it's a powerful itch, and so I scratch!

"Fire is sacred to all the Rajputs, but especially to the desert people," Prayag Singh said to me. "It burns within us, and never dies."

"Is that why you say you have the hottest chilies in all of India?" I asked jokingly.

"Yes," he said with a straight face. "You will see, perhaps, tonight in the village." He spurred his camel to a quicker pace, and we followed suit, eager to reach the village of Samrau before dark. We had been warned that "naughty men" sometimes roam the caravan trails at night. It seems the Spice Road has always attracted its share of the unsavory.

I was in Rajasthan, northwestern India with my cohorts, the brothers Paul and Bruce Harmon. The ancient fortress of Jodhpur was far behind us and we had just mounted the high dunes of the Great Indian Desert in a quest for fire and spice, and history, and for a fine and mad goal I had taken on during a stopover in Thailand.

"You won't believe it," Sven Kraus had said. Sven was a Swiss-trained chef at a Bangkok hotel. "I was working in Saudi Arabia," he continued. "There was a wedding of some sheik or other. And you won't believe what they wanted me to cook."

I knew in my gut, in my gastronomic soul, that what I had long hoped was true. That it wasn't just some wild traveler's tale designed to stir the imagination and not the pot. The ultimate cookout was a reality. The only thing that could possibly be greater would be to spit-roast a T. Rex. My wildest culinary dream could come true. Sven, Allah bless him and may his tribe increase, had done it.

"I tell you no lie," he went on, sipping a cold one. "They wanted camel. I roasted a whole camel on a spit."

He told me how it took twenty-four hours to cook, and that he served it on a silver platter in the shape of a recumbent camel. He related how the tribesmen who were the sheik's guests then attacked it en masse with their knives, feasted with their bare hands, and ate the meat down to the ivory.

"Sven, I'm going to Rajasthan in India. There lives the largest camel herd in the world. I intend to roast me one of them. I'll give a great feast to the Rajputs. I'll invite all the local potentates and nabobs and other Indian poobahs. Tell 'em to bring their families and harems and seventh sons. This is the Holy Grail for me, Sven. This is my golden fleece, my windmill to topple. Bless me, Sven, you who have done this mighty deed."

And now I would try it. And why not here?

Across this desert and across the centuries have traveled the camel caravans that carried the luxuries of the East: silk and myrrh, gemstones, medicines and ointments, gold, and those commodities that were worth their weight in gold—spices.

I was here in India on a quest that would take me, ultimately, around the globe in search of these ancient routes. How many men down through the millennia have traversed this same track, by these same means, for these same interests? Tens of thousands? Hundreds of thousands? I'll never know. But I know that fortunes and lives have been spent in the journey. The fates of individuals, armies, even nations have passed over these mountains of drifting sand on the way to Jaisalmer and beyond. In A.D. 410 Alaric laid seige to Rome, and was persuaded to depart with a ransom that included 3,000 pounds of pepper. India was the only source of pepper in those days. Was Alaric's ransom transported over the same ground on which I now hurried my camel to beat the night's approach? The Byzantine empress Theodora regularly imported silks and spices of all kinds from India. Did her goods pass this way? Did the myrrh delivered at Christ's birth come from here, and perhaps the wise man who carried it?

Here in Rajasthan I had come to follow in the tracks of those innumerable traders, soldiers, merchants, and "naughty men" who through the ages made the Spice Road the ancient superhighway. And here in Rajasthan was the India I had most longed to see: the India that came into being as the waystations of that rich, old route. Not the twenty-first century nuclear power, nor the Third Word famine threatening to happen. Not the remnants of the British Raj, the Himalayas, or the Taj Mahal. But the India where past glory lives in the present day and proceeds to the future; where both echoes and new voices commingle; where the descendents of horse- and camel-mounted warriors remember the passionate songs of their grandfathers and still wear antique swords to formal occasions, and turbans every day. A place that has seen civilizations come and go, conquerers rise and fall, and yet the world makes only those impressions upon her that she chooses. A place where a visit to the spice bazaar is as common as a visit to the grocer.

The hilltop fortress of Jodhpur could have made a backdrop for *The Man Who Would Be King*. The battlements rise straight up from the crown of the hill like a Persian-inspired acropolis. Crenelated and carved with arabesques it is a jewel in the desert. Below it nestles the famous "Blue City." The aromas of cardamom, clove, cinnamon, and pepper floating up upon the sounds from the market bespeak the spice-laden caravans that have passed this way for centuries. In the medieval square a dancing girl dripping with bangles and swathed in flowing robes did her wild, fiery Rajput dance. She teased the eye and whispered, "Baksheesh, Sahib, baksheesh." Baksheesh is loosely translated as "tip" and Sahib as "my lord." The word Sahib is pronounced "Saab," like the car, not "Saheeb" as it is in so many B movies about India.

To steal a look into the loosely veiled faces of these darkling women is to see back as far as human experience. And yet they are a mystery. Theirs is a deep darkness like night and the unknowable. I found myself ogling them, searching for something familiar or revealing. But that delicious dark mystery still remained. In all of Rajasthan I did not see one woman in modern dress. City dwellers and country girls alike wear brilliantly colored saris and festoon themselves with gold and silver jewelry, and paint their sacred markings upon their brows. At least half go barefoot and wear rings on their toes and chains on their ankles. Fantastic gold filigree stretches from their nostrils to their earlobes in chains, disks, and charms.

While many of the women might be called handsome or statuesque, few would be called pretty by our current Nordic-inspired standards. They tend to be heavy, especially in the middle. Even virgins and old women look pregnant. Of course many of the women are, or have been recently. And a big belly is still a status symbol in a land where hunger resides in living memory.

A family of musicians entertained us on the grounds of a temple. The man played a stringed instrument, the woman sang through her half-opened veil and the two daughters, ages four and six, danced. For this they earned thirty-three cents. The mother was hauntingly, disturbingly beautiful, and I couldn't tear my gaze away from her. I put on my sunglasses and gawked at her obliquely, so as not to upset her. As she sang for her supper, and that of her children, I admired her unusually lithe and slim body. It came home to me with special poignancy that when you don't know where your next meal is coming from an ample belly is good security.

It was in Jodhpur that we met Prayag Singh. His people are camel breeders and drovers from Jaisalmer, near the border with Pakistan, and he agreed to help us organize a caravan to his hometown and be our guide and interpreter. We had planned to camp along the way but Prayag advised against it, as did everyone we spoke to, citing, as I mentioned, the "naughty men."

"We can stay in the villages," he told us. "The desert people are most hospitable. They may ask us for a token to sleep in their houses, but they will feed us for nothing."

"Spicy food?"

"Very spicy. With the hottest chilies in all of India. Perhaps it will be too hot for you."

"Not bloody likely! While we're on the subject, how long have the Rajputs been using chili?"

"Maybe two or three hundred years. They came to us from a place far to the South. When our ancestors first tasted them they thought it was a gift from the fire god. Fire is sacred to us as is the camel."

"The camel?"

"We are Hindu. But in the desert there are now cows, so we revere the camel."

"You don't eat them?"

He just looked at me as though I were mad. Damn! That was one goal that would have to wait.

We secured camels for the four of us (for riding only) and the services of two drovers to help along the way. Prayag taught us how to tie a Rajput turban and we costumed ourselves accordingly. We left Jodhpur on a cloud of music, excitement, and spicy aromas.

Our second day out we drove the camels hard in our attempt to reach Samrau before dark. The land smoothed out and we made good time, raising the village on the horizon with plenty of time to spare. As we approached the village we came upon a goatherd who tended a flock of about twenty. His name was Naglaman. He was amazed to see three camel-mounted foreigners and with grand gestures invited us to tea. As we dismounted he disappeared into a little shelter he had made of twigs and desert scrub, and reemerged with his "tea service": one battered old pot, two metal cups of different origins, and a couple of desert palm leaves. The leaves he tore into pieces, then folded expertly into conical cups, disposable and biodegradable.

Over tea mixed with wild honey and goat's milk I asked Prayag what we could expect for dinner in Samrau that night. "*Chapatis*," he said. *Chapatis* are unleavened flatbread made from wheat or, among the desert people, millet.

"Of course. Anything else?" I asked.

"Oh yes. Vegetables."

"Just like the last one. Are the desert people vegetarians?"

"No no. But they eat meat only on special occasions, because it is very dear."

"How dear? For instance, how much would one of these goats here cost?"

I settled with Naglaman the goatherd for 400 rupees (US$12.50 at the time) for his fattest kid. He was very pleased with the bargain until I said, "But I gotta have a receipt. It's a business expense." His smile faded when Prayag translated. "It's not that I don't trust you," I said. "It's just that I have to keep careful records or the taxman will complain."

"But, Sahib, I don't know how to write," he said, and looked at the ground.

"Oh. I see." I took out my pen and notebook and said, "I'll write it out for you and all you'll have to do is sign it." I wrote it out and handed it to him saying, "There. Just sign your name. Can you do that for me?"

He looked even lower, and lowly said, "I don't know how to write my name, Sahib."

I felt like I had just stripped the man naked and whipped him through the streets. Prayag was speaking to him softly in Marwati, his native tongue, when an idea came to me. "Naglaman," I said, "my great grandfather couldn't write either. But he would sign documents with his thumb. If I ink your thumb with this felt pen can you sign the receipt that way?"

The idea that he, an illiterate, nomadic goatherd could actually sign an official document suddenly raised his spirits, pumped up his chest, and put the smile back on his face. Raising my pen I said, "Let's have your thumb." He stuck it eagerly in my face. I inked it well, making sure to cover it all, while he looked on with something approaching wonder. I then held the notebook for him and he painstakingly rolled his thumb onto the paper. Prayag wrote across the thumbprint, first in Marwati and then in English, "Naglaman: his mark." The goatherd was now an honorary member of the order of letters.

I tethered the goat to my camel and we mounted and rode on into the tiny village. Our arrival caused quite a stir, though a happy one. We were conducted to a shade tree to sit and relax while the village headman was summoned. A group of villagers sat around us and we chatted with them through the voice of Prayag. One of them pointed to me and said something that caused them all to giggle. Prayag reported that the villager had pointed out that among the desert people the color of my turban was the traditional color for widows' weeds. The villager jokingly asked if I were a widow. I said, "No. But just like a widow I have no husband." If any ice needed breaking, that did the trick.

Soon the headman arrived and we were formally welcomed, told where we might sleep if we cared to stay, and invited to share their dinner. The headman's name was long and difficult for us to pronounce, but we were invited to address him as "Baba," a term both affectionate and respectful, rather like "Uncle." He called us all "Sahib." All the while the people had been hungrily eyeing my goat, which Bruce and Paul had nicknamed "Jimmy."

"Why Jimmy?" I asked.

"We call any animal we kill and eat Jimmy."

"Then call him Jimmy the camel."

"Prayag. Tell Baba that everyone is invited to the feast of Jimmy. As long as they agree to teach me how to cook him in their traditional way."

The unexpected feast threw everyone into a flurry of preparation. The women went immediately to work in the communal kitchen preparing *chapatis* and vegetables, which they cooked over a slow-burning fire of dried camel dung. Men gathered firewood and set up a kitchen and dining area in a wattle-and-daub enclosure that opened out onto the central yard. Prayag introduced us to a man in a bright yellow turban, explaining that he would cook the meat. "Only men may cook meat," he told us. "This man will teach you his way." We called the man "Yellow Hat."

In a far corner of the yard, near where our drovers were feeding the camels, some men were laying down a pile of twigs and straw, and scraping a wide, shallow depression in the ground next to the pile. Baba appeared before us bearing a long, heavy, and ancient looking sword. Two men led the goat into the depression where he began to munch on the straw. "The purpose of the straw is not for him to eat," Prayag explained, "but to prevent the blood from touching the earth."

"Who will kill the goat?" Baba asked, holding forth the sword. "It must be done properly, according to the ritual we call *Jhatka*. I will teach him."

"Bruce," I said, "you're the strongest among us. Kill me this goat."

Baba gave Bruce a lesson in the proper use of a Rajput sword and the *Jhatka* ceremony of slaughter. He led him to the goat, and all stood quiet as he intoned a brief prayer. Bruce raised his powerful arm, the big sword flashed, and the goat never felt a thing. The feast was on.

As Yellow Hat, wielding a Ghurka knife, did the butchering, some men spread a layer of earth about two feet wide in the enclosure, set a pile of sticks for a fire on top of it, and placed a circle of rocks around that. On top of it they set a brass cooking pot with a concave lid. From somewhere a bottle of white lightning appeared and it was being passed around, leaving a trail of broad grins in its wake. When it reached me I took a long pull, and to my surprise it didn't taste half bad. It burned on the way down, but I like that. "The fire burns within me," I joked to Prayag.

"And here it never dies," he said, again with that straight face.

When Yellow Hat had finished the butchering and had the meat and organs arranged in a tub, he summoned me to follow him into the enclosure. From a wooden chest he took out his ingredients and through Prayag he spoke. "I'm cooking this goat in the way of all the desert people. We use the spices that the caravans have always carried, and the red chili powder. We grow the chili in Rajasthan and we use it all in Rajasthan. The caravans have never carried it because other people find it too full of fire."

Another man brought out flint and steel and tinder, and while all the men watched in reverent silence, he kindled the fire. Yellow Hat poured what looked like a pint of red chili powder into a brass bowl. I tasted it, and it was indeed full of fire. It wasn't habañero, but it was still powerful stuff. On top of that he poured half as much turmeric powder. Atop that half as much *garam masala*, then half as much salt. Over the mound he sprinkled a layer of sweet paprika. Then he mixed them all with his gnarly fingers. Into the pot he poured oil and when it was hot threw in a handful of anise seeds and cooked them till they all popped. Then he stirred in his spice mixture with some water.

The liquor bottle made its rounds and some of the men were singing songs of old battles and long rides. Yellow Hat put the meat in the pot but kept the organs aside. He put the concave lid on the pot and filled it with water. When it was well heated he stirred it into the pot. He repeated this process till the dish was done. The liquor bottle was now a dead soldier but his replacement soon reported for duty. A boy brought in several small heads of garlic and Yellow Hat and I peeled and separated them, and using our fists crushed them against a flat stone, then set them aside. As the new bottle made its rounds and jokes and stories circulated, the yellow-toqued *chef de cuisine* laid the organ meats directly on the fire and let them roast, turning them now and then. They were quickly done. He laid them on a plate and sprinkled them with a little of his cooking liquid, then offered me first choice. I used his Ghurka knife to claim half the heart. I also took one Rocky Mountain Oyster. All the turbaned heads nodded their approval at my choice. I wondered what they would have done had I selected some other combination. If I had taken a chitlin' and an eyeball would they have thought me gauche? If I had declined the offer altogether would I have been invited to a duel? Such are the little minefields we tread at foreign tables (or, in this case, the floor).

The last thing Yellow Hat did was to stir in the garlic and some yogurt and let the mixture cook another ten minutes. At about the same time some women arrived bearing the *chapatis* and vegetables. When they noticed that we now had two dead soldiers and one about to die for the cause, they set the food down, drew their veils across their faces, and wordlessly disappeared till morning.

Dinner was served. Each man laid a *chapati* on a brass plate and Yellow Hat dished out the stew upon it. It was fiery stuff, washed down with more local hootch. But I've never eaten more flavorful meat. The spice blend brought out its natural flavor rather than masking it. It made us all break out in a sweat. But we fed richly on the fire.

It was growing late, but Paul, bless him, capped the feast perfectly. From his bag he drew a bottle of California Cabernet Sauvignon. The desert men had heard of wine, but they had never seen the exotic liquid. They gathered closely and with rapt attention listened as Paul let it gurgle into their cups. They sipped it like nectar and sniffed it like roses and pronounced it the most excellent gift to follow the most excellent feast. With full bellies and full hearts, and a pleasant buzz, we all moved close to the fire. We sang a few songs, Marwati and English. We tried to translate jokes, though the effort was funnier than any punchline.

All would rise with the sun, and so the men began to drift away to their homes. Some others brought us travelers *char-*

poys (roughhewn wood and rope beds) and asked where to set them. "Would you like to sleep in here, next to the fire, Sahib?" the headman asked. I looked out into the yard and saw that the night was fine and said I would like to sleep there. Paul thought that was a good idea too, and so two of the beds went outside and the others came inside. Somebody brought blankets, though the night was so warm they seemed useless. A man scooped up half the cooking fire and poured it between the two outside beds.

All was quiet and dark as I lay down, the only light being the cheery glow of the coals that burned by my side. A mist rolled in over the dry, dry desert, a silvery, delicate, gossamer mist. I closed my eyes and let its tingly fingers caress my face. "Are you sleeping, Sahib?" I heard the deep voice of the headman speaking through Prayag.

"No, Baba. It's too pleasant to sleep." I opened my eyes a crack. In the darkness I could make out his white turban, and great white *mustachio* that moved as he spoke again.

"Sahib, from this night, you will be long remembered among the desert people."

"Thank you, Baba."

"Sleep well, Sahib."

The mist thickened. I pulled the blanket over me, not because of cold, but to keep my clothes dry. I thought of pulling it over my head, too. But the mist was like liquid silk and felt good. I slept, waking now and then to luxuriate, till dawn. And despite the ever increasing moisture in the air, and the hours that passed, the fire never died.

11 *M u r d e r e r ' s   E g g s*

WHAT IS IT ABOUT DESERTS THAT DRAWS ME? How is it that the barren places of the earth can be so full of potential? Perhaps because the land itself is so stripped down to its bare minimum, so become we. We have fewer needs, fewer distractions. And so we are better able to see and seek the adventure of life, to embrace it and not let go. And to just have fun.

After leaving the pavement of Baja's transpeninsular highway, I had some trouble locating the arroyo. It was dusk and the features of the land were all beginning to look the same. I made rapid drives up two or three openings in the terrain only to encounter rock walls. Finally, in the last of the light, I recognized a distinctive portion of the skyline of jagged hills up ahead that could lead us through the arroyo and into a valley. Across that valley, another arroyo leads past the remains of a deserted, old *rancho*, then into a canyon where lay the long abandoned Mission San Borja, Lucrezia Borgia's legacy to the New World.

I was traveling with Garrett Culhane and Matt Tully, two friends from school. Matthew is five foot eight, with a beautiful physique and a perfectly silly looking tattoo of a cherub and a crescent moon on his right shoulder. His shoulder-length hair and trim beard are both flame red. His hair is so thick and curly it looks like a seventeenth century cavalier's wig. If he traded his gold-rimmed glasses for a rapier and a dueling pistol the picture would be complete. He's a fun guy, but he tends to forget that there is a tomorrow.

Garrett grew up on a ranch in the California Central Valley, but he looks like he stepped out of an E. M. Forster novel about turn-of-the-century England. He is tall, lean, and angular with black hair and a neat mustache. His jaw juts forward handsomely. His favorite cloth is tweed. He is cerebral and reflective and tends to preface his questions with "Well now, Richard, let me ask you something." He likes to have philosophical conversations that often become so convoluted he gets lost in them. He is also a first-rate mechanic.

Garrett and Matt were behind me in Garrett's rebuilt 1959 Willys jeep, paneled version. I led the way in my four-wheel drive vehicle, the Argo. The normally clear skies were full of January clouds and a mist had risen from the ground. The sun had fully set and the darkness was so dense and so thick it was palpable. It gobbled up my headlight beams in mere yards. The recent annual rains had turned the dry watercourses into gooey bogs and we would have to cross them in the dark. We crept along in low four-wheel drive, keeping in close radio contact.

We had been rolling for over an hour when Matt radioed "Argo, be advised we are overheating."

"Cause?"

"Unknown. Will keep you advised."

Within minutes he called again to say, "Argo, Argo! We've got to stop, we've got to stop, we're redlining!"

"Ten-four," I answered. "I'm coming to help." I judged from the lights in my rear-view mirror that they were about forty or fifty feet behind me, so I cut the engine and hopped out and began walking toward the Willys. The mist was not uniform like a fog; it was a crazy mist, hanging in clumps and swirls with currents of clear air between them. It puffed up from the watercourses and slid down hillsides and curled itself around the cacti and *cirrio* (*Idria columnaris*, also known as the boojum tree) and other solid objects. It made the Willys seem much closer than it really was. I turned around and could no longer see the white form of the Argo.

When I reached the other vehicle the guys had the hood up, and in the reflected light of the headlamps I could see a stream of hot water drizzling down to the ground and making a big, steamy puddle. "Have you isolated the leak yet?" I asked.

"No," Garrett said. "It's almost dry now. We'll have to fill it up and try again. Let me ask you something, do you have plenty of water?"

"Five gallons. But from the look of that stream it won't get us back to the highway."

We filled the radiator and turned on the engine. Water gushed from a broken seam in the radiator's exit port. The damage could hardly have been worse. If it were a broken hose we might have fixed it, as we carried a few spares; but this situation required our removing the radiator and then having it repaired by a welder. The nearest welder was in Guerrero Negro. I would need a full day to get there, a day to have the radiator repaired, and a day to get back. I would have to take Matt with me in case I should have some break-down; or injury; or end up in jail; or who knows what. Garrett would have to keep his own philosophical company in the desert for the next three days. Happy New Year.

Somewhere in the mist a dog barked. "Was that a dog?" Matt asked.

"Must be a coyote," I said. "Got to be a coyote. No dogs out here." The dog barked again. In the headlamp beams a puff of drifting mist began to darken and take form. As it came near it assumed the shape of a man with rifle. A dog shape trotted alongside. When he was still a silhouette he stopped and hefted the rifle in the crook of his arm.

"*¿Quien es?*" he hollered. Who's there?

"*Amigos,*" I answered. "*Hombres que necesitar ayuda. ¿Quien es usted señor?*" Friends. Men who need help. Who are you, sir?

The shape paused. He said something to his dog, who then sat down and licked his chops. He came forward and with each step divested himself of mist. He came to within arm's length and stopped. He was a short, dark man, strongly built, with a curly beard. He was scruffy and dirty and lost-looking, and he eyed us with curiosity and delight, especially Matt's bountiful cascades of firehair. He thrust a stubby hand out to anyone who would take it and said, "*Manuel, me llamo Manuel. A su sirvicio, señores.*" I am Manuel, at your service, sirs. He spoke no English, so I translated introductions. He told us he was living in the ancient *rancho* a few miles from the mission. He lived alone.

"Why are you carrying the rifle?" I asked him.

"Because I thought you might be cattle rustlers. I have a few head and I thought you might be after them."

"Cattle rustlers, out here?" I asked.

"Who else would come here?" he shrugged. "Tell me, sirs. Why, in fact, are you here?"

We told him of our quest to San Borja, and then we told him of our trouble. He looked very excited and said, "Oh let me, let me." He took my flashlight and crawled under the hood, half his body disappearing between the V-8 engine and the radiator. He fingered the breach, then came up smiling. I told him it needed "*soldadura,*" welding. "Maybe not," he said, gesturing up the road. "At my *ranchito* I have a paste, an epoxy, that I mix together and use to repair metals. Maybe it can work to fix your radiator."

I translated this to the others. Garrett looked hopefully at Manuel and said, "Right now?"

"*¿Ahora mismo?*" I asked Manuel.

"Please, gentlemen, it's dark. It's no time to work, or to drive in the desert." Eagerly he said, "But I would be delighted if you would be my guests tonight. I can fix you some dinner. I can give you fresh eggs; I have chickens. You like coffee?"

"Hey, I'm for it," Matt said. "I'm starving." Matt is never not starving.

"How far is it?" Garrett asked. "Will we have to leave the Willys behind?"

The *rancho* was only about fifty yards in front of the Argo. Manuel ran ahead. When we rolled up a few minutes later he was rousting his chickens for all the eggs he could find. "Come in, come in," he said with a sweeping gesture and a grin, as we walked into his kitchen. "Sit down. Be comfortable." His little house consisted of this room and a bedroom. It was lit by a kerosene lamp and candles, and at the sink he drew water with a hand pump. All was dirt and dishevelment but, putting a hand on his heart and a pious look on his face he said, "I have very little; but what I have I give with all my heart." Matt pulled a bottle of wine out of his jacket; Manuel glowed.

Manuel had collected six fresh, brown eggs, very large, and set about preparing them on his kerosene stove. "I have no tortillas, I hope you won't mind. I'll make you something similar to *huevos rancheros*. It's my own dish." He made a soupy *ranchero* sauce of onions, chili peppers, garlic, and tomato sauted in *manteca* (lard*)*. To that he added cooked macaroni. He broke three eggs into the pan of sauce. The others he broke into another pan and fried them, again using *manteca*. The eggs in the sauce were poached semi hard; those fried were sunny side up and the yolks ran when cut. He served us each a fried egg and a poached egg, both covered with the macaroni salsa.

I pushed some of my macaroni over onto the fried egg. I cut the egg up and swirled it, letting the fat, yellow yolk coat the pasta. The pasta was still hot enough to cook the yolk into a tasty glaze. On the other side of my plate I cut up the poached egg and mashed the yolk into the piquant sauce, making it thicker and more savory. The *manteca* gave the whole dish a rich smoothness and produced a warm and satisfying full feeling in the belly. Matt poured the rosy red wine and we feasted.

Manuel beamed and politely tried not to guzzle the Cabernet Sauvignon.

After dinner we decided that whiskey was called for and Garrett brought forth a bottle. Manuel was agog at his good luck. He had been living out there for months, he said, "with no comforts." Garrett poured healthy drafts all around and Manuel asked us to tell him our story. We described our lives to him, told him of work, school, travel, war, and peace. He followed each story with interest, he savored every detail. He had been starving for human company and this was nourishment for him.

He became effusive with good cheer. "My friends," he said, suddenly inspired, "we have a custom where I come from. When men are friends, and they enjoy each other's stories and food and drink, they exchange *mustachios*." So saying he reached up to the corner of his mustache and, grabbing on to several whiskers, gave a snappy tug and yanked them out! Grinning, he held them forth between thumb and forefinger, the white roots like little flower bulbs at the ends of black stalks. "For you," he said. Not knowing what else to do we each took one, muttering a confused "*gracias*."

Manuel sat there grinning, looking at us each in turn, waiting for a response. With a shrug, Matt reached up to his mustache and ripped out a shard of hairs that made a sound like grass being pulled from the ground. "There you go, Manuel," he said, "and one for all of you, too," and he passed them around.

Garrett seemed to think the whole thing hilarious and said, "Ha ha. And here's some for you," as he reached for both ends of his mustache and tore out his offering, sharing them with all. Manuel collected his mementos and promised to keep them in a special place. I was so glad that I was the only clean-shaven member of this bizarre ritual of male bonding and said, "Damn! I wish I had a mustache!"

Lest this go any farther and we start driving nails into our arms or slicing off bits of our flesh, I asked Manuel to tell us his story. He sat back for a moment and took a breath, as though gathering his powers. He requested a refill. Taking a sip, and rolling it on his tongue pensively, he spun out a long tale. He began: "I'm here, my friends, for gold." We leaned closer. Taking another sip and gauging our interest he said, "I know gold. I know how to find it. It's here, my friends, in these hills. The Spaniards, they were no good at finding gold. They built the missions and found souls to save but they weren't good at finding gold. That's why it's still here," he whispered, "and I'm going to find it." He looked at his empty glass. Hands rushed to fill it.

He drew a lump of ore from his pocket and set it on the table. For a moment the only sound was breathing. "Look," he urged. "Look. If you know gold, you can see I'm going to be rich." We all leaned toward the quartzy piece of rock and peered into its interstices, as though it were a crystal ball, looking for a golden future.

"Let me have a closer look," I said. "When I was seventeen I worked in a gold mine." I picked it up and, turning it over said, "Mmm."

"Does it look like good stuff?" Matt asked as Manuel sat proudly looking on.

"Mmm."

"Well, what do you think? You think it's the real thing?" Garrett asked.

"Mmm."

"Good eh?" said Manuel.

"Uh...mmm...er...I can't tell. It's been a long time since I worked in the gold mine, and that was just during summer vacation."

Manuel took the ore and said, "I'll show you." He got up, a little woozily. Having been so long without "comforts" he was getting "comfortable" pretty fast. He dug through a wooden box and came up with a battered pair of binoculars. Looking through the big end he focused on the ore with the small end and said, "Here, look." We all looked. We saw nothing, but said nothing. We just nodded, not letting on that we didn't "know gold," and wondering how you could know it by looking through the wrong end of a pair of binoculars. Manuel helped himself to more whiskey.

The liquor coursed through him, and he waxed expansive as he described all the things he was going to do when he was rich, all the places he would go, all the women he would have; they would all be blondes. Then he suddenly changed the subject. "You see that saddle over there," he said, pointing to a ruinous-looking pile of old leather. "Pancho Villa rode in that saddle. It belonged to him. You know Pancho Villa, the great general?"

"Oh yes," we all nodded. "Pancho Villa, the great general."

"He was from Sonora." Manuel told us. "I'm from Sonora, too." Lurching across the room he picked up his old rifle. I noticed that the butt was cracked and held together with electrical tape. He brandished it at us and said, "And this rifle was used in the Mexican Revolution. It killed many men. Many men."

Matt looked like he was going to hide the whiskey, but I grabbed it and poured Manuel the stiffest drink his glass could hold. "*Salud*," I said. "Let's drink to Pancho Villa, the great general!" Patriotically, Manuel drank the health of the general, draining his glass. I refilled it.

"My friends," said Manuel, "I told you I'm from Sonora. You know why I'm now in Baja California?"

"For gold," we all said.

"Well, yes. But you know why I'm also in Baja California?" Cradling his rifle he sat down and eyed us all dizzily. Absentmindedly he reached into a pocket and pulled out a handful of bullets.

"Let's drink to Sonora!" Matt said. Manuel, rifle in one hand and bullets in the other, considered his glass. He put the bullets back in his pocket and drank to Sonora. I refilled his glass.

Manuel continued, "I'm here because I killed a man in Sonora. He was an Indian. I caught him cheating me at cards.

I didn't have my famous rifle with me," he said, patting it on the breach. "So I killed him with my knife. He was a big man, but I'm fast, and my knife was big. I don't have the knife anymore because I left it in the Indian. Damned Indian," he muttered.

His rifle was getting heavy so he leaned it against a wall and turned his attentions to his glass which I kept full. "Yes, I had to run from Sonora. The police wouldn't get me because they're my friends. I had to run from the Indians! So I went to Sinaloa. And what do you think? I killed another Indian, over a woman! This time the police wanted to get me, so I ran away to Baja." His head drooping low, his face inches from the table, he murmured his last words of the evening: "And now I'm going to get rich and find gold."

He sank into a little heap of whiskey-soaked flesh. We laid him in his lumpy bed and covered him with his filthy blankets. We looked at each other and sniggered. Pancho Villa's saddle, a revolutionary rifle, two dead Indians and a lost gold mine all in one night; we'd never heard whiskey talk so much.

The next morning Manuel was up and about, hung over and still drunk at the same time. After giving us his epoxy he kept getting in the way of things, so we dispatched him quickly and painlessly with a few more drinks. After making our repairs we set a big lockback knife, as a present, on his table and left him sleeping. About a week later, in Bahía de los Angeles, we met Don Guillermo, who turned out to be *el dueño*, the owner of the land Manuel occupies. "Was he kind to you?" Don Guillermo asked.

"Oh yes. He gave us dinner. And we gave him whiskey," and we all chuckled.

"You gave him whiskey?" Don Guillermo asked with visible concern.

"Uh...yeah. After all, he was very hospitable to us."

"*Senores*. You should be very careful whom you drink with around here. Manuel can be violent when he's drunk. He's already killed two men, that we know of."

So, O.K., Manuel is, indeed, a murderer. He has conducted two of his fellows out of this world untimely to the next. *Qué vayan con Dios and amén.* But when he follows them he will, at least, have left behind his single, humble contribution to the happiness of the living. His little culinary offering stays active in my recipe file, where it frequently satisfies the appetites of my friends and garners me much praise. It was no less a personage than Brillat-Savarin, the great eighteenth-century gastronome who said, "The discovery of a new dish does more for human happiness than the discovery of a star." Even if the telescope is wielded by a man with the curse of Cain, the discovery is a worthy one.

1 2 *Death's Journeyman*

I WONDER HOW THAT SON OF CAIN, MANUEL, went about the business of death. I cannot imagine that he killed in cold blood using a knife. Such an act, so close that you could feel your victim's last breath on your face, is too intimate for cold blood, for calculating thought. To stab a man in the heart would take blood that boils. And though men might not absolve you of it, it would be a deed for which you could go to the priest, or pray to God, and say, "Forgive me. I have sinned. I burned with a passion so hot that I surrendered to my raging desire to quench it."

But what of deathly works done coldly: planned, practiced, done again and again? Done on a massive scale? Done in the comfort of the notion that while the death of one is a human tragedy, the death of a million is mere statistics? What do you say to the priest then? What then is your prayer of contrition? Do you say, "Forgive me. I banked the fire"?

Dealers of Death: the name we gave ourselves. That was a good name, Dealers of Death. And we sailed a ship known as the Gray Ghost of the Nam Coast. God, that was a good name! And we were death to the gooks. Man, we killed some gooks.

I don't know the name of the place we were at that day. Somewhere south of Haiphong. The gooks know the name of the Gray Ghost in Haiphong, from the time we steamed into the fortified harbor. We went in early in the morning with the sun at our back, battleflags flying like medieval knights, guns announcing our name. We shot the place to pieces, leaving it all smoke and chaos. All a part of Operation Linebacker II. A good American name for a good American operation. You've got to have good names. LBJ's Operation Rolling Thunder was a flop and its name was too pretentious for Americans. But Richard Nixon's Linebacker had a good name, and dealt the gooks a serious blow.

So it was somewhere south of Haiphong. And we were pumped, because we were some gook-killing sons of bitches. And we were Dealers of Death, and we sailed in a ghost ship and now we were linebackers as well. And we all had cool-sounding nicknames like Chopper, the Bear, Doobie, Radar Love, and Petty Officer Monsoon. We had such good names.

So there were these gooks in a bunker on the shore south of Haiphong and we blasted 'em. We hit 'em with four triple salvos from the heavy forward turret with its six-inch bore guns. Twelve rounds of heavyweight frag. Then we used the five-inch dual mount and fired a few incendiary rounds, just to flame their gook ass.

And we cheered. We could see 'em. They were close. "Yaaah! Fuckin gooks! Ha! Look at their gook arms and legs fly like matchsticks." Yeah, that's what they looked like: tossed and burning matchsticks. And we sent 'em all to their gook hell.

And we all worked at it together. Black guys, white guys, guys in between, even guys who looked like the gooks. People have trouble understanding that. There were a lot of tensions between us in those days, and sometimes they spilled over into fighting. I guess it was mainly black versus white, but there were tensions between us all, over lots of things. But not when it came to killing. Killing transcended things. Race, religion, class, education, hometown; these distinctions had no meaning in the business of killing, for Death respects none of them.

That night we killed some more. We found a target we had been looking for at the time we came upon the bunker. The gooks had a surface-to-air missile battery hidden away in some hills and they were giving the Air Force a bad time. And the Air Force couldn't seem to pinpoint it, or they couldn't hit it, so they called the Ghost Ship. And we found it, electronically. Because you don't hide from the Ghost. We didn't know at first if it was the site we were looking for, but we had a language officer on board who could speak gook, so he patched into their radio traffic and identified them. "Yeah," he said. "These are those bad boys."

We launched two of our homing missiles at them. They were well over the horizon so we couldn't see, and it was a trick shot, but our telemetry seemed to confirm we'd done the job.

Then we sailed away to rest up. Because maybe I make it sound easy, killing gooks, because of the way I tell it; but it's not easy. It's hard. You've got to have skill, and know-how, and teamwork. Everybody has got to be good at his job, and do it right all the time. When the moment comes to close the firing key and send those projectiles or those missiles off to their target, there's no turning back. There's no chance to correct errors, change your mind or lose your nerve.

And it's hard to kill gooks because your days are full of labors and your nights are so often sleepless. It seemed like the gooks never slept. And you had to hit 'em when you could, day or night. And they would make it all the harder. They would run. And they would hide. And they would shoot back, too. Cocky little fucks. So don't think it's easy.

A day or so after the missile launch we heard from the Air Force's aerial reconnaissance operation, known as Operation Big Look. The Bear brought the news down from the radio shack to the weapons control shack where some of us were maintaining our gear.

"Hey, I just got the skinny from Big Look," he said. And we dropped everything.

"Wha'd they say? Wha'd they say?"

"They say we kill taksan gooksan."

"No shit!?"

"Fuckin' aye! They said there were so many they couldn't count 'em all. That makes taksan in my Japanese dictionary!"

"The Gray Ghost kicks ass!" we all cheered. "She's the ass-kickin'est ship in the whole fucking navy." And we chanted our pride in our ship: "Haze gray and under weigh, this motherfucker is a-O.K.!"

Then we imitated the marines and said "Uuragh!" a few times. Man, we were pumped. We were some death-dealing, ghost-riding, linebacking, taksan-gook-killing sons of bitches. And when the cheering died down we were flushed and quiet a minute, and Gunner Rodino said "Gentlemen, that was a difficult shot. But attaboys all around. You've all done a good piece of work."

You see, that's what we called what we did. That was the name we gave to the thing we practiced. It was work. It was your job. And you remembered that, because sooner or later it would happen. It was like it was inevitable. Some civilian you met on the beach would ask you. Or some high school friend who went to college when you joined up would send you a letter from campus and demand to know. "How does it feel?" You know what I mean? "Do you have any objections to killing people?" Jeeze! And there were the real pain-in-the-ass types who would put it in terms like "angst," and "taking of human life," and "gestalt." Gestalt!? Jeeze. Assholes.

So what do you tell 'em? What can you tell 'em? You tell 'em the truth: Just doing your job. You tell 'em there's a war on, and this is your job in wartime. You tell 'em you're a highly skilled individual. The U.S. Navy has put a lot of time and money into you, to train you, and bring you up to do this job. You're a petty officer of the line, that's the name you bear, and this is what you do. And you make sure those civilians know that the line we're talking about is the battle line. Like in "ship of the line." Because you're the man. You're the one who operates these weapons. You close the firing key. When you take the rest of the whole U.S. Navy and you put it all together, it has one task. And that is to get you to the place where the work is done. And you make sure to tell 'em you do good work.

So that was my job. See? That was my work. Like people have work everywhere, military and civilian too. Like, say a guy is a carpenter, that's his work, and you call him a worker. If he's good, maybe you call him "a hard-working man." That's a good compliment, "hard-working man." Or say a guy's a preacher. You could call him a worker in God's vineyard, or say that he does "good works."

Well I never worked to build anybody a house to live in. And I never worked in the vineyard. But I worked. I worked hard, and I was good at my work. I did good work. I did. I was a hard-working man. You can't say I wasn't!

13 *The Perfect Punch in the Face*

WAR TEACHES MANY USEFUL LESSONS TO THOSE willing to learn them. Lessons about how to achieve goals, how to focus yourself, how to bring your powers to bear. It can give you perspective, so that you can know which things are truly important and which are not. Even the arts of peace and the arts of love can be improved upon by the skills and experience of the warrior. We learn how to make little wars, that harm none. We learn that not every combat is deadly, or hostile, or even unpleasant. There is ample field of endeavor for the Happy Warrior.

I have a friend named Rod. He's a master cabinetmaker. You can see his mastery in his self-confidence, and that part of him that is always far away, occupied with lofty things, like his craft. You can see the mojo in him. To be admitted to his workshop, his sanctum sanctorum in Sonoma, California, is like being admitted into a matador's dressing room before the fight. To be able to watch him work is like being given a private concert by James Brown. And he makes huge money, as master cabinetmakers do.

"What do you want for your birthday?" he asked me, thinking he would show largesse with an expensive gift. "You want a Rolex?"

"I want a snuffbox made by you," I said. He seemed disappointed. I told him, "You're a master craftsman. It's what you do. It would be a piece of you and your tradition, going back to, what, Jesus when he was a carpenter. If I have something just for me, made by a master, then I'll feel a little like a master, too. I'll feel privileged."

So he made just for me the best cherrywood snuffbox the world has ever seen. Just holding it in my hands I can feel the mastery, and feel I'm holding something Jesus could have made when he was a carpenter in Nazareth. Jesus would have made nothing but the best.

So what, you're wondering, has this got to do with a punch in the face? Pinky Gomez and I trained in the same boxing gym in East San Jose, California. Not such a nice neighborhood, but a good venue for fighters. He was pro, I was amateur. He was magic. It was what he did. To watch him train or fight was to watch a master craftsman at work. I knew, if his mojo held, that in him I was watching a champion being born. I was watching the history of the sport I love being made. I wanted some of his mojo. And that was in his fists. Girlfriend was appalled. What can I say?

But there was more in Pinky's fists than mojo. I learned that he had sparred with Sugar Ray Leonard. Had even tagged him a few times. And Leonard had given Pinky a shiner. Now think about this: Leonard had punched Pinky. Before that Tommy Hearns had punched Leonard. The champ before Hearns had punched him; and on and on back in history. On back to Jake LaMotta, through Sugar Ray Robinson. Back, back to Hammerin' Hank, first holder of a Triple Crown. Back, back through the ring record to the first championship fights under Marquise of Queensberry rules in New York and London, back to the 1890s when John L. Sullivan fought Gentleman Jim Corbett in the first major fight with gloves and three-minute rounds. Back when "the form" had first been established. In Pinky's fists was a physical, living, blood-pumping link with the history of modern boxing.

"I think you're great, Pinky," I told him. "How 'bout layin' one on me? Right in the face." Pinky grinned. He knew what I meant. Because of our different weight classes we would never meet in the ring. It was this or nothing.

"You want it with the glove or without?"

"Don't risk your knuckles."

A looping right cross sheathed in a nine-ounce leather glove slammed into my left cheekbone, just under the eye. Pinky did it just right. Not hard enough to knock me down, but hard enough to leave a mark. My eye swelled. My head buzzed. And I was one more link in the chain with Pinky and Hammerin' Hank and all the others. It was a perfect punch in the face.

14 All at Sea

T HE CAFE ALMEJA LIES ABOUT TWO HUNDRED yards from the mouth of the Rio Mulege and the town's outlet to the sea. Here the fishing boats dock and land their catch. If I've just finished lunch and have nothing else to command my attention, I'll take a walk down to the harbor to watch the boats tie up. Some of them are quite new and spiffy looking, ship-shape and all. Some are just old rust buckets. And some are a bit sad looking.

It is sometimes the sad looking ones that most catch my attention. We always refer to sea-going vessels in the feminine, as "she." And these ladies in the little harbor are virtually the only females I know in Baja, other than Claudia, and she's both off-limits and foreign. There really are no "women of Baja." At least none in life. This is a masculine place for me. But when I see the sad looking boats, I'm reminded of another place to which the Spaniards came in their age of conquest, on the other side of the great blue Pacific. And I'm reminded of a certain female character, there in the faraway Philippine Islands.

She had one of those names that are so common in the Philippines, like *Lucy* or *Linda*. Maybe it was *Dinah*. I can't remember. I met her on the Manila waterfront. True to what I had been told, she did look a bit of a tramp, and an older one at that. You might even have called her mannish for her shape. But she was a she to the core, as all good ships are, which I discovered when I boarded her. I'll speak no ill of her. Under the maritime subdivision of the Masculine Code, it is a bad thing to defame virtuous females, whether terrestrial or marine.

I was going to ride this cargo liner to the southern islands where I could relax in a place where nothing ever happens, and feel nostalgic. This was one of my many return journeys to the countries of the South China Sea since the end of the Vietnam War. It was in this region I came of age, and lived many years.

I was almost too young when I was sent out to this end of the world in the final years of the war. I was that guy everyone called "the kid" in so many old war movies about better wars. This is not a war story, so I'll just say that in the battles without and the battles within there was plenty to make a man crazy, I mean really truly bad crazy, unless he had something with which to ground himself. Some men got religion. Some took drugs. Others wrote songs or poetry. Still others just went crazy.

Me, I was lucky. I was able to get away frequently to the Philippines, Thailand, Indonesia, all over the South China Sea, where I took my comfort with women. It was the Tribe of Women who kept my mind and spirit whole. I found I could sail to the antipodes, fight all the hordes of Ho Chi Minh, live in fire, go without beer, if I could but lie in the arms of a woman. I drank deeply from their cup, and their female powers sustained me. And there didn't always necessarily have to be any sex involved, although that was certainly a plus. Indeed, I remember times when the woman whose arms I would have most preferred were my mother's. Maybe you'll find it questionable that a grown man wants to nestle in his mother's arms, but any man who has been in war knows whence I speak. We all know stories of men dying in battle with the word "mama" on their lips. You may be sure the stories are true.

So there I was in the islands again, roving southerly in a tramp steamer with no particular destination, and ready to put ashore on any island where a lady might find me good company. My cabin was located port side amidships and contained a bunk, wardrobe, sink and toilet, a little desk and chair, and a porthole. We had been at sea several hours when I decided to tour the vessel. I started at the bottom and began working my way up the decks, having the bridge as my ultimate goal. When I reached the level of the crew's quarters and the chart house I noticed a closet-sized space that held a swivel chair. A cigar box full of scissors, combs, and other supplies sat on a makeshift shelf. A hand-lettered sign above the door read, "Barber and Beauty Shop."

I kept climbing upward intending to reach the bridge. One level below my goal, I found a small bar. "Hot damn!" I thought, and walked in; the bridge be damned. The place had a porthole on each side, but otherwise no access to outdoor light. No electric lights were burning so the room was pretty dim. It was seedy looking, kind of like the ship itself—a tramp bar. Only a few passengers were in there. I figured it was mainly for the comfort of the crew. It looked like a waterfront dive. But I had drunk in many a waterfront dive, so that was O.K. with me.

I took a seat at the counter and ordered a San Miguel beer. The sleepy looking barman served it up with no glass but it was icy cold, and I downed it quickly then ordered another. I was taking my time with the second beer, gazing out a porthole when I heard someone sit down near me. I didn't turn around, but I heard a woman with a husky, Lauren Bacall voice order coffee in a Philippine accent. I heard the cup set down on the bar, the spoon tinkling in the cup as it stirred in sugar and milk, then short little sipping sounds. I realized that she was sitting right next to me. And all the other barstools were empty. I made a quick, silent prayer to Aphrodite that this woman be attractive, then turned, as casually as possible.

She was dressed in a kind of jumpsuit, but the sleeves and legs were short. It looked clean, but rather old. She was very slim and lithe looking, in the manner of one of Balanchine's dancers with their characteristic small breasts and hips. Her skin was the same color as her coffee with milk. Her hair was shoulder length and fine. She had big brown puppy dog eyes. She was not beautiful, but in no way was she undesirable. To my eye, her most remarkable features were her hands. They were very graceful and expressive, and looked like they belonged to a sculptor. In one hand she held her cup and saucer, in the other, her spoon, with which she drank her coffee, just as a child might do with a cup of hot chocolate. She held the cup close to her mouth and looked at me over its rim. Her name was Luz.

A lot of women in the Philippines are named Luz. In Spanish *Luz* means "light," as all Filipinos know from their time as a Spanish possession. In the islands Luz is short for Luzviminda, a contraction of the names of the three island groups that comprise the Philippines. Luz, then, is a female patriotic name with a lovely double meaning.

"Are you going to Cebu?" she asked in her Lauren Bacall voice, and took a little sip from her spoon.

"Yes," I answered. "Are you?"

She nodded a yes and said, "But I'm not going to be stopping there. I work here in the ship. I have my beauty shop."

"Oh, yes. I noticed that."

"Do you want a haircut?"

"No. Thanks."

She put the spoon into her mouth, upside-down, like a lollypop, and drew it out slowly between pursed lips. We made small talk. I offered her a beer but she declined, preferring more coffee. "Do you have a girlfriend in Cebu?" she wanted to know.

"No. No I don't. I'm just on a pleasure tour. Do you have a boyfriend? In Cebu?"

She looked into her coffee for a moment, stirring thoughtfully. "No," she said. "I don't got no boyfriend no more. I leave him because he's always hitting me."

What do you say to something like that? I tell you, it always upsets me to hear about men who beat women. I come from a long line of cowboys and lumberjacks and frontier sheriffs and other Neanderthals who have the quaint and outdated notion that men are to protect women and guard them against abuse. I have brawlers aplenty among my kinfolk in the Tribe of Men, but from earliest times I can remember their admonition: "Never hit girls, even if they hit first. It's a bad thing to do." I take it near personally when I hear of men who violate the code. You can call me old-fashioned, patronizing, patriarchal or sexist, but there it is. And I don't care.

I mumbled something I hoped sounded sympathetic, because I was, and because what else could I say, and she said, "Don't worry. That's O.K. He's not going to hurt me anymore because I leave him forever."

"Good for you," I said.

She sipped another spoonful of coffee and then slowly licked the spoon, her puppy dog eyes on mine. We made some more small talk. I drank more beer. She even bought me one. Now and then, with the back of her spoon, she painted her lips with coffee and then licked the sweet creamy brew from them. She did none of these spoon maneuvers blatantly. Rather, each action was very subtle, as though she had learned to do it in some kind of finishing school where young ladies of position study social comportment, and how to snare a man.

At length she said, "Can I come visit you in your cabin?"

"When?"

"After they serve the dinner."

"Why not have dinner with me?"

She shook her head. "We're not allowed to do that. But I will come to visit you after the lights are out. After ten o'clock."

After dinner I killed some time in the bar and by walking on deck. At 10 P.M. all the ship's white lights were extinguished and only her running lights shone on the exterior. The moon still made plenty of light, and it reflected brightly off a mirror-calm sea. In the enclosed passageways the claret-red nightlights were on. I smiled as I remembered from navy days about red lights. They preserve your night vision, in case you have to go quickly between exterior and interior, where such a sudden change in light could temporarily blind you.

I returned to my cabin and waited. I opened the porthole and the moist scent of the warm sea filled the room. Only the dim reading lamp above the little desk was burning. Not long after, Luz tapped on my door. I opened it, and her silhouette stood in the dim passageway. She wore a sleeveless pullover and a full-length cotton skirt, sandals on her feet. In the night vision claret light I could faintly see the gleam of her lip gloss. I stood back as she entered the region of languid light in the cabin. She reached across the desk and turned off the reading lamp. "I'm shy," she explained in a curiously small voice. I closed the door. The moonlight streaming through the port-hole would be enough.

We sat on the bunk, not touching, leaning against the wall. "Did you enjoy your dinner?" she asked.

"Yes. It was very good. And there were a lot of interesting people to talk to." My eyes were adjusting to the moonlight and her features were becoming clear.

"Yes, I meet many people in the ship. Sometimes they send postcards to me. I like to see a view of other places." She slipped off her sandals and curled her legs up on the bunk. I know my breathing was coming deeper, and I could see her bosom rising higher. Her features, although muted in the shadowy cabin, as though in sepia, were clear now. Her head was inclined toward me, and she twirled a lock of hair in her fingers. She looked up at me in a sidelong glance.

"Maybe you think I'm bad," she said.

"Maybe you think I'm bad," I countered.

"No. You're not the bad kind of guy. You don't hurt no-body."

"No. I don't. I try not to, anyway."

She shifted the weight of her body in my direction. A few inches of space lay between us, yet I could feel her body. That tactile zone that surrounds the human body, lying normally close to the skin, was expanding outward, as it does in times of passion or tenderness. That special sensory reaching-out was in play. A shiver ran down both our bodies and our tactile zones swelled out to engulf each other. I became aware of our mouths, sealed together, breathing in humid kisses. Lips pressed urgently. Breath came short. I thought to break away for a moment to recover my composure, but neither my body nor hers would obey anything but desire.

Our mouths inseparable, I reached behind her and caressed her buttocks, then up under her pullover to caress her back. I realized she wore no bra, so I reached around the front where I cupped a willing breast in my hand. It was unusually firm and the skin quivered at my touch. I held the nipple between thumb and forefinger and began to squeeze, ever so gently at first, but with increasing pressure. She moaned and almost sobbed into my mouth.

Suddenly her mouth broke away from mine with a gasping sound and she desperately began kissing my neck and chest. I tore at my shirt buttons while she, shaking, wrestled with my belt and zipper. My groin was throbbing so intensely, pressing so hard against my trousers that I was in near pain. Luz pulled the trousers down to my knees. She grasped through the cotton underwear with her sculptor's hands and I cried out with excitement.

She tugged my underwear down to my knees. She knelt over me for a moment, looking, panting, collecting herself. She brought her head slowly down to my breastbone and kissed. She followed the line of hairs that grow from breastbone to navel, kissing, biting, kissing, biting. I could feel her hot breath at my crotch. Her mouth poised over me and she waited,

waited, waited until her desire was so strong that her will gave in and she fell upon me. Using one of her hands she forced me into her mouth as deeply as I could go, pressing me to the back of her throat. She trembled, and little desire sounds emanated from her. The universe contracted upon itself and all that there was were Luz's sculptor's hands, her mouth, me, and the little sounds she was making. It all spun dizzily.

I felt that I was going to come at any moment, and that was too soon, too soon. Shakily I sat up, reaching for her skirt. Luz's mouth uncoupled with a wet sound as I pulled her skirt up and reached for her panties. She gave a little cry of protest, as though she were menstruating and didn't want me to see. But it was too late. I had the panties down below her crotch and was kissing upward when I plainly saw the little shriveled, flaccid cock and balls made lifeless by long use of estrogen.

I told myself I was seeing shadows, that it was the dizzy effect of passion. I touched to make sure. My hand recoiled of its own accord, snake-bit. Nausea billowed in my gut. My own tool went quickly as limp as Luz's. Luz's? Hers? His? I stood up in haste and pulled up my pants, zipping and buckling them securely. Luz sat on the bunk, adjusted his underwear and covered his legs with his skirt, demurely. He sat there, hands on his lap, face down but eyes looking up at me, mortified, ashes of sepia. He trembled. His lip gloss was smeared and I knew that it was also smeared on my cock at that moment. I could feel it shriveling and withdrawing into my body.

With the back of his hand Luz wiped the saliva that had flowed out of his mouth and across his cheek and chin. "Spit that gushed out of his mouth while he sucked my cock!" my thoughts roared. "The pukey little lying, perverted faggot!"

I hit him, open handed. I slapped him full across the face as he sat there, and the blow jerked his head to one side. The smacking sound was satisfying and the stinging in my hand told me I had hurt him. But it wasn't enough.

Luz had made no sound, but sat there quietly, his head slightly awobble. I hit him again, this time on the other cheek.

It was the one that had the passion spit on it and the residue came off on my hand. It felt like poison and I wiped it off on Luz's hair saying, "There! Let it poison you, you little queer!" Luz's head bobbed with the force of the wipings.

He stared straight ahead as I punished him, making no sound, no protest, no defense. A fat tear welled out of one of his eyes and ran in a stream down the hot cheek I had just slapped. "How dare you sit there and cry after what you just did to me," I spat. Then I slapped him again, as hard as I could. I grabbed him tightly by the hair, drew back my arm and spun my body towards Luz so as to put all my weight behind the blow. It landed perfectly on the cheek I had first hit and I felt the impression of the jaw and cheekbones on my palm. It landed with enough force that it made Luz finally cry out. It knocked him over, too, and he would have landed on his face had he not thrown out his hands to break the fall.

I took a step back, and watched as Luz slowly, effortfully sat back up. He put his hands on his lap and stared straight ahead, eyes not seeing. He took a deep, shaky breath. And so did I. Both his eyes were streaming tears now, silent ones. They were pain tears, yes, from the punishment I had meted out to him. But even in that dim light, nothing but the moon through the porthole, I saw the pain that went much deeper than his cheeks. These tears were the distillate of suffering, rejection, and abuse. Luz's mouth quivered, but then set firmly. He swallowed hard. "At least he's taking it like a man," I thought. "At least in this he's honest."

But he had lied to me to get me into bed. I recalled something I had read by Gloria Steinem. She wrote that seduction was rape by other means. I had given it no thought at the time, perhaps even scorned the idea. Now I knew what she meant. Luz had seduced me, willingly misrepresented himself. He had violated me, stolen from me. He had taken a chance, doubtless not for the first time, and it had turned out badly for him, equally doubtless not for the first time. But at least he had the guts to take his medicine without complaint. And it was bitter.

"Why did you do it?" I asked sullenly.

In a misty voice he said, "Because...I want to. Because when I see you...I like you."

"You shouldn't have done it!" I insisted.

Luz just nodded his head and turned his gaze to the deck. He looked very small. Regarding him now, I noticed the telltale signs of the pre-op transsexual whores I had seen and resolutely ignored as they prowled the waterfronts of a dozen ports of call: larger hands, broader shoulders, narrower hips than most women; an Adam's apple. None of them in themselves meaningful, but taken together with exaggerated gestures and a low voice they're pretty suggestive. I looked at Luz's breasts. One was larger than the other; they pointed in different directions. "Must have had a back-alley surgeon," I thought. "Couldn't afford anything better. Probably saving what money he can to get chopped and channeled by the same guy or one like him. I wonder how often he gets beat up?"

"What's your real name?" I demanded.

"Luz," he squeaked. "Luzviminda."

"Isn't that a girl's name?"

"Luzviminda," he quietly insisted. "Luzviminda."

I went to the tap and filled a cup with water. I gave it to him and he said, *"Selamat."* Thanks.

I watched as he drained the cup. A realization came to me that made me shudder: I felt sorry for Luz. Some part of me even wanted to reach out and kiss and caress this crazy confusion of genders and make it better, for his were crazy-maker pains, pains he had to bear alone, with no one to comfort him, neither men nor women. A deep and unknown part of me even wanted to let him have his pleasure with me, let him have his way if it meant so much to him. After all, the damage was already done, he had already deflowered me, as it were. It wouldn't hurt me, and it seemed a world of satisfaction to him. But how could such a thing be? I quickly banished such thoughts.

He gave me back the empty cup. I took it, looked into it dumbly. I turned away and rested my hand on the little desk.

And I stared at the wall, inches from my face. There in the half light I stood mutely facing aft while he, or maybe she, sat facing midships, drying his, or her, tears.

"Look," I said in the direction of the steel wall. "Look …uh…why don't you go back to your cabin now. It's late."

The clock stopped somehow. We shared a long long silence that didn't seem to register in time. The moment just hung there and stayed current.

"Before I go," Luz finally said in a small voice that yet filled the room, "will you embrace me? One time?"

I know I did not quite hear those words at first. But they echoed in my mind until they finally registered on my ear. "Embrace?" I thought. "Embrace him? Embrace her? Embrace whom?" Luz looked awfully pitiful, and in need of some comfort. Like a wet puppy. I would have known what to do in the case of a wet puppy.

I would have known what to do if Luz were a man. I could have put one arm around his shoulders, given him a brotherly punch somewhere and said, "It's O.K. now. Your buddy is here." But Luz sat there in a dress and woman's underwear.

I would have known what to do if Luz were a woman. I'd have gathered her to me gently, stroked her hair, and held her closely until the pain subsided. I'd have kissed away her tears. But Luz had a cock and balls, and no breasts of Mother Nature's making.

On the other hand, I could just throw Luz out. I knew how to do that. I'd just open the door, grab the nearest body part, and walk the intruder out. After all, I had had enough trouble. Hadn't I? Hadn't I? The code gave me no guidance, but this seemed the nearest possible solution.

I do not know what moved me. Certainly it wasn't thought or knowledge. But I do know that my mother, whose principal motive is to nurture, would be disappointed if her son caused or allowed the needless suffering of a fellow creature, however crazed or confused. And while I am a man, my father's son and a warrior, so am I my mother's son.

And so my arms reached out. My hands found their way to either side of Luz's face, to those same hot cheeks that those same hands had so recently assailed. I lifted up his tear-wet face, and drew him to his feet. I gently pressed his head to mine, temple to temple, and stroked his hair. Luz trembled delicately. Then, as though it were the most natural thing in the world, I inclined his head forward, pushed back his bangs, and kissed his forehead. And then kissed him again. It did not seem a bad thing.

I lowered my arms and allowed them to encircle his waist. Whatever bosom Luz professed, I drew to mine. He lay his head upon my shoulder, and sighed many sighs. And I watched through the porthole as miles and miles of moonlit sea slipped gently by; the good old ship, the *Lucy* or the *Linda* or maybe the *Dinah*, sailing smoothly on, bound I knew not where.

15 *Reconciliation*

DARKNESS WAS THICK ON THE MEKONG RIVER delta that night, making it difficult to keep my bearings, but I was able to orient myself by the light of shell flashes to the west, near Saigon. The larger bursts were like camera flashes, and my eye took pictures, etching onto my memory the siren-song beauty of the land we were about to quit in defeat. A hundred or so Vietnamese refugees crowded the open deck of our vessel as we made our way past the Vungtao Peninsula and out to sea. They were exhausted and dispirited after the chaos and tumult of evacuation and the losses they had suffered. I was bitter and angry. As a military man, a U.S. Navy weapons specialist since 1971, I was bitter at our failure and the sudden haste of our withdrawal. At the blood, the treasure, the hopes, and plans and all else we left behind. As an American I was in anguish over the ugliness we had visited upon a land and culture too beautiful for my powers of expression. It was the night of April 29, 1975, my last night in Vietnam, the last night of the war.

In my anger I cursed the enemy, and I even cursed the land. I cursed the war and defeat, and all the politicians and generals on either side. I swore I would never return. Though veterans often visit their old battlefields later in life, I vowed I would not. I would leave behind forever the land whose presence I had grown up with, and had come to both love and hate.

But while I might leave Vietnam, she would not leave me. For nearly two decades afterwards, the Land of the Ascending Dragon invaded my dreams. I awoke from them with the stink of cordite in my nostrils and cries in my ears. A friend has told me that I sometimes walked in my sleep, uttering Vietnamese words that had long faded from my conscious memory. In California, Vietnamese restaurants would send their culinary siren songs wafting through the streets, never letting me forget. They awoke a thousand sensual memories of the urgent fragrances of chili and garlic, the New Orleans-style charm and exuberance of Saigon streets bursting with color, of steam billowing from little noodle shops and of the taste of life being savored in defiance of an evil war.

My memory flooded with visions of women in the *ao dai*, the Vietnamese dress of a knee-length split tunic and sheer trousers, worn with a limpet hat or a parasol to guard the lady's tea-and-cream complexion. There was never a garment designed to better flatter the female form while still covering the woman from neck to toes. The *ao dai* makes a woman at once as modest as a nun and yet winkingly provocative. It is to me the very metaphor of the land that has held a grip on my imagination since I was in seventh grade.

In that dizzying rush of events in 1975 there had been no time to give a proper ending to the long relationship between America and Vietnam, and between Vietnam and me. For me it began when I was thirteen. My Dad was on his first tour there. I watched for glimpses of him or his unit on the news every night. I told my mother that I wanted to serve in Nam, too, when I came of age. "Don't be silly," she said. "Wars don't last that long."

But it lasted so long it almost became an institution, a fact of daily life. The looming presence, and my subsequent experience of Vietnam became a part of my psyche, like a tempestuous and demanding lover. And the severance was so quick, the parting so sudden. There was no time to say good-bye. After a long and frenzied night I awoke and she was gone. No chance to say "I'm sorry," or "I'll miss you. It was good while it lasted; it was hell while it lasted. I love you and I hate you." I left behind a great, unfinished business. And I left behind a part of me.

The writer Maxine Hong Kingston has said that Homer causes Odysseus to wander for so many years because it takes a long time to bring a warrior home, fully and completely. That is how long the human mind and spirit need to come to grips with something as large as war. Little wonder then that it was not till the 1990s that I felt the stirrings to return to Vietnam, to somehow finish the unfinished. And to stop the dreams. For as long as I walked through Vietnam in bad dreams, I was not yet fully and completely home.

I chose Tet, that span on the Vietnamese calendar where over a period of days the old year blends into the new, as the time to bring my odyssey to a close.

Because of the U.S. economic embargo at the time my two traveling companions and I had to send to Mexico City for visas, and take a circuitous route through Thailand and Cambodia. We arrived at the Vietnamese border by car from Phnom Penh. I felt like I was sneaking in through the back door. "Don't let anyone know I'm a veteran," I told my non-vet companions. "Not till I know how people are going to respond." I was sure that response would include hostility, and I dreaded it. Not only what might be directed at me, but my own reactions to it as well.

As we left the border crossing behind, I closely surveyed the greening land. For a place of so many memories it seemed strangely unfamiliar, for I saw no soldiers, no convoys, heard no shouting and smelled no smoke. And then we crossed the iron bridge. Below us flowed a branch of the Mekong River. The river that I had navigated in wartime, as my Uncle Thomas had before me, and my father before him in the seemingly endless years of war. My cousin Joey, a childhood playmate, had flown helicopter missions over it and took the bullet in the spine that left him on crutches to this day. Now I knew where I was.

As we crossed the bridge the rutted and nearly empty Phnom Penh highway gradually smoothed out and filled with trucks and small cars hauling goods and crops, and with people buzzing around on countless motor scooters. Approaching Saigon at thirty miles per hour two young men on a motor scooter pulled up alongside, smiling and waving.

"Hello!" the one seated on the rear shouted. "Hello. Are you Americans?"

"Uh...yeah, yes we are," we shouted back.

"Veterans?"

Before we could respond the bike's driver swerved to miss an onrushing truck. Three days would pass before I told anyone that I was a veteran.

Busy, bustling, and pulsating with life, Saigon was a stream of consciousness made corporeal. Trees grew in their countless numbers, cathedral tall and stately. Sycamore, palm, and cypress provided a vast canopy of green held aloft by wooden columns. Restaurants and food sellers were almost as numerous as the trees, and gave the city a festive air. The elegant French Colonial buildings and grand hotels with their terraces and curved corners blended easily with Chinese-inspired temples, schools, and theaters. So many motor scooters filled the wide boulevards that we laughed to see the occasional motor scooter gridlock.

Though the city was obviously maintained with pride there was a great shortage of cash in Vietnam then, leaving many of Saigon's buildings in need of paint and trim. Plaster needed fixing and walls needed shoring up. But, then, the city was not as garish as she had been either. The GI girlie strip, Tu Doh

Street, renamed Dong Khoi Street, was lined with apartment houses and small shops. The wretchedness that used to be so common and the desperate poverty were fading. Violent crime was and is now almost unknown. What few police I saw went unarmed. They didn't even carry nightsticks! The city was like a lovely woman who needed to put her make-up on, as though she had just risen, hair in confusion and sleepy-eyed. But when she is made up she will dazzle you.

Alongside all the newness and optimism in Vietnam are the veterans of the old regime: the ARVN soldiers. One of them is Tran. He drives a pedicab, a three-wheeled "trishaw" and earns about twenty-five cents for pedaling his passenger across town. Decades ago he was a soldier, young and strong with a straight back. Nowadays he is bent with his labor, and with the weight of defeat. He will never do any other kind of work. There are very few good jobs in Vietnam, and they belong to the victors.

He drove me to my hotel on the third day and en route mentioned that he had been a soldier. He said it was the best time of his life, until the end, at Vungtao. The very name of Vungtao struck a nerve, and arriving at the hotel I asked him to tell me his story. Standing almost at attention he related the course of his unit's final retreat across the Vungtao Peninsula to the beach where he was captured. His description of the place perfectly matched the sheltered cove I shoved off from in '75. I remembered seeing a disorganized column of ARVN soldiers streaming past it, as though pursued. With a shock I realized that our paths had almost certainly crossed in those last hopeless days. Not noticing the knot of people that had gathered around us I told him who I was, that I had been there too. It was the first time I had told anyone in Vietnam I was a veteran. He looked to the little crowd, pointed to me and said something excitedly. I recognized the word "GI." They all grinned saying, "GI, GI, veteran!" Some of them clapped their hands. I reached into my pocket to pay Tran and pressed a fistful of bills into his hands. "For a veteran," I said. He stuffed them into his pocket, and then we shook hands, saying nothing, for a long moment. Finally we stood back and exchanged a salute. All our lookers-on applauded and patted us both on the back. Tran remounted his humble vehicle and rode away like a soldier on parade, back straight.

Soon after it was out that I was a vet it seemed the whole neighborhood knew. ARVN vets came to see me, carrying their medals and old I.D. cards. They asked if I knew so-and-so, pressed letters into my hands for relatives or friends, asked if I could help them get to America. A man who had trained at Mare Island, California, near San Francisco, wanted to know if Carol Doda still danced at the Condor. When the hotel manager learned who I was she told me that an American man on the fifth floor was ill and asked if I would look in on him. She was worried. Another American had sickened and died in the hotel a few months earlier. It seems there are a number of quiet American seekers after-they-know-not-what in Vietnam.

Thinking the guy had a normal traveler's complaint or was suffering from the heat, I bought a bottle of drinking water and some aspirin, then went up and knocked on his door. A Vietnamese boy of about eight years answered. He spoke no English, but he quietly gestured me in. A tall, fortysomething white man with a crew cut lay motionless on one of two beds. I could see he was breathing, but his eyes were open and rolled back. The boy sat on the other bed and resumed his quiet watch over the man.

"Hey, buddy," I said. "Hey, can you hear me?" He made no move so I reached out to his shoulder, shook him and repeated my call, "Hey, buddy." Gradually, he came to.

"Are you all right?" I asked.

Groping for speech he said, "Yeah, uh huh. It's just my medication."

"What are you taking?" I asked.

He recited a list that sounded like a pharmacist's inventory.

"This is my boy," he said, still groggy, pointing to the kid on the other bed. "I'm not his real dad, but I'm gonna adopt him. I'm gonna adopt his brother too, if I can find him. This is my second trip here, since the war. I was in the Americal Division in '69. My name's Terry." We shook hands.

Terry told me his story. It was one of war trauma, drugs and alcohol and treatment centers, wife beating and divorce, remarriage and divorce, more drugs, bad dreams. He lived on veteran's disability. When he told me of his bad dreams, I told him of my sleepwalking. He said, "Hey, man, tell the VA. You can get disability too. I get $1,200 a month, tax free. And there's no charge for the medication. I've been getting it for years."

I left Terry, telling him that I would come back and check on him again. When I did, he gave me the name of a doctor in the States. "He can help you get the disability," he said. "You deserve it, man. Don't forget." I left Terry to his schemes and medications.

I don't think Terry will ever notice, because of the drug fog he wanders in, but Americans are quite popular in Vietnam. Throughout the south we three were received almost like prodigal sons. Outside the city of Hue the entire village of Thuan An turned out to greet us when we arrived with letters from relatives in California. In the north we were greeted cordially and with respect, quite in contrast to the scorn reserved for the few remaining Russians. A popular story was making the rounds of the few Western tourists in the land: Two Americans were chased through the streets of Hue by an angry mob shouting "Lien Xo!" (Soviets!) The people in the north seem to regard the Americans as true foes, and the Russians as false friends, there being honor in the former. It reminded me of the John Wayne movie *McLintock*. In it the Duke and an old Indian chief had fought each other in the wars of their youth. Now, as elders in peacetime, they greeted each other warmly as "honored enemy."

Everywhere in the Socialist Republic of Vietnam we saw capitalism and Americana displayed, worn, sung, and praised. People wore hats with American flag logos. T-shirts with English words were hugely popular. It didn't matter what they said or if they made sense as long as they were in English. Typical messages were: "Sentiment Boy = American Dream Staff," the very popular "Inmutation is your sweetness: U.S. difference of information," and my personal favorite, "Three-Bear Boys have a top sense feeling!"

In Hue, the citadel, the old imperial seat, had been a symbol of Vietcong resistance. Now a souvenir shop in the audience hall sells facsimiles of U.S. military rings. All the service academies and numerous divisions, air wings, and ships are represented. When I confusedly asked why the citadel would carry U.S. military facsimiles I was told, "Because we ran out of the real ones."-

At first I thought all this American iconography was being worn like war trophies. But the people simply like Americana. "People want to have style," the ring sellers told me.

In Hanoi I found that the single most popular icon of any kind, more than Marx, Lenin, or Ho Chi Minh or a Catholic Jesus was the Marlboro Man. People cut his image from magazines and taped it up on walls, doors, windows, and inside automobiles as though all the folk were members of a new religion and he was their patron saint. I have even seen his manly gaze directed to his votaries from the ceiling.

One evening I noticed him regarding me from the window of a Hanoi cafe. A familiar fuzz-tone guitar riff reverberated through the open door. Looking in I saw people of many ages drinking bootleg Pepsi at tables in front of a big-screen TV showing a video of the Bangles playing "Walk Like an Egyptian." In my pocket I had a copy of the new constitution of Vietnam, purchased from a souvenir stand at Ho Chi Minh's tomb. The document enshrines the right of foreign capitalist enterprise to do business, make a good profit, and be free from seizure.

My mind went back to the first week of May 1975 as we sat for a few days off the coast of Vungtao waiting for refugee transport to Guam. I struck up a series of conversations with Captain Long of the late South Vietnamese Air Force. In a wistful moment, tongue only partially in cheek, he said, "You know, you Americans did it all wrong."

"I guess so," I said, "since we lost."

"That's not what I mean. Instead of sending Hanoi bombs for years, you should have sent them Coke and Levis and rock 'n' roll albums. Then they'd be begging to join you."

In Hanoi there was something I was very keen to see, and it had been on my mind since our arrival. A few weeks after the fall of Saigon in '75, a journalist in Manila told me an intriguing story: The United States had had a consulate in Hanoi until 1954, when the country was partitioned pending the elections that never came about. The Hanoi government, he said, had kept the consulate intact, all through the days of partition and through the long war, for the day when we should return to occupy it. "They always take the long view," he said. "They've always had to."

One morning I went to the foreign ministry to ask if it were true, and if so, where I might find the consulate, so eager was I to see this anomaly. I found the foreign ministry to be a combination of Byzantine, Socialist, and Mandarin; in practical terms, the answer to any question is: "My supervisor is not here today."

Having received the same answer several times, and not always politely, I found myself standing in the courtyard, frustrated. A refined looking Vietnamese man of about fifty came out of the building and approached me, limping slightly. "May I help you?" he asked. His warm voice and smile were tonic after the bureaucratic coldness I'd just met with. I told him what I was looking for, and he said a public affairs officer in another building would be available at 2 P.M. if I cared to come back.

"Thank you," I said, "you're very kind. I'm afraid I haven't been having any luck with your colleagues."

He nodded for a moment, then said, "You are a veteran, aren't you?"

"Of the Vietnam War? Yes, yes I am," I answered.

"Well," he smiled wryly, "we call it the American War."

I pointed to his weak leg and asked, "Did you fight the Americans?"

"Oh yes. And my father, he also fought the French. My brother fought the Cambodians and lost his eyes. My son fought with the Chinese. We're happy that he came back well. Did you lose anyone?"

I told him of my cousin Joey, and that my Dad has become a recluse since the war's end. He nodded thoughtfully and said, "That's too bad, too very bad."

I told him I'd come back at two o'clock, and thanked him once more. He patted me on the shoulder, almost like father to son, wished me luck, then limped back into the mandarinate. He made me think of the words of Thomas Hardy: "Yes; a quaint and curious thing war is/ You shoot a fellow down/ You'd treat if met where any bar is/ Or help to half a crown." I never did see the consulate. But I heard from a member of the U.S. State Department on the matter. It really was still there.

The one place I had to screw up my courage to visit was Vungtao. It was there I had had my last, long look at Vietnam. It had been a scene of death and smoke and roaring. The vision provided the backdrop for most of the bad dreams I've had since then. It symbolized the mess we left behind, and the breakage of people and promises. I'm embarrassed to say so, but I've long felt culpable for what we did there. To those self-righteous opponents of the war who blamed me and other vets personally for it, I've always maintained that I was a military man discharging my military duties in the lawful manner. And that is true. I have nothing personally to be ashamed of. And yet...and yet deep inside I felt the need to say "I'm sorry," for myself, and for all of us, every one.

I rented a Czech-built CZ Jawa motorcycle and made the drive to the coastal resort town of Vungtao. All along the way the sounds and smells of my dreams followed me. The wind in my ears screamed horribly. The roar of the bike's engine was the roar of helicopters and trucks and landing craft. Its thick, clinging exhaust carried that special acrid stink of war smoke. A couple of times the engine failed and I wheeled the bike to one of the many shade-tree mechanics who set up shop along the roads. I wanted to use the occasion as an excuse to turn back. I told myself I had made the effort, that I didn't know how much farther it was, that I might get lost. But I had crossed too many miles and too many years to turn back.

I continued until I smelled the ocean very strongly and saw gulls circling in the near distance. Dreading what I might find, I drove on to the beach whence I had shoved off eighteen years before. I expected to see a deserted, pockmarked, and dirty wasteland. But I found it pristine, clean, and fully restored. All of its wounds have healed. On this occasion I saw no warriors and no refugees. I saw families on picnics. Kids playing ball, making sandcastles, and laughing. The weather was the same as before: warm, brilliant, and calm. A gentle surf sighed easily on the shore. I dismounted and walked down the shore to the waterline and listened. All I could hear were the natural sounds of a tropic beach. I snuffed at the air and smelled only warm, moist cleanliness. I tried to conjure up the scene from so long ago, but it would not come. I was simply unable to imagine it. I heard someone approaching from behind and turned to see a pretty girl, no more than eighteen years old, greeting me in strained English. She chatted me up for a while to practice what she called her "American." She had a musical giggle, and she gave me a flower as a souvenir which she pinned to my shirt. As she walked away, down the beach and back to her picnic, the spirit of the place seemed to wrap itself around me, softly, and I could hear a voice within say, "It's O.K. now, it's all over. No more bad dreams. You can go home now. But come back also. You now belong here, too."

In 1999 I again went to Vietnam to do some shooting, but it was strictly peaceful. I took part in a television documentary. TV shooting had been going well. I demonstrated to the world how to eat a duck embryo, discussed love potions with an herbalist, held forth on various strains of rice, and drank lots of beer. So far, so good. Then the director had the crew tape me having breakfast with a former Vietcong spy.

The scene was difficult, even after all these years of peace. The man is in his eighties and is highly decorated for his service in "the American War." They call him Grandpa Toai. During the war he ran a restaurant popular with American planning officers. As they dined he listened in to their conversations. He gathered intelligence and took it upstairs to a conference room where he and his comrades would plot actions against our forces, including some of those whom he just overheard. Nobody knows how many Americans died as a result.

He still operates the restaurant, Pho Binh, and that's where we did the scene. I felt uneasy on the way there, like I was about to enter the lion's den. War memories are still close to the surface. He didn't know that I am a veteran, and upon meeting treated me very cordially and correctly. He seemed to me just a nice old man, but I couldn't get it out of my head that he had done in a lot of my fellows. I know, we did in even more of his, and trashed his country as well. But emotions don't always comport with such logical symmetry. I couldn't help but see dog tags and body bags as I looked at him. I couldn't help but be aware that Americans had doomed themselves, at his hands, merely by entering the room I was now in.

Still, I was polite and cordial, just as he was. Opening old wounds is in no one's interest. As we finished the scene I took my leave of him. Speaking through our interpreter I decided to give him a surprise. I offered him my hand and said, "Grandfather, I am a veteran of the American War. I'm happy to meet you now in peacetime." He paused, looked up to my face and regarded me with a searching look. Then he put his arms around me, and drew me to him closely. For a moment he simply held me tight. Then he said, "It is my honor to receive you."

We stepped back. We rendered each other a salute. I said, "Goodbye, old soldier." He said, "Please come visit me again, before I die." Then I sought the refuge of our van, so no one would see me bawl.

1 6 *B r o t h e r h o o d*

WHAT SEPARATES US IN THE FIRST PLACE, HOW does it happen? What are the processes that drive us apart, and then bring us back together? Sometimes I think I know. But then in moments of clarity I admit that I do not. Where do we belong in the wide world? In our birthplaces or foreign fields? They say home is where you hang your hat; home is where the heart is; home is where, when you go there, they have to take you in. Is home on the range? Home sweet home. Where do we belong? And with whom? Do we really have the power to choose? Or do they choose us?

It was my first trip to Africa and I had stepped into a neighborhood bar in Nairobi, Kenya; the kind of place ordinary guys stop in on their way home from work, or use as a respite from normal cares. You know: an African "Cheers" kind of joint. The place was crowded with regulars so I gingerly shouldered my way to the bar.

"*Jambo!*" the barman said, giving me the national salutation.

"*Jambo* back at ya, pal!" I said. "How 'bout a large Tusker lager?"

Tusker is a fine brew, and easy to spot among the others by the elephant head motif on the label. As I waited for my beer the guy sitting to my right said, *"Jambo!"*

"Jambo to you, too," said I.

"Would you like to buy me a beer?" he asked. I had quickly found this to be a common question in Kenya. No sooner would they *jambo* me than they'd ask for a drink. Even a woman accosted me so, out on the street in broad daylight. And she wasn't even pretty! She was an ugly, tobacco-toothed, over-the-hill, bone-in-her-nose National Geographic magazine cover girl in a Western-style dress, the kind that Richard Pryor has been known to call "a floppy-titted zebra bitch." She cornered me between rush hour traffic and a gaping open manhole. And I don't think she even stopped to *jambo* me, she just smiled her tar-and-nicotine smile and asked me to take her out for drinks. Drinks! Plural!

So by the time the guy in the bar asked me for a drink I was practiced in my polite refusal. "Thanks for the offer," I said, "but I'll pass this time." And I turned the other way. In front of me now sat a another man.

"Uh...*Jambo*," I said.

"Jambo, friend!" he said with a broad smile. "My name is Patrick Chege. Are you from America?"

"Yeah, from California. Does it show?"

"It's easy to tell. You Americans all stand at the bar like cowboys."

At that moment the barman set the Tusker lager in front of me, and Patrick nonchalantly laid down forty Kenyan shillings to cover the cost. He said nothing, just smiled. "Well here's something new," I thought. I picked up the one-liter bottle, toasted him and took a long pull. Aarrgghh! I had forgotten to specify *cold* Tusker. Kenyans generally drink their beer at room temperature, holding the belief that it's unhealthy to drink ice-cold drinks. I'm sure it's something they contracted from their former British rulers who taught them how to make and drink lager-style beer. As we all know, the

Brits quaff their suds at room temperature. But a British room normally requires the wearing of woolens and huddling next to a coal fire. Your average Kenyan room sits a few degrees from the equator. And when it's packed with Kenyan good ol' boys and the odd American tourist, it can be sweltering. Beer is one of the most important things in daily life to me. It is one of the eternal verities and high virtues of civilization. I know and acknowledge that there are people in the world who use and enjoy it in ways different from mine. But I do not like their ways. I respect them, but I do not like them. It was only by an effort of will that I was able to swallow.

"We make a pretty good beer here in Kenya, don't you think?"

"Oh yeah. Good."

Patrick and I talked about our lives for a while, sharing our very different stories. I told him I was eating my way through the world and writing a book about it.

"I'm in the food game, too," he said. "I ship beef cattle to Saudi Arabia. We have very good cattle here."

So we chatted about the qualities of good beef and where to find the best. And I grimaced as I choked down more of the equatorially warm Tusker. Somewhere in the ebb and flow of our warm and beery chat a jolt of realization struck me. Though I had been in Africa, been in Nairobi, for three or four days, this was my first awareness of it: Every face I saw was black, except for mine.

Now, I live in Berkeley, California, the epicenter of political correctness (it's where the term was coined) and racial rhetoric. And only a few minutes walk from Oakland, birthplace of the Black Panthers. I can hardly walk out the door of my home without being acutely aware of the "racial heritage" of everyone I see, including myself. Right-wing radio-talk führers and whining minority malcontents make it their mission in life to keep me so informed. And the blondest of blond, guilty, white liberal speechifiers and wavers of placards will take pains to remind me that I am "melanin deprived" and that others are not. And if I were to stumble into an "African-American" bar in the wrong part of Oakland, well, I would likely stumble very quickly right back out. And as long as I'm telling the truth, any American who found himself the possessor of the only black face in a cowboy or biker bar would feel the same as I would in that bad-ass Oakland bar. For that matter, he might not feel at ease anywhere in North America except at home, behind locked doors, and maybe not even there.

We don't like to talk about this sort of thing. But there I was, at least three days in Nairobi, at the bottom of the tourist season, seemingly the only paleface in town, and in a bar full of "young black males." And I had only just now noticed! It had taken at least seventy-two hours to notice that I was the lone European sort of guy in a sea of African sort of guys (and gals...grrrls...women...O.K., Womyn! Don't hurt me!).

As I was being stunned by this revelation Patrick said, "You know, my younger brother is in your country."

"Oh?"

"In Texas. He studies there at the university. There are many Kenyans there. Oh yes. They all like to go to Texas, where the cowboys are."

"I guess cowboys are popular everywhere," I said, in something of a daze.

"Yes. But he says the Kenyans encounter a lot of racialism there."

"Uh..." Had warm Tusker lager destroyed my cowboy poker face? Was Patrick now reading my thoughts?

"Do you think there's a lot of racialism in Texas?" he asked.

Racialism. Damned British tutelage. Always got to stick in an extra syllable. "Well," I said tentatively, "I suppose it might depend on the region. I hope the cowboys aren't giving him too much trouble."

"Oh, it's not the cowboys. The cowboys are first-class fellows."

"Then it's the KKK?"

"The what?"

"Never mind."

"Actually, it's the black Americans that cause him the most trouble."

"Huh?"

The world was suddenly upside down. Here was I, perfectly at ease as the only white among a multitude of blacks; and there was Patrick's brother in Texas (in Texas, damn it!) getting grief from the "black Americans." (His words, not mine. I never heard an African-African say "African-American.") I took a slug of Tusker. Jesus, it's awful when it's warm! And I was beginning to wonder if it were a ticket through the looking glass.

"Um, I'm afraid I don't quite understand, Patrick."

"My brother writes to me that the black Americans discriminate against him because he is African."

Now this was just too much. And warm beer, too! I felt sure that if I took one more swallow of the hot suds it would cast loose all my moorings. Fortunately, Patrick called to the barman, "*Jambo!* Two more Tuskers."

"Make mine cold!" I shouted with an urgency that Patrick noticed.

"Oh, yes," he said, "My brother reminds me that the Americans insist on cold beer."

He laughed as he threw down some more notes, tipping the barman 10 percent. The two Tuskers appeared before us, and I could see from the beaded condensation on mine that it was as cold as a witch's tit, and as soon as I nursed on it all would be right with the world. I took a long pull and let the coldly warming liquid foam down my throat in an icy, reassuring froth. My balance restored, I said, "So, Patrick, would you kindly explain your last remark?"

"Well, my brother enjoys the company of the cowboys. They take him riding and teach him many things. This is good because he will come home to be in the cattle business like me."

"Uh huh." And another fortifying gulp of the cold one.

"But the black Americans shun him and the other Kenyans because they are ashamed of their African roots."

"No. No way. I see black Americans all the time wearing African medallions, and African clothes, and taking African names. And, and, oh, all kinds of stuff."

"Yes, yes. These things are all well and good. But when they meet an African they have another opinion."

"I don't get it." We each took a long bracing swig, the warm and the cold.

"When they meet an African they meet a Third World person. They meet someone from a country that has 50 percent literacy, 30 percent malnutrition and, I hate to say it but, a government that cannot or will not govern. A poor country that's going to stay poor a long time. They are ashamed to be associated with such a country. And I cannot entirely blame them. But when they meet a Kenyan or other African they make sure to tell them that they are Americans. And they make the Africans feel badly about it. Of course I'm not saying that all of the black Americans are this way. Maybe only a few. But enough to make the Africans feel badly, and to write some sadness into their letters home."

This gave me pause. And I recalled a brief item I saw in that morning's newspaper about a group of African-Americans in a popular Nairobi restaurant. They felt they weren't being waited on quickly enough, so one of them stood up and proudly shouted, "We're Americans!" According to the report, they got quicker service.

"You know, Patrick, I finished reading a book recently. It's called *Schindler's List*."

"Oh yes. I saw the movie."

"Isn't it curious how some of the Jews helped the Nazis to pursue other Jews, because they were different kinds of Jews. Isn't that crazy?"

"Yes, of course. But then, I think we are a crazy species."

We took a thoughtful sip of the warm and the cold, rolling

it over our tongues, enjoying it each in his own way, and lost for a moment in our private thoughts.

"Do you have racialism where you live, in California?"

"Uh..."

How could I tell him the truth without a social science treatise? How could I explain the racial balkanization of my home state without making it sound like race warfare? How could I tell him that the short walk to Oakland was a problematic, possibly dangerous affair, but the worst of the long walk to Africa was the occasional warm beer? Could I explain the oppressive idea of political correctness without sounding like a neo-Nazi, conservative, sexist, racist, homophobic, patriarchist, straight white male oppressor of women and people of color and the gay-lesbian-bisexual-multicultural alliance?

"Not officially," I said. "We have laws against it."

"Do the police enforce the laws?"

"Do the police enforce the laws here?"

Patrick laughed and said, "I'll ask you no more, my friend. *Jambo!* Barman! Two more Tuskers. And make them both cold. I'll try it your way this time."

1 7   *The   Crowded   Hour*

How does that saying go? "Beer will get you through times of no food better than food will get you through times of no beer." I don't think I agree. The one without the other is less than one. And without the company of like-minded individuals the two are insufficient. But bring them all three together, throw in some bad luck and some good luck, and you've got all you need.

Garrett, Matt, and I were together on the road again. This time on the Sea of Cortez, and we had arrived at Bahía de Los Angeles. Garrett's rebuilt 1959 Willys jeep was performing well off-road. The Argo, my modified Toyota 4x4, was in its element. We called the two vehicles our "desert ships." From Bahía de Los Angeles we planned to cross the Llano de San Juan portion of the desert to Bahía de San Franciscito, to the south. It's a small bay at the tip of a wide cape; an out-of-the-way place in an out-of-the-way land. We had heard that the fishing and diving were good and that a man and woman lived there year round. We mapped out a route that would take us in a great semicircle, first going inland, to westward, then wheeling south and finally east, back to the coast. Another route, from the west is the preferred one, as the road is tolerable and clearly marked. The way we chose is poorly charted and the region was abandoned by its few rancheros many years ago. The only remnants of their dwellings are melting adobe walls and some rusting utensils. A score of wild asses, descendents of those left behind, survive.

We filled every empty vessel we had with water. We bought all the gasoline we could from a man who sold it from oil drums on a flatbed truck. We strained it through a cloth, but in spite of that it clogged Garrett's fuel filter so badly we had to change it. I bought what fresh groceries were available in the local tienda (shop), including a nice, fat barnyard chicken, fed on corn. Ice was in short supply but we were able to buy two blocks. We got six cases of beer. Our desert ships were soon provisioned, fueled, and made ready for their voyage across the Dry Sea.

Judging from our chart, we determined that if we left early in the morning—and didn't tarry or encounter any problems—we could arrive by late afternoon. We departed at 7 A.M. The road out of Bahía de Los Angeles is a very badly corrugated dirt track. The going was very slow. But the Dry Sea is beautiful, and no one was voyaging on it but us. We spliced the mainbrace (sailor talk for having a cold one) at 10 A.M. Shortly after, I noticed up ahead a small stone building with bars on its windows next to a fifteen-foot-high heap of slag. We stopped next to the little blockhouse. A bearded man in dirty coveralls appeared from behind the slag heap and waved us over to him. Rounding the heap we saw a wall tent and the stranger disappeared into it. We followed. He stood in the middle, half-smiling, saying nothing. *"Buenos dias,"* I offered.

He said, "Howdy. Have seat."

"You're American?"

"Yep," he drawled. "What are you boys doin' way down here?"

"We're on our way to San Franciscito. How about you?"

He allowed himself to smile and said, "Ha. Well, boys, this

here just happens to be the Las Flores mine. Me and my buddy work it."

The Las Flores mine was on our chart, but it was listed as having been abandoned long ago. He put his thumbs under his armpits and said, "This ain't really the best way to get to San Franciscito. You ought to go by way of El Arco. Know where that is?"

"Yeah," I said. "But we want to go this way. We'll go out through El Arco."

"Look here," he warned. "I been down that way. This road peters out in a few miles. Then it's just tire swale. After that it's nothin'. There was an earthquake a few years ago and then the winter rain washed away a whole hillside where there might have been a road. You'll never get them rigs through."

I didn't tell him how the Argo is equipped. I just smiled a little and said, "We'll get through." I thought of saying something like, "The road may be bad, but we're badder," but I didn't.

"Don't think I'm just blowin' smoke, here!" he said impatiently. "You won't be the first ones I seen walkin' back." The tent door parted and his buddy walked in, another bearded man in dirty coveralls. "Miguel," the American said in heavily accented Spanish, *"Di les a los hombres como malo el camino es."* Tell these guys how bad the road is.

Miguel grinned and shrugged and said, *"Que camino? No hay camino. Se termino hace unos anos. Ha ha."* What road? There is no road. There hasn't been a road for some years. He bubbled a little laughter.

"We'll make it," we said, and got up to leave.

The gringo called after us, "Oh yeah? Well I'll be waitin' for you when you come walkin' back! If I see any buzzards flyin' that way I won't wait up!"

"Adios, muchachos!" Miguel called gleefully. *"Buena suerta. La necesitaran!"* Good luck, boys. You're going to need it. And he cackled. We climbed back aboard our vehicles and left the two men behind, the one scowling, the other laughing.

The weather was fine, clear skies and warm. Here and there a roadrunner scouted ahead of us. We stopped now and then and Garrett and Matt would light cigarettes. The air was so still that their smoke rose up in thin, straight columns. Garrett had installed a detachable sunroof in the Willys and a man could stand up in the hole. We called it the turret and took turns riding in it. When Matt rode the turret he pretended he was reviewing his troops and would return their salutes. I pretended I was seeking the northwest passage to the Indies. Garrett thought deep thoughts.

The level terrain began to roll and undulate into low hills. As we progressed the hills became steeper and more pointed at the top until they became rows of enormous knives thrusting up from the ground, towering over us and sharp enough to rip the belly of the sky. The road did peter out, just like the man said. After that we followed the tire swale until it ended abruptly where a hill had come sliding down. Earth movement or rain, or both, had broken off the knifepoint hilltop and tumbled it down across our path, leaving truck-size boulders to block our way. Even a mule would have trouble getting through.

We scouted left and right. Either way led to more broken, boulder-strewn ground. We backtracked some distance, then probed left and right again. We found a faint, old track that wound its sinuous way through the mountainous blades. We followed it, twisting and turning, for two or three hours. Here and there other faint tracks crossed it. Or was it crossing itself, and we were traveling in figures of eight? The sawtooth hills all looked the same. I remembered another time, lost in the desert's sameness of terrain and confusion of old trails. Someone had laid out markers of three stones that showed the way at each juncture. I had no idea where they led, but I was in nowhere and they were leading to somewhere. I followed and came to safety. Here I looked in vain for markers.

After a very long time the road came to a stop where the land dropped steeply away and settled into a broad, flat valley.

We needed to know where we were so Garrett and I got the big chart and laid it out on Argo's hood. With compass and ruler we took bearings from all directions. We were able to determine our general area, but the quality of our chart and the riotous topography made it impossible to pinpoint. Matt, who had been busy shooting pictures, came over and asked, "So where are we?"

Without looking up from the chart I said, "We're lost, Matt."

"Cool," he said. And he meant it, and went on shooting pictures.

I trained my binoculars on the valley floor, looking for roads, fences, any sign of humans. I saw two bleached-looking lines running east to west. I couldn't tell if they were roads or rock ribs or something else. They started and ended within the confines of the valley, leading to no place. In Baja there are many old roads that lead to no place; and many places near no road. I studied the valley's surface. It was thickly grown with cactus but the earth looked smooth enough to drive over. If we could gain the other side, we thought, we might find a way out. It was that or go back. We decided to press on.

Getting down into the valley was tricky because the slope was so steep and the surface loose. The Argo, which weighs only twenty-one hundred pounds, slipped and slid several times. The Willys, however, when fully laden, weighs two and a half tons. It came down the hill like a snowplow out of control, mashing any cactus in its way. Garrett's jutting jaw was set so tight I thought it would crack, and Matt was yelling, "Yahoo! Ride 'em cowboy!"

On our safe arrival we cut engines and spliced the mainbrace. We strolled among the tall cactus. The valley was very deep and at the bottom the air was palpably warmer. It felt thick in my lungs. It lay still and heavy, and the dust we had kicked up hung in it without moving, as though weightless. It muffled sounds. We had to shout to each other, even at short distances. Walking about, we blundered onto an old track. It was so dim it looked like a giant hand had come down and tried to erase it, tried to rub it off the face of the earth so that no one would come this way.

We remounted and followed it, weaving among the cactus to the other side. Here a still loose, but gentler, slope rose up out of the valley. We climbed it, hubs locked in four-wheel drive. As we crested the top the air cooled in an instant and filled my nostrils with the tang of the sea. "We're near!" I cried. "I can smell the sea!" A breeze was drifting easily in from the Sea of Cortez. We scanned the horizon, and though we couldn't see the water, we could see a smudge of blue reflecting onto the bottom of a distant cloud.

The dim track developed into a tolerable road as we made way toward the sea. Within an hour we could hear the surf. When we arrived at the shore we saw a white beach stretching for a thousand yards, but no one was there. It was not San Franciscito we had come to. It was a graveyard. The bones of marine mammals lay all around us. Some were scattered and solitary. Others lay in piles, or cairns, as though the dying had thrown themselves on the heaps of their fellows to die among them. Still-rotting carcasses offered their stench up to the air.

We took out the chart again, and again took many bearings, and noted the lay of the shoreline. This time we were able to fix our position exactly. The semicircle we had driven was short by a third. We still had miles to go. I looked to the western horizon and measured the sun at two hands high. "We've got about two and a half hours of light," I told the others. "You want to spend the night here or press on? We can make a nice enough camp and have a good meal tonight."

"Press on! Even if we don't get there by dark. Let's go."

We pressed on, and the road steadily improved. By sunset we were sustaining a speed of ten miles per hour. I called Garrett on the radio. "We must be getting pretty close, G-man."

"Yeah," he answered. "I think I could make a little more speed. How about you?"

"Yeah, I think so. It'll be bumpy, but at least there's no traffic."

We gradually increased our speed. By dark we were doing twenty-five to thirty. The Argo was in the lead and the Willys close behind. It was bumpy, and sometimes I caught air, but we were closing in on our goal and were eager to make it. In the corner of my left eye a dark shape zipped past me. "Must have scared a coyote," I thought. "Had to be a coyote, even though it didn't look like one. It couldn't have been a..."

"Argo, Argo!" the radio blasted. "We just lost a wheel!"

"You mean you've got a flat?"

"No, we lost a wheel!"

"One of those spares tied to the roof came off?"

"No! A wheel, a wheel! The front, driver side wheel just snapped off and went flying!"

I stopped. "So I guess it wasn't a coyote," I said to myself. I turned my truck around and flicked on the high beams. Matt was out in the cactus with a flashlight picking up pieces of broken metal. Garrett stood on the side of the road with a beer in his hand, thinking deep, dark thoughts. The Willys, amazingly, was not on its side or upside down. "Maybe it's too heavy to flip over," I thought. It was on three wheels and a spindle. The entire wheel assembly had broken clean off. As I drove up I could see that the spindle had driven into the dirt and dug a furrow thirty feet long. I could have planted a row of corn in it. I got out of the Argo and walked over to Garrett. Thus began our crowded hour.

"A bit of metal fatigue," he said grimly. "Would have happened sooner or later. Guess it's better here than on the freeway."

Garrett was shipwrecked, run up on the reefs and shoals of the Dry Sea and listing badly to port. We gathered up the broken bits of his desert ship. We jacked it up and put the now retrieved wheel underneath to level it out. We solemnly spliced the mainbrace. Then came the storm.

The narrow Baja Peninsula, and the adjacent, equally narrow Sea of Cortez, form a thin barrier between two great weather giants: the North American Desert to the east; the Pacific Ocean to the West. When pressure differences occur between the two, their natural tendency is to equalize. But the thin wall of Baja prevents it, until the pressure builds high enough to crack the barrier. When it cracks, the winds come raging through without warning, as if to make up for lost time. That night the barrier cracked.

With a mighty *whoosh*, a spinning cloud of dust leaped up from the ground and stung us in the eyes and filled our mouths with earth. The blast picked up the light, dry cactus thorns that lay on the desert floor and sent them whirling through the air in a swarm of tiny darts. Choking, I dropped my beer bottle and ran for cover in the lee of the Willys. The others followed, hacking and coughing. Matt motioned to us to follow as he opened the rear doors and we scrambled in, battening the doors behind us.

The inside of the Willys was as dark as a cave. It was all a-jumble with gear thrown about in that bumpy, final, thirty-foot ride. Our lantern was in the Argo, so Garrett lit a match and dug out a storm candle he carries for emergencies. He lit the candle and hung it from a cross member on the ceiling. As the Willys shook in the teeth of the wind the candle swung, casting kaleidoscope shadows. We rearranged some of the gear and did what we could to make things tolerably comfortable. We sat on, and were surrounded by, cases of beer, ice boxes, backpacks, camp tools and all the other jetsam in the hold of Garrett's desert ship. We were so cramped our knees were touching and one man could feel another's breath when he sighed. The storm candle swung.

Garrett was very quiet. The flickering shadows on his face were dark and deep. "Don't worry, Garrett," we told him. "We're going to get out of this. Even if we have to drive the Argo all the way to San Diego and back for parts. We'll get the parts and fix this beastie. If it takes a week!" He forced a smile and a wink and nodded.

"Is there anything to eat?" Matt asked.

"Yes, indeed, I could go for something," Garrett said, perking up. "I don't think I've eaten all day."

"Ricardo?" Matt said inquiringly. "Chef? Chief cook and bottle washer? Do you have something up your sleeve for hungry castaways?"

I remembered that nice, fat, barnyard chicken. I had planned to marinate it, then barbecue it over some hickory chips I had brought along and serve it with *fettucine al pesto* and grilled onions. "None of that now," I thought. "But what? A good dinner would be the perfect spirit-lifter right now. And cold rations from a can...from bad to worse. But what can I do in this space...?"

My first inkling of what to do came when my imagination's nose smelled the finished product. "Of course!" I thought, adding from memory the cheerful pop of a champagne cork.

"Matthew," I said. "I'll need your help, bring your flashlight. Garrett, make sure we have access to the iceboxes. Watch our light through the windshield. When you see us coming back, stand by to let us in."

Matt and I crouched near the rear doors and took hold of the handles. "Ready, Matt?"

We broke open the doors and leaped out into the storm. The doors slammed shut with a *whump*. The cold wind screamed in anger. It flung the Dry Sea's dusty spume, stinging our bodies and wearing the paint work off our vehicles. We squinted and covered our eyes.

We ran, listing into the wind. When we reached the Argo we threw up the hatch and clambered in, closing it behind. "O.K. Hold the light for me," I said. I found a canvas bag and began digging through the compartments. I gathered wine, vegetables, both fresh and canned, and some things from the icebox, including that nice, fat, barnyard chicken. In my dry goods box I found the seasonings and pasta. I had a full load so I held the light while Matt gathered my little one burner propane stove, skillet, small stockpot, colander, and small utensils.

"What are we going to eat, Ricardo?" Matt asked.

"What all castaways eat," I said with a satisfied smile. "Ship's biscuit. But oh, what a ship."

Using the flashlight, we signaled Garrett that we were ready to return. We held our goods close, lifted the hatch and ran through the choking blast again. We stopped in the lee of the Willys and banged on it. As soon as the rear door swung, we threw in the supplies and leaped in after.

Garrett had rearranged the gear to make a little more room for cooking and provide a bit of shelf space. We had no room to move or turn about, but at least everything was in arm's reach. From my canvas bag I drew out a bottle of Codorniu Brut, Spanish champagne. "Here, Garrett," I said. "Ice this down."

I set up my little kitchen in the space Garrett had made between me and the rear doors. It was about a foot square. My cutting board went on a case of beer, the stove on the floor, spice box in Matt's lap, and the canvas bag hung from the wall. While the bubbly cooled I poured water from Matt's canteen into the stockpot and set it on the stove to boil. I borrowed the G-man's pocketknife and quickly boned the chicken —removing the skin—and cut it into bite-size pieces. I sliced some scallions, thin.

When the water boiled I dropped in the pasta and cooked it al dente. Then came the tricky part: draining boiling water from pasta inside a cramped, six-foot square space with a raging storm outside. I was sitting cross-legged and could do no other, but I was, at least, near the rear doors. Matt was able to get to his feet, though bent over at the waist 90 degrees, lean over me, and grasp the handle of the windward rear door. If he were to slip and fall on me there would be hot water and pasta to go around. At my signal Matt lunged at the door and opened it about ten inches, forming a lee in which I could operate. A little dust got in but, at that point who cared? Colander in one hand and pot in the other I drained the pasta, returned it to the pot and tossed it with butter. "There!" I said. "Cover that with something so it won't get cold and give me some champagne."

Garrett had the bottle out and was twisting the cork, letting it ease out ever so slowly so as to prevent a too-rapid expansion of the bubbles and a ricocheting of the cork through our little cabin. When the long cork had almost wholly cleared the bottle he gave it a tug, and the pop echoed off the metal walls. The sound cracked the vessels of mirth and let it gush forth. A canteen cup and two coffee mugs did good service as crystal flutes. The happy liquid gurgled in the bottle as it tumbled into our cups and frothed over.

"To the storm!" Garrett offered.

"Yes!" I agreed. "To Meteora!"

"The bitch," said Matt.

"She's in a snit now, Matt," I said. "She doesn't like being pulled back and forth by the two giants on either side here. She'll rage tonight, but come the morning she'll be beautiful again and charm us out of our beds. Just you wait and see."

I lit the fire again, and in the skillet melted unsalted butter. As it foamed, its sweet, dairy smell filled the cabin. Into the pan I put the chicken, sprinkled it with salt and pepper, and began to brown it. We all stopped talking for a moment to listen to the sound as it sizzled; that warm, familiar sound of sizzling meat that says, "Here there is succor." To the meat I added the scallions and we savored their pungent fragrance. The swinging light of the storm candle was too dim for me to judge the meat's doneness so Matt held the flashlight for me. Garrett poured more bubbly.

When the chicken was thoroughly browned I added tarragon, a can of mushrooms with their liquor, a box of frozen artichoke hearts (they had thawed days before but had kept well on ice), some chicken bouillon and a good splash of vermouth. I brought it to a boil, then reduced the flame and let it simmer. I set the pasta next to the stove to keep it warm. The vapors rising from the pan filled the cabin with moist warmth and spread the delicate, yet earthy smells of mushrooms and artichokes and the subtle, sometimes elusive licorice aroma of tarragon. Outside, Meteora was venting her spleen, but the inside of our cabin began to glow.

When the liquid in the pan had fully reduced I added sour cream and a spoonful of Dijon mustard, stirred it well, brought it quickly to the boil once more, and it was done. We had left our plates in the Argo but the forks were in my spice box. We stirred the pasta into the creamy sauce and set the pan between us on an up-ended box of tools. From my bag on the wall I drew out a bottle of red rioja, in keeping with the Spanish sparkler. We poured the wine into our cups and toasted the sailor's toast: "To those at sea; and so, to us."

After dinner I had one more thing in my canvas bag: a bottle of Warre's Warrior port. This we passed around and drank from the bottle. The air was chill but I could feel the warmth from the bodies of my two mates. We sat as close as conspirators plotting an escape. We talked of women, we talked of friends, of cars, of things lost, of things won. We talked of women again. Several times we stopped to sing for each other. Garrett sang old Irish songs about great loves and failed revolts. I sang from old movies, such as *The Wizard of Oz*. Matt's favorite music is that of the Rolling Stones. We decided it wouldn't sound good a cappella, and so he played Master of Ceremonies instead.

When the port was gone, our songs were all sung and stories were told enough, we sat in quiet comfort. The candle was burning out, flickering its last. Our eyes drooped, heads nodded. We wriggled and snuggled and yawned one more time. In our ears Meteora's howl faded to a whisper, the sound retreating to some far horizon. A murmur sounded, "Don't worry, Garrett. We won't leave your ship behind."

"Somehow we'll fix it."

"I know."

The next morning the storm was finished. The hammerforce winds had become perfumed little sighs, smelling of the clean sea not far away. One or two little dust devils, the size of cats, scampered across the ground, then melted into air. The sky was cloudless and the sun was warm.

I began to make coffee on the tailgate of the Argo and lay out some fruit for breakfast. Matthew came over looking for my little folding shovel, the one I call the toilet handle. "Remember the part in *Ulysses*," he asked with a glint in his eye, "where Leopold Bloom goes to the outhouse?"

"Uh, yeah. I think so," I said, clutching a handful of bananas.

"Do you remember what Joyce says?

"What?"

"As Bloom sat there he felt a gentle loosening in his bowels."

So saying, Matt picked up the shovel, stuffed some TP into his shirt pocket and said, "I go now, Ricardo, to loosen gently." He turned and walked, whistling, into the cactus, juggling the shovel like a ninepin. Moments after he had disappeared, I heard him shout, "Ulysses!" Only a cavalier like Matt could turn a humble bowel movement into a literary experience.

After breakfast, and more literary experiences, we held a council of war. We decided that Matt and Garrett would stay with the Willys and do what work they could on it. I would go on to San Franciscito and see what aid might be available. If we were lucky, the ranchero might have a rig big enough to tow the Willys to shelter. Then Garrett would be able to stay there until Matt and I went to San Diego for a new wheel assembly. There would be no chance of getting the parts in Mexico; Willys jeeps have never been sold in Mexico. It would be difficult enough to find the parts at home, considering the vehicle's age. It would take us a day to reach the highway, then a day or two to reach San Diego, probably a day to find the parts, and then three days back to Garrett. We had no idea how long the repair work would take. We would leave all food and drink and other supplies with Garrett, taking only money and fuel.

I reached the little bay in about forty-five minutes. I first saw it, and the rancho, as I came up over a rise. Out on the tip of a cape, it juts out into the sea and catches a lot of wind. A gust blew a swirl of gritty sand through my open window, forcing me to close it. I saw that the rancho was composed of about six buildings, some of wood, others of thatch. I could see no people, even through my binoculars. I rolled slowly down the hill, looking for any signs of life. I reached the first building, cut the engine and got out. I listened, but the only sound was wind. "I wonder if that's Meteora laughing at me?" I thought. "It would be a shame to have to leave Garrett out there in the desert for a week, this close to shelter."

I made my way along the buildings, stopping at each one to check for occupants. In one I saw a rusty old car frame and what seemed to have been a workbench. "Maybe this was their garage," I thought. "It might be useful to us. Although there's nothing left of that car. Like buzzards strip a corpse; not a thing left but the rusted frame and the wheels. Can't even tell what make it was." Then I saw the rusty, dirty, faded label. It said "Jeep."

I found a man, his wife, and three of their cousins living at the rancho, and told them of our plight. With the enthusiasm of an Italian soccer team they sprang into action, removed a wheel assembly from the old Jeep and mounted a three vehicle convoy to the Willys. When we arrived on the scene, the look on Garrett's and Matt's faces told me they knew we were saved.

The three cousins went to work on the wheel and it quickly became apparent that we didn't have all the necessary parts and tools. But necessity is a mother, and all that. Living and working in the desert, where all things are rare, had made the three guys brilliant jury riggers. They made a clamp from an old spring. Then they made a spring from an old clamp! They supplemented their tools with rocks and nails and boot heels, and they shimmied and shimmed, pounded and prodded everything into place. They did so much with so little, I became convinced that they could do anything with nothing. Matt said, "Richard, they can jury-rig a Jeep as well as you can jury-rig a dinner!"

After six hours of mechanical marvel they presented us with a bill for $500. They wanted $250 for the part and $250 for labor. Between the three of us we had maybe $200.

"Richard," Garrett said, "let me ask you something. Didn't you agree on a price ahead of time?"

"Uh...Matt," I said. "Didn't I hear you talking money with them earlier?"

"Money?"

Two hours of hard negotiation and a few rounds of beer brought the price down to $100. Not bad for a rare old part, imaginative jury-rigging, and eighteen man-hours of labor. We figured the repairs would last us till we returned home, maybe a little farther, but that was fine with us. In the end, Garrett drove on that wheel for three years. And the dish I prepared that night of the storm resides in my recipe file as Jury-Rig Chicken. All in all, a victory. A small one, to be sure, in the grand scheme. Born of the crowded hour.

The crowded hour, and the human response to it, is the essence of the experience of war. There are many kinds of war, and many ways to make it. Battle may be joined with weapons or without. The conflict may be in the field or in the soul; between nations or armies or ideas. The foe might be soldiers, or the elements, or the self, or other players in grand warlike games. It requires only the challenge, and the presence of Homo Agonistes: what Theodore Roosevelt called "the man in the arena." He with the blood on his face, sweaty and begrimed. Ready to continue, to press on regardless. To victory, or defeat as fortune may cast. When this man stands ready for the buffets and the blows, ready to persevere, and to prevail or fall, only then does the god of war open his eyes. Only then does he breathe fire into the combatant. And thus begins the crowded hour.

1 8   *G a m e s*

Saigon has always been a lady, and a beautiful one, but a lady with a touch of sin. There is a game you can play here when you are tired of more mundane pastimes and hanker after a contest of wits and nerve. It is not inherently dangerous, but neither is it a game for the faint of heart. Much is at stake. For in this game the hunted becomes the hunter, and the predator turns prey. I should say that there is currently an Englishwoman residing at the 333 Hotel with her left leg in a cast for a torn ligament. But her's is the only injury I have ever heard of. And she played at three o'clock in the morning after an evening of drinking. And she played rough. Many beginners do. I did.

So you must not play this game when you have been drinking, or ill, or in a bad mood. Your senses and your reflexes, and your powers of observation and decision must be in top form, because you, the visitor, the amateur, will be going up against the pros. But you can win at this game. If you follow my advice and learn from me you can win almost every time. In fact, I haven't lost yet. Although in fairness I'd have to say that the outcome of my most recent encounter was very dodgy and too close for comfort. And I had put too much at stake. But I won. The game is called Trolling for Pickpockets.

Trolling for pickpockets, as a Saigonese contact sport, was invented during the Tet New Year celebrations of 1992 by Bruce and Paul Harmon and myself. We were wandering the Ben Thanh market on Le Thanh Ton Boulevard one fine morning. The holiday crowd was dense and there was much rubbing of shoulders. Two unsavory looking guys walking side by side approached me head on. I knew I was their mark. Their appearance alone tipped me off. The best players look like the woodwork. Just before contact they parted like waters and went to both sides of me, bracketing me hard. I felt hands as they slid by.

I am very aware of hands in this country. In Vietnam it is impolite and unseemly to touch strangers. Most people don't even observe the Western custom of shaking hands. Children will sometimes touch you as you walk by, out of childish curiosity at someone who looks nothing like them or theirs. Or they will run up from behind, touch you and flee. But they're just playing a game of "counting coup." They know it's naughty, but the fascination of foreigners overcomes their good manners. Or they might be pickpockets in training. But certainly an adult who touches you on the street is at least being disrespectful, and could be trying to get your goods.

So that morning in the market when I felt hands, my own right hand went instinctively to the small bag I carry on my hip, slung to my belt like a holster. My hand brushed a strange hand that instantly snapped away. At the same time my left hand, almost of its own accord, shot through an undulating press of bodies and grabbed a fistful of shirt front. The guy on my right melted into the crowd. But on my left I gave a tug and jerked the wearer of the shirt to front and center. I relieved him of my sunglasses. Maintaining my grip on his shirt I told him in no uncertain looks and tone that I would eat him without salt if he should make me his mark again.

At this point Bruce and Paul, having seen what happened in

the brief encounter, came rushing to my aid, ready to help me pound the culprit into the dirt like a railroad spike. But I let the lad go, sent him back to school to study his lessons a little harder. After all, he had nothing of mine. And I had one of his shirt buttons. To my amazement I wasn't even angry at him. I felt no sense of outrage at the attempt on my person and property. I had no desire to haul the bad guy off to the pokey and demand justice. I didn't thirst for his blood. Rather, I was jazzed. Yessss! I was pumped. I was mighty. I had won.

"Richard," Paul said. "That was beautiful. You caught that guy like a fly ball!"

And Bruce said, "Damn it! I want to catch one too!"

And so the sport of trolling for pickpockets came into being. We immediately set our hooks with bait: sunglasses, banknotes, pens, and so on hanging provocatively from our pockets. And then we went watchfully on patrol. Bruce was the first to bag one. He was a solo operator who foolishly went for Bruce's front pocket, the most easily defensible. Obviously a rank beginner, and Bruce should take no undue pride in hooking him. Bruce's response to the guy? No shirt-grabbing or nasty looks of intimidation. Just an openhanded straight right to the chest. Doesn't sound like much, but Bruce is a powerful man. It sent the cutpurse three or four steps back and almost onto his ass. A troupe of cyclo drivers lounging nearby saw the encounter and nearly rolled on the ground laughing. Cyclo drivers are poor, and nightclub entertainment is beyond their means. But Bruce had amused them mightily. So much so that they wanted more. Knowing who some of the local pickpockets were, they encouraged them to try their wiles on us. We all bagged our limit, and by midafternoon the Ben Than market was cleansed of pickpockets, and the people were secure.

Paul had the most dramatic capture. As we were new to the game we didn't know that skillful players can get through even the strongest lines of defense in the forms of buttons, zippers, locks, and so on. Only the most alert vigilance is proof against a good player. The brotherhood of cutpurses and pickpockets even has a saying on the subject: "You can't steal a man's goods when he's thinking about them."

Paul carries his expensive camera in a holster with Velcro, buttons, and a zipper to secure it. Seems safe. But a senior member of the opposing team actually got through the defenses, grabbed the camera, and was on the lam by the time Paul realized what was up. He gave chase with a hue and cry. Bruce and I followed about twenty paces behind. We ran passed the cyclo drivers, who cheered us on. We ran passed the fabric merchants who cursed us for the disruption. Rounding a corner into the food stalls Paul was closing in when the thief lost his breath, or heart for the chase, or just slipped on a banana peel. He went crashing into a stall selling deep-fried spring rolls. His impact knocked over a huge wok full of bubbling hot oil which spilled down his back, across his ass, and down his thighs. In an instant he was airborne. Almost before his feet touched the ground he was gone in a flash, leaving behind Paul's camera, the echoes of his screams, and a curious odor reminiscent of deep-fried pork skins.

Crowned with many victories we repaired to our digs at the Prince hotel, at that time a favorite of backpackers and other budget travelers such as we were on that occasion. We told everyone then gathered in the bar of our exploits. But they were not amused or impressed. A pious Swede even scolded us. "You shouldn't do that," he complained. "These people are poor!"

"And they're gonna stay that way if they try to make a living out of our pockets," Bruce said.

"But they're socialists!" the Swede cried.

"Huh? What? Socialist thieves?" Paul wondered aloud.

"Socialists!" the man reiterated, trying to get it through to us why it was a bad thing to toy with commie crooks.

"Hey," I asked him, "with that kind of individual initiative and free-enterprise spirit, wouldn't that make them capitalists?"

The Swede shook his head in despair. The backpackers shifted uncomfortably in their printed t-shirts and Indian-made, cotton pajama-style trousers. They tugged at their blond dreadlocks and stared into their watery budget beer and thin herbal teas.

Note to players: Don't share this game with backpackers or Swedes. They have no fire in the belly. Australians make good players. Any nation that has an annual dwarf-tossing contest will make good players. Texans and Yorkshiremen are good for trolling. As are Nepalis, especially if they have a bit of Ghurka background. I spent a pleasant afternoon last week with a guy from Ghana. He told me that he plays the game at home! (I guess it's like the wheel: been invented many times.) I suppose it's not so much where people come from that counts the most. It's that gleam in their eye that tells you who will make a player.

Now I don't want you to get the idea that Saigon is a dangerous place. In fact it's one of the safest cities you can visit. Far safer than San Francisco, Los Angeles, or New York. I can nearly guarantee that you won't get shot in Saigon (unless it's by the authorities); that you will not get raped (unless you pay someone to do it); that you will not be hit on the head and have your poke pinched; you won't be kidnapped, murdered, stabbed, gassed, poisoned, or fed bad food. This is generally a nonviolent society. The criminal urge is expressed in the con, the counterfeit, the card sharp, the stock swindle, the pickpocket, and the cutpurse.

Now there are exceptions to every rule, and one of them hangs out near my hotel. I've recognized him as a player and a mean sort, too. We've never spoken but we have exchanged some hostile glances as I've passed by his station. We know each other, and we both know we know. A few days ago he made an attempt on me as I made my way home.

I was hot and tired and in no mood to play. For the first time in all my encounters I got angry. As soon as I felt him make his move I wheeled around and threw up my fists in a proper boxing stance and challenged him to "Try it again if you dare, you SOB!" At the same instant he assumed a kung fu-type pose, curled up with one foot off the ground, ready to release a kick. We had a standoff for about two or three seconds, and we had begun to draw attention when I decided that he had just rendered a good performance. Most pickpockets would have slunk away at the prospect of a punch in the nose. I laughed and offered him my hand, and we shook. Then I turned to go and the creep tried me again! I swung around to backhand him, but by then he was gone. Fast man. Dangerous player. But I still won.

In playing this game the ideal conclusion to any encounter is so subtle that only you and your fish know that it happened. You troll through a market or fair or promenade where you know that they school. Your baited hook is out, not too obviously but temptingly. (And of course you're not carrying anything you can't afford to lose.) Your senses are heightened. You see, hear, even smell with intense acuity. You are very much alive to all around you. You watch for any unusual or sudden movement, especially at the periphery of your vision. You listen for sounds of breathing and the rustle of clothing or bags, or the soft footfalls that tell you it's about to happen. But most of all your sense of touch is so acute that you can feel odors afloat on the air. You're aware of the slightest change in temperature. You know the texture, weight and fit of your clothing. For it's your tactile faculties that will most likely tell you that the hand is at your pocket and you've just hooked your fish.

You now have one, maybe two seconds at most, to win the game. That's not much time, but it's you who has the advantage of surprise. Your quarry doesn't know that you've been lying in wait for him. He thinks you're easy pickings. So now! Wheel around! Make your move small and without show, but make it sudden and swift for the fright it will give him. Grab for the wrist whose hand has your bait and hold firmly because he may try to bolt. The trick is not to wrestle with him, but to make eye contact as soon as possible. Nine times out of ten it will make him freeze. He knows the jig is up, might even realize he's been had. And being the nonviolent, nonconfrontational sort that he is, he submits. You hold him for a second or two, just for emphasis. And just to appreciate his racing pulse. Then you quietly let him go. Just catch and release. He'll scurry off to hide somewhere, perhaps to be cuffed and scolded by his master who was watching from a fair vantage point. Score one for the visitors. Yesss!

There is one class of pickpocket that bears warning of. He is the same type that provided the Englishwoman in the 333 Hotel with a cast for her leg. He is known as a "cowboy." He rides a motorbike with an accomplice passenger behind known as "the snatch." They ride up alongside you, usually from behind, and grab whatever protrudes, then they're off across town. Because of their speed, power, and clever tactics they are the worst you'll ever go up against. The trick with them is simply to step aside as they pass and let the snatch grab nothing but air.

But when a cowboy and his snatch made their move upon the Englishwoman she was feeling cocky, and thought she could drop the snatch to the ground by hanging on tight to her boodle. But at 3 A.M. and full of drink she was in no shape for combat. They dragged her for a few yards until she let go and slammed into a tree. She cursed them loudly, and if their feelings were hurt it would be a good thing. Now she plots a better game, while the cowboy and his snatch live well.

In all my years in Southeast Asia I never once personally encountered a cowboy. Until last week. I was in a cyclo driven by a guy I hire often. He's a good guy with a sense of humor and we get along well. I can't pronounce his name, nor he mine, so I call him Joe. He calls me Kieu. I don't know if my spelling is correct, and he can't tell me because he's illiterate, but I'm sure it's close enough.

We had stopped at an intersection for a traffic light. The light was just about to turn green, and I could feel Joe taking a strain on the pedals of his cyclo, preparing for the mad free-for-all that Saigon traffic is. Cars, motorbikes, and cyclos lined up behind us were doing the same.

I am blessed with good vision. It's 20/10, which means that I can see twice as far as most people. I'm also just an observant sort of guy. Most writers are. I saw to my right on the cross street, and heading into the intersection, a red and white motorbike driven by a t-shirt clad man, and another riding pillion. The one on the rear was looking straight at me and hollering something to the driver. No alarms tripped until I saw him suddenly bank left and accelerate into the turn. The computer in my head that does idle geometry and lead computations as I observe moving objects ran a quick calculation on the bike's curve. It wasn't heading for the middle of the opposite lane. It was heading for a close encounter with *moi*. A cowboy and his snatch, at last! My time, rate, and distance computer was now running millisecond updates. I had three seconds till impact.

One Mississippi...

The snatch's eyes are locked on me, watching intently for dangers and opportunities. I know if I make any move of preparation or defense he will abort his run. I keep my face forward, watching from behind dark lenses. Joe's cyclo lurches into movement. I have to know what the snatch is going to go for. I have to know ahead of time in order to make my move quickly enough.

Two Mississippi...

I've got a shopping bag at my feet, some miscellaneous stuff hanging out of my shirt pocket, a leather folder on my lap. Wearing no jewelry. So he's got three options. But I can't tell where his focus is. Damn! This is going to be close. Look to his grab hand. It's open and ready, waist-level and rising. So it won't be the shopping bag. I'm holding stone still. He's closing fast and on schedule. There! I can see his eyes. I can see the whites of them.

Three...

He seems to be looking me in the eyes. Is he going for my shades? They'll steal anything, if only just for practice. I can hear the cowboy's engine, he's still winding up, accelerating. They'll make the grab and be gone in a heartbeat.

Miss...

There! I see it: the vector of the snatch's hand and eye. He's going for my hat! The bastard! My $80 handwoven-in-Ecuador, genuine Panama hat! That changes the whole game. It's one thing to nick a man's briefcase, but his hat is just too damned personal. He who steals my purse steals trash; but he who messes with my hat gets punished.

issi...

So now I want to hurt him. But how? I could stiff-arm the driver and spill them both onto the pavement. But they're coming too fast, I could dislocate my shoulder. His hand is up for the grab and I've got to decide. I could spit in his eye. But I might miss. Never been a good spitter. I could have tossed the shopping bag at their heads, but there's no time now. Head butt them? Scratch at their eyes? Call 'em names?

POW!

I high-fived the snatch as hard as I could. I know it was solid because it stung my own hand like frenzy. The force and surprise rotated the snatch's body counterclockwise around the axis of his spine more than ninety degrees. The motion translated the speeding vehicle's forward momentum into one wild and crazy ride. The driver almost lost it to the right, over-compensated to the left and straight into oncoming traffic. He slalomed back and forth across both lanes for one hundred yards, the snatch screaming and cursing like a jilted Latina.

Both Joe and I laughed our heads off. "How do you like that, you SOBs?" I hollered after them, waving my hat. "I win, you bastards! I win!"

"You win, Kieu! You win!" Joe shouted and laughed.

Joe didn't know precisely what game I had been playing, but it was abundantly clear to him that I had won. Hands down.

1 9 *Male of the Species*

 As I've said before, Saigon is a lady. But even as you can turn the tables on her cutpurses, she can turn the tables on you. When she does, take it like a sport, and she will welcome you back time and again.

I met two Aussies on one of my many flights into Saigon from Bangkok, and I forged a grand alliance with them. We immediately became mates. Rob is the tall one, a typical blond Aussie beach boy—a beer-chugging, ball-playing good fellah. He's the quieter of the two, but always ready to shout "Aussie Aussie Aussie! Oi Oi Oi!" Leon is the other side of the coin. He is everywhere mistaken for an Israeli commando on leave. Until he opens his mouth and says "G'day."

Together we three became Mighty Men about the town. We strode the boulevards with large steps. We showed largesse to the poor and to all the pretty girls. The pick-pockets feared us, and the dames loved us. I even taught a barmaid to address us as Mighty Rob and Mighty Leon and Mighty Dick. (Well she couldn't pronounce "Richard," could she?)

The Mighty Men went to dinner one night, and we still glow with the achievement. Half a mile north of the Apocalypse

Now bar, on Thi Sac Street, lies a cluster of densely packed sidewalk restaurants alive with feasting. Choose any one with an open table. They're all good. But be especially aware of the one with a second-story terrace overlooking the scene, for that is the one we Mighty Men call Restaurant No.

We had picked our way through the crowd, climbed the steep and narrow stairs, and emerged onto a terrace happily strewn with lobster and crab shells, awash in beer, and afloat upon a thick cloud of hubbub and bustle. A short, slim, intense waiter beckoned, nay commanded, us to sit at a table from which he was sweeping the remnants of the previous meal onto the floor.

We took the proffered seats and ordered "Beer!" But before the monosyllable was out the young cur had disappeared, off to order some other diner to do his bidding. Then he returned with a single menu, dropped it on the table and ran. "Beer!" we shouted to his receding back. Some minutes later he returned at a near run, handing off bottles of beer like relay batons as he sped by. Mollified by suds we relaxed while I perused the menu. Rob and Leon declared that since I was the Indiana Jones of gastronomy, and since we had only the one stingy menu, I should order for all three of the Mighty Men.

At length our surly servant returned with pen and order pad. He had spoken not word one to us since our arrival and even now stood sphinxlike, poised to take our order. "Well," I began. "We'll have..." And the beggar ran off again to some distant call! "Beer!" Rob hollered after him. Miraculously he returned with more beer. I reopened the menu and glared at him, as if threatening to trip him if he should try to escape again.

I pointed to chicken on the menu and said, "This one." He nodded and wrote in his pad. And wrote and wrote. Perhaps he was noting my particulars for some future police lineup. "And we'll have this," I said, pointing to water greens with ginger. Again he wrote and wrote. And by now Rob and Leon were beginning to snigger at the whole scene. "And we'll have..."

whereupon the miscreant turned around, hurled a stream of Vietnamese curses, and ran off to punish some other diner!

When he returned I held him firmly by the shirtsleeve, and pointed to "beef in sauce" on the menu, and said, "Give me that." He wrote and wrote, then moved to leave. But I held him fast, and pointed to fish and said, "That. Bring me that."

"No!" came the reply, his first and only word.

"What?! What?! Waddaya mean, no?!"

"No!"

"But I want fish. Fish! Fish and be damned, you rascal!"

"No!" Then he pointed to all the other items I had ordered and nodded, as if to say, "You may have that and no more."

"Blast you! Fish!"

Again he pointed to the other items. And now Rob and Leon were laughing out loud. "This is like Fawlty Towers with you as John Cleese and he's Manuel," Leon guffawed.

"I am speaking English pronto," Rob mimicked.

It occurred to me that the restaurant might be out of fish. In a conciliatory tone I pointed to a dish of pork cooked in a clay pot.

"No!"

"What, you're out of pork too? Then this one."

"No!"

"Then this one."

"No!"

"You can't be out of everything! I want this," I demanded, pointing to yet another item.

"No!"

"Then I want this one!"

"No!"

"I want it I say!"

"No!"

"Then I want to fuck your mother!"

"No!"

"I know seven virgin nuns that want to smoke your pole!"

"No!"

"Bastard!"

"No!"

With the boys doubled over in laughter and me on the verge of apoplexy, I pointed to the last item on the menu and swore, "Bring me this you son-of-a-gun or I'll black your eyes!"

"Yes!"

"Waddaya mean yes you...oh...uh, yes?"

"Yes!"

"O.K.?"

"Yes!" And with that he snatched the menu from my hands and dissappeared.

"Churl!"

Rob and Leon were still chuckling when a Vietnamese fellow diner at the next table leaned over to me grinning and said in fine English, "The reason he says no is because he's afraid you won't be able to eat all you order. If there are any substantial leftovers, he has to pay a penalty. But he doesn't know how to say that."

"Awww. And I thought he was just being a prick."

"We'll have to make sure we clean our plates," Rob said.

"We'll eat every bite," Leon promised.

And for my part, I resolved to grant the waiter a thousand pardons and to not tell the guys that the last dish I had been able to order was cock's testicles braised with garlic cloves.

The waiter, whom we had dubbed "Young Dr. No," arrived unbidden with more beer and the chicken. It was a whole bird, though rather small, like a game hen, but roasted and spiced to a state of gustatory poetry. I prodded it with a chopstick and found it meaty and fat for all its puny size. Then came the water greens with ginger, dusted with the black pepper that is unique to Vietnam. It's less biting, flowery, and almost sweet to the taste. It's nearly good enough to eat by itself. Then the beef in sauce swaggered fatly to the table, redolent of some fine liqueur, done to blood-rare perfection, graced with slivered onions and garlanded lordly with fresh green herbs. Fluffy white rice sat chastely beside. And lastly came a dish of glistening gonads.

They were piled on a six-inch silver serving dish mounted on a pedestal, rather like a Victorian candy dish one might see on some grandmother's sideboard or locked in her china cabinet. A twist of lime and a sprig of cilantro balanced the presentation. The garlic with which the balls had been braised were fat, snowy whole cloves. And the several roosters' family jewels were very like the cloves in size, shape, and color. Indeed, I had to look closely to tell which was which, and they were about equal in number. The testes were distinguishable only by a more rounded appearance, rather like that of kidney beans. I was surprised and impressed at the very size of Foghorn Leghorn's endowment, I say I was impressed and surprised, son, and thought it should give enlarged meaning to the term "cock o' the walk." I paused to wonder about the dimensions of his other apparatus, but the time had come to taste.

Rob had noticed the strange dish and recognized the garlic cloves. "Ah. Giahlic," he said in Strine (Aussie dialect). "Smells good."

"I love giahlic," Leon concurred.

Lifting my chopsticks I gingerly fished out a rooster's best and brought it beneath my nose. The scent of garlic roiled up, mingled with some undefinable masculine aroma. I slipped it into my mouth and rolled it around between tongue and palate. It was firm yet pliable, like a grape. I probed its envelope with my incisors and determined it to have a resistance a bit more than that of a plump kernel of corn, perhaps with the same creamy richness within. I rolled it over to the right side of my mouth, positioned it between my wisdom teeth, and bit down. The outer surface stretched and strained, and under the pressures of the omnivore's generalized dentition that is the result of a million years of evolution, the little DNA factory burst, and spilled itself across the surface of my tongue.

In texture, consistency, and taste, the rooster's physical connection with eternity was not unlike that of a mild and smooth goose liver paté, expressing a bit of juice. Knowing as I do that human taste buds are distributed according to a set pattern, I spread the contents of what *Grey's Anatomy* calls an "organ of generation" evenly over the tasting battery so as to discover its composition. I found the bird's instrument of continuity to be a bit salty, though you might have guessed that, with echoes of sweet, sour, and bitter in such proportion as to obtain the sort of balance aspired to by the Chinese cook's philosophy of yin and yang, or the ancient Greek's "golden mean." It was rich and creamy, and I suppose you might have guessed that, too. It went down as easy as oysters.

Leon and Rob were helping themselves to the other dishes, so I picked up a testicle and put it in Leon's rice bowl. "Oh, thanks, mate," he said, and popped it into his mouth and began to chew. Then he looked somewhat confused. I told him what it was. There is a certain gravity in the term "cock's testicle" that makes it impossible to be a joke. If someone tells you that you have one in your mouth you know instantly that it must needs be true.

Rob asked, "So how do you like the sperm packet, Leon?" Leon continued to chew, but almost imperceptibly slowly, as though weighing his options. Rob reached across the table and took a morsel from the dish, chewed experimentally, and pronounced, "It tastes just like giahlic."

"That's because you just ate a clove of garlic, " I said. "Here." And I served him the genuine article. He boldy chewed, swallowed, then reached for another gonad saying, "This puts me in mind of how they 'nad sheep in the outback. The old timers just pick up the little boy lambs by the hind legs and chomp off their balls with their teeth."

I looked at Leon, who was now still more indecisive. "Come on, Leon," I prodded. "Just think of it as a rooster coming in your mouth."

That did the trick. Leon choked, swallowed involuntarily, then turned pale. "I'm glad to see that you're a swallower and not a spitter," I told him. Leon took a long drink of beer. I selected the most garlicky looking gonad in the dish and handed it to him saying, "Here, try the garlic now."

"Oh, cheers, mate," he said with relief, quickly followed by "You bastard!" But by then his mouth was no longer virginal, and he gamely swallowed. And so we feasted. We ate the small but plump and juicy chicken. We ate the aromatic water greens. We ate the blood-red beef and the wedding-white rice. And we ate the pungent lily and *poulet's* privates. We quaffed more beer. In the end the table bore only clean plates, a little pyramid of chicken bones, and twelve empty beer bottles. Young Dr. No would pay no penalty this night.

As I sat in the afterglow, the fellow diner at the next table asked, "How did you enjoy your dinner?"

"It was magic," said I. "Although we could have ordered more with no danger to the waiter. That chicken was very small."

"Oh, but it's large for its type," he assured me. "It's a small breed but this restaurant serves only the male of the species so that you always have the biggest possible."

The male of the species. That it might have been either one sex or the other had not occurred to me. So it was a rooster then. It was a…well, suffice to say, on that night, the Mighty Men ate cock and balls. And we'll lick any man who says aught against it!

2 0 *L o n g i n g*

IN JOSEPH CONRAD'S SHORT STORY, "THE Secret Sharer," a tall ship eases her way through the warm night, toward the coast of an exotic tropical kingdom. The captain secretly assists a mysterious man over the side and he swims to the leeward shore of the "Cambogee." Nowadays we call that land Cambodia.

Years ago, as a sailor plying the "China coast," I often slipped past that spot where Conrad's hero bade farewell to his secret other self. Every time I saw that blue-green, palm-lined shore, the Cambogee, a land of lost temples, colorful ceremonies, and beautiful women beckoned. Many a time I had planned to drop anchor there and attend the magnificent feast of the Water Festival. Old shipmates reported that at Phnom Penh and Sihanoukville they had acquired some of their fondest memories, and tasted a unique style of spicy cookery that might well have been the best in the East.

But the map of life would lead me elsewhere, and in that time the long night of Pol Pot and his Khmer Rouge fell upon the land I would always call the Cambogee. In the years that followed I read what little news trickled out of the country. I listened to secondhand tales of refugees, and sorrowed for them. I still passed the Secret Sharer's landing, gazing longingly at the now forbidden shore. I greatly missed the country I had never visited, as though I had known her well, as though I, too, had shared her secrets.

Cambodia's nightmare is now largely over, and the veil has lifted. There is regular air service to the country, although most roads, other than the one leading to Vietnam, are usually closed, and there is now a U.S. diplomatic presence. And despite the passage of the years, the Cambogee's tropic siren song still reached my heart. And one day I obeyed its call.

With a friend and a photographer in tow, I hopped a plane to Thailand. At Bangkok's airport a Russian-built charter plane from the Cambodian capital of Phnom Penh was on the tarmac, revving up its engines for its return flight. Fast action and a credit card got us on board. In less than an hour, we landed at Phnom Penh's Pochentong airport. After a twenty dollar visa fee, three photographs, and ten minutes in line, we were out the door. I was in the Cambogee, at last!

The first Khmer, or Cambodian, king was Kambu, and the kingdom he established, in the ninth century, was known as Kambujadesa: the Sons of Kambu, or Kambuja for short. The land of the lower Mekong river valley became a confluence and focus of immigration, trade, religion, and culture. From the Sri Vijaya empire of Indonesia came Hindu conquerors, missionaries, and scholars. Though the country has been Bhuddist now for over four hundred years, the modern Khmer system of writing is still based on Sanskrit. From the east, by way of Annam, came the Chinese; from the north came the Thai and the Lao; from the west, the Malay; and finally, from afar, the Europeans. Each brought their influence in literature, science, the arts, and in the kitchen.

Curry from the Hindu, noodles from the Chinese, basil and other aromatic leaves from the Thai. And from the Europeans? Bread, of course, attributed to the French, as well as wine and beer. But the most common, most important and pleasing contribution of the Europeans to Khmer cookery is the chili pepper.

We don't know precisely when or by whom the chili was introduced to this part of the world, but it is logical that the credit belongs to the Spanish or Portuguese in the late sixteenth century. The first documented official contact between the Cambogee and the West took place in 1596. The king of Angkor, Barom Reachea, feared an attack by his neighbors. He sent an embassy, which included a Portuguese adventurer, to the Spanish governor general at Manila to request the assistance of his musket-armed soldiers. Seeing an opportunity to extend Spanish influence, the governor sent two small expeditions. They presented themselves to the king in 1596 and 1598. We don't know what the expeditions' supplies, provisions, and gifts for the king included; but one hundred years after Columbus, the Spaniards were well supplied with capsicums from the New World. It is delicious to speculate that though the military missions came to naught, a culinary mission enjoyed great success.

Angkor must have made the Spaniards swoon with amazement. Approaching from down wind you can hear it before you see it. The wind moans and sings and whispers in the ancient towers, calling, calling. Maybe Conrad's man was hearing it. Maybe I was for all those years. As the monument comes into view its stunning massiveness can overwhelm the visitor; and coming close, so can the echoes of its former beauty. And closer still, so can the echoes of its former ugliness. The pockmark scars of bullets mar so many walls and freizes. The well-marked paths tell of the land mines that still lie nearby. Most telling of all are the men, women, and children who walk on one leg, or don't walk at all; who hold out a remaining hand for alms, or stare with darkened eyes.

Built over a span of centuries beginning in the ninth, what we refer to as "Angkor Wat" is actually a city and temple complex, with one of its principal temples or "wats" being Angkor, located about a mile and half outside the walled city of Angkor Thom. Inside the city is the Bayon, a temple every bit the equal of Angkor Wat. The former faces east, the latter west. The best viewing and photographing are at sunrise and sunset, respectively.

The Bayon is covered with the famous friezes that depict the history and culture and even daily life of the ancient Khmers: battle scenes full of soldiers and elephants; women grooming themselves or each other; merchants, fishwives, and cockfights; royal processions.

Angkor Wat tells the story of the Ramayana in a bas-relief that wraps around the temple for over two thousand feet. The Ramayana is the Hindu classic that vividly depicts the battle between good and evil. The scars of twentieth century battles continue to tell the tale.

Pol Pot's legacy doesn't end at Angkor. In any village of size, and especially near the capital, walk in an empty field and you may see buttons or bits of cloth pushing up from the ground. Outside Phom Penh, at the place we have all come to associate with "the Killing Fields," it's hard not to step on human teeth. Because the Khmer Rouge favored iron bars and other blunt instruments as their murder weapon, it saving them bullets, any crowbar, reinforcing bar, or sledgehammer you see may have been turned to Pol Pot's work. Images of death are so common in this land that I was daily astounded at how vibrantly alive it is.

Today the capital is a once gracious and beautiful city, continuing to emerge from under the rubble. Broad, tree-lined streets, designed by French colonial planners, ring with the sounds of construction and recovery. Monks, once banned and marked for death, color the city saffron. On city streets we were often followed for blocks by giggling children, the product of Asia's highest birthrate, who wanted nothing but to tag along. Also among the most common signs of life and recovery are the innumerable restaurants, cafes, food stalls, and snack sellers on every sidewalk, street corner, and dusty country crossroad, and the joy the people take in feasting.

Having dealt so much with death, they find that the best ways to reaffirm life are making babies and eating.

I can't advise you on the best places for making babies, but one of Phnom Penh's most memorable eating establishments can be reached by following the main boulevard, Monivong, as it leads north out of town. Near the outskirts it narrows to a rutted asphalt track not quite two lanes wide. From here it turns straight for a mile and a half, bordered on both sides by closely spaced houses big and small. It curves westward past a great heap of field guns, old tanks, and armored vehicles and other war stuffs being reduced to plowshares by busy men with cutting torches. Snaking through a clump of leafy trees, it arrives at a meadow where it intersects with half a dozen other roads and pathways. In the daytime this confluence is deserted, but by sunset it is a bustling carnival of portable restaurants.

Little bakeries on wheels, butchers on trucks, produce sellers bearing baskets on yokes, and whole kitchens set up on wooden tables clog the gathering of roads. Glowing paper lanterns hang from posted wires that zigzag and crisscross throughout the field. Families, packs of young men, gaggles of girls, day laborers, soldiers, beggars, and farmers come here to dine in community. For in the Cambogee, despite its recent violent history, dinner is still a shared ritual, one that must please both the flesh and the spirit. It reaffirms the ties of family and friendship, and of us humans to the natural world. That and making babies should cure many ills.

2 1 *M r . D i s g u i s e*

GARRETT AND MATT AND I ONCE ROLLED INTO San Quentin on the Pacific coast of the Baja. It was sometime between Christmas and New Year, we had a bellyful of beer, and I was wearing a big, bushy, fur hat from the city of Saint Petersburg, Russia. And I was also wearing a beard with a handlebar mustache. I looked ever the Cossack. And Matt could not help himself. As we entered the bar, without even consulting me, he used his primitive Spanish to introduce me to one and all as a visiting Russian professor who spoke no Spanish, but he, Matthew, would be glad to translate for anyone who would like to meet this exotic foreigner. Of course I do not speak Russian, nor he. But could I refuse the challenge? Nyet! Matt and I spent a boozy evening speaking mock Russian that might well have been appreciated by Danny Kaye, while Garrett regretted his lack of facility in phony foreign languages. The best part of the evening was when one of the Mexicans taught me, "El Russo," some colorful Spanish profanities. Disguise can be seductive.

I arrived in Saigon on a Saturday afternoon, seven hours late from Hong Kong. Nobody here had ever seen me with a beard, and most knew me with a shaved head, the guy who does the Captain Picard impression. I resolved to fool them all with my newly shifted shape.

I donned big sunglasses, pulled my hat down low over my eyes, and slouched into Headquarters (Hien's Bar) like a private dick working a case. Outside the tropical sun blazed and glared with painful brightness. But inside the bar the shadowy gloom wrapped around me like a trenchcoat. There she was, behind the bar. Gorgeous as usual, dressed in one of those silk *ao dai* she always wears. She still had that pouty look she gets when no one is there to tell her what a doll she is. Yeah, it was her, the divine Miss Hang. When she turned and looked up at me a lock of her thick midnight hair fell over one eye, Veronica Lake style. "Ha," I thought. "I've got her blindsided. She'll never recognize me now."

I took a seat at the far end of the bar. Without a word she turned and walked toward the cooler, and through the split tunic of her garment offered me glimpses of those long, long legs that start at the surface of the earth and go all the way up to Paradise. She opened the cooler and, as if reaching for a switchblade, grabbed a cold one. Off came the top in one flick of the wrist, the spent cap clattering on the marble floor and worshipping at those platform-shod feet. All as if to say, "I do that to guys like you all the time."

She walked slowly down the length of the bar, pouring the suds into a tall glass as she moved. With a cool hand and a keen eye she lifted the bottle ever higher as she poured and walked, skillfully building up a creamy, frothy head that threatened to over excite itself and foam over the top to lave her hand in its whiteness. But at the last possible moment she stopped her tease with a skill born of innumerable such non-conclusions. She set the bubbling frustrated drink down in front of me. "Why you get hairy face?" she demanded. "And why you gone so long?"

"What? Huh? You recognize me?"

"And you get new hat, too. I like the other one better."

"But I'm in disguise."

"You don't disguise from me. You think I don't know how you walk? Besides, you got a big head. Anybody can see. You want to play Jenga? I beat you again like always."

"But I'm in disguise."

"Where your friend Garrett?"

"I'm Garrett, damn it! I'm in disguise!"

"You drink your beer, Mr. Disguise. I get the Jenga game. Beat you again."

After losing three straight games I decided that I looked down enough in the mouth and could walk in a sad enough shuffle to fool someone with my disguise.

I went to the Hot Chile bar. There the Russian-speaking Miss Huyen burst out the door at my approach, threw her little body at mine for one of the Russian bear hugs she learned at school and hollered, "Tovarich! You come back!"

"You recognize me already? But I'm in disguise, da?"

"Nyet. You very bad spy. Better you drink beer."

I drank beer. Then I went to all the other usual spots. Everywhere my brilliant disguise was of no use. It was as though I hadn't even gone to Spain, grown my hair and beard, and bought a new hat. It was as though I had just gone to the men's room and stayed a little longer than usual.

Finally, in total defeat, I went to the Rolling Stone bar. I walked in and told Miss Thuyet to set me up with the usual. "What usual?" she asked.

"The usual usual," I said. She just looked at me quizzically.

"Don't you know me?"

"No," she said, looking closely.

"Bless you."

Her look of intense scrutiny began to soften. A gleam appeared in her eye and a little smile began to curl her lips. She opened a BGI beer, poured it into a mug and set it before me, and winked.

"Welcome back, Richard." Case closed.

2 2   *I r o n y*

O<small>N EVERY OTHER STREET CORNER OF</small> C<small>AIRO A</small>
medieval Arab squats almost obliviously on the
sidewalk as the twenty-first century rushes by. Men
both in suits and djellabas stop their business, set all aside and
face Mecca to pray. Most of the city is the color of the desert
over which it spreads out: a dusty tan. Brighter, lively color is
in the interstices, the nooks and crannies, the twists and turns
of the great city's guts. There the food sellers hawk their colorful, aromatic wares; there the men sit in masculine
communion in the coffee and tea houses, puffing contentedly
on their imposing hookah pipes, playing chess and dominoes,
and cussin' and discussin'; there the scarved and veiled women
avert their eyes from the gaze of strange foreign men and
hurry about their business; there the beggars beg and the kids
play in the street and the ceaseless commerce of daily life is
transacted as it has been in this city for a thousand years. The
huge stone metropolis is honeycombed with innumerable cells
of human goings-on; the snaking alleyways are rivers and
rushes of bustle; the labyrinthine Old Quarter is the true setting for the *Thousand and One Nights.*

It's here in this face of the city you will find the ancient bazaar called the Khan al Kalilli. Through all its medieval twists and turns, amid the carpet merchants, hookah sellers, touts for worthless souvenir gewgaws, and purveyors of finest silks and jewelry snake the heavy odors of spice and perfume, frankincense and myrrh. There is no older spice entrepot in the world than Egypt, and no grander spice bazaar than Cairo.

The Egyptian cooks come here, not to the grocer, but for spices. They all have their steady merchants, often having provided to one family for three generations or more. This is the place to buy bohar, an essential of Egyptian cookery. It's a blend of spices that strives to balance the hot and the sweet. Sweet is represented by such spices as cardamom, nutmeg, and cinnamon; and the hot by black and red pepper. Searingly hot blends like many I found in India are rare. The *fellahin* (Egyptian common man) prefers a slow burn, or just a teasing reminder of the chili pepper's presence. No two merchants have quite the same blend, and many of them refuse to divulge. But I was able to watch several in the weeks that I wandered this city in the shadow of the pyramids. You must buy your spices whole, and it's the grinder who determines the final proportions, making adjustments for the age, origin, and quality of the stock. I came to know the city by its smells and, passing familiar restaurants, felt sure I could recognize the work of this or that grinder of "the Khan."

Though Egypt is predominately a Muslim society, it has several religious and ethnic minorities. The result being that they make a very good beer here. It's called Stella. And the best place to enjoy it is in the Stella bar in central Cairo (next door to the famous Felfela restaurant at 15 Sharia Talaat Harb). It's a place full of *fellahin* good ol' boys, laughing, backslapping, bragging and lying and holding forth for the amusement of all present. Few of them speak English, and I speak no Arabic, but I made it a regular stopping place and became friendly with the staff. They called me Monsieur and I called them

Senor. They always gave me the same table, and would tell the other patrons, "That's the American writer. He comes here all the time." (Or so one of the English speakers told me.) Instead of beer nuts and pretzels every patron gets a dish of salt beans and a dish of raw veggies. And when the mood strikes them they serve the most delicious spicy dips and spreads (which they call salads). My favorite is white cheese and tomato: goat cheese, olive oil, garlic, and fresh chopped tomato blended with spices and eaten with bread. Egyptian cookery is replete with this sort of dish for making bread go a long way. And in the desert heat its coolness and lightness are most welcome. Goes good with a Stella, too!

After about a week I realized something remarkable about the Stella. I was sitting writing my journal and having a cold one. And it dawned on me. My journal entry for that day reads: "Everybody in there looks like somebody! A dead ringer for Anwar Sadat is drinking brandy with the mirror image of Eddie Murphy. Sergeant Rutlege is here, right out of the movie, smoking heavily. And Mahatma Gandhi's alter ego has drunk too much. A look-alike of Naguib Mahfouz, the Nobel prize-winning Egyptian novelist is here (then again, maybe it is Naguib Mahfouz!). Two men at the bar, who seem to be brothers, look like sons of Omar Sharif. But then I've seen a lot of guys in Egypt who look like sons of Omar Sharif. From what I hear of Omar, they might all be! Holy smokes, the barman is the jolly fat merchant who sold the tribbles on the Star Trek episode of the same! If he calls me "Friend Klingon" I'm outta here. Hugh O'Brien just walked in. Not the old Hugh of the *Wyatt Earp* TV show, but the new Hugh, after his face-lift and hair coloring as he appeared in the movie *Twins*. Naguib is sitting by a window. He uses a cigarette holder, wears a gray silk jacket, black shirt, and coordinated tie. A literary gangster look. Iron gray hair, black mustache. A fastidious drinker. Brandy on the rocks. Doesn't stick his pinkie out, though, or wear a pinkie ring. Watches intently through the window by which he sits.

"Am I the only one here who doesn't look like somebody? Where does that leave me, the only real guy in a room full of images? How lonely it feels! Like I'm the phantom and they are the real. I'm gonna tell the barman my name is Kirk, James T. Ask if he'll tribble himself to get me another Stella. And a double brandy, too. There's nothing else for it when you're the only guy in the Look-Alike Bar who looks like nobody."

How can you go Egypt, to Cairo, and not make the short trip across the Nile to visit the pyramids? It would be like going to Terlingua, Texas and not taking in the Chili Cook-Off!

There are many theories about the design, construction, and layout of the sphinx and pyramids of Giza. Eric Von Dannegen says they were homing signals for ancient astronauts. The Rosicrucians say that the Great Pyramid marks the center of the world, or the universe, or the way to San Jose; something like that. And certain assorted numbnuts think the whole scene is the focus of planetary powers, or vaults containing the secrets of life, or portals to other dimensions and lots of other dementia. Having visited the place, I think the pyramids and the sphinx were designed and laid out, at least in part, for aesthetic appeal.

Their stunning massiveness, and their simple, elegant symmetry are overpowering. The sphinx looks almost alive, a benevolent giant who might take you in his great stone arms and protect you. The pyramids are so enormous that to view them up close is like standing at the mouth of the Grand Canyon and feeling the immensity of the universe. Beneath their huge, towering enormity all your troubles seem suddenly small. Their balance, order, and harmony argue order and purpose in the universe.

All around the pyramids of Giza lie villages that have been occupied by Bedouin families since time out of mind. One of them is the family of Amdi Nasr el Nahes. They have been camel and horse breeders for generations. I met Amdi in a coffee house in Cairo where he had come on some family business. I invited him to share coffee and a hookah pipe with me and we became friends in a day. Two days later in the family village I was adopted. It's amazing what some coffee, a pipe, and a little hospitality can do in the right place. Amdi and his brother Ali took me trekking across the desert with their camels. "How many years has your family lived here?" I asked Amdi as we packed our gear. He looked at his brother, they both shook their heads.

"I don't know," he said.

"Approximately," I pressed him.

"I don't know, Brother. Since pharaoh time. How many years is that?"

The morning of our first day out across the Egyptian desert, Amdi and Ali saddled a camel for me whom I had named "Clyde." My friends thought the name hilarious and laughed every time I uttered it. When Clyde was ready to be mounted Ali said, "Now we must teach you how to ride."

"No problem," I said. "I learned how to ride a camel in India. I'll show you." I mounted the seated beast and braced myself for the sudden rise of his hind legs, which can tumble an unprepared rider head over heels. "*Khush*, Clyde," I said, speaking what I thought was pretty good Camel. "*Khush!*" (which means "Get up, you lazy camel!") "*Khush*, Clyde!"

Clyde suddenly raised his two left legs, rolled over onto his right side and spilled me on the ground with a "whump." Clyde laughed his camel laugh. It was a sound I would come to know well. Though I had crossed the Great Indian Desert on camelback, and thought myself quite the "camelteer," Clyde was out to teach me otherwise. Later on he took to nipping at me with his teeth, as though he would rip out a piece of flesh and eat it in front of me. Miserable beast. "Clyde is very bad sometimes," Amdi said. "I think we will get rid of him soon." It couldn't have been soon enough for me.

When we returned from the long trek I thought I would never be able to sit down again for the saddle sores Clyde had given me. I also checked repeatedly for broken bones. I was about to depart Egypt in a very sorry state. My spirits soared, though, when Amdi and Ali told me they would give me a great feast of farewell in their village. They even said I could bring along some friends I had met earlier in Cairo. "That's great!" I said. "And what's on the menu?"

It was Clyde. Oh yes. It was Clyde.

Apparently my expression, that of having stumbled upon El Dorado, didn't mean quite the same in Arabic, and Ali hastened to assure me that, "We eat camel often. Yes. You will find it delicious. Especially camel's foot stew! It will make you very strong."

"It will?" said I, dreamily.

"You will see. The camel butcher is our cousin and he will be at the feast. He eats camel's foot stew every day. And he has three wives and nine children. Yes, it will make you very strong."

"Can we roast him?"

The whole village turned out, and it was said to be the most magnificent feast that anyone had ever attended. Amdi's mother supervised the preparation, and sent Clyde to us in many guises: roasted, stewed, grilled, braised with vegetables, made into soup. I stood by with a notebook, as Mother directed her daughters and daughters-in-law, writing down the recipes. And the anticipation! It was as savory as the meat itself. The Ultimate Cookout was happening before me, in the shadow of the Sphinx, and in my honor no less. And every bruise, every indignity, saddle sore, and near miss with his teeth would fade with every morsel of Clyde. Ah, Clyde, Clyde. I bear you no malice anymore. You were a bad camel, Clyde. But in the end, you were oh so good. Though I never did get a coat of you.

I spent my last night in Egypt in the Look-Alike Bar drinking ice-cold Stella and eating *babaghanoush*, a spicy eggplant puree served with bread and raw vegetables. A local journalist, who looked like yet another son of Omar Sharif (may his tribe increase) spoke good English and we had a brief chat over a couple of Stellas and a double brandy. He asked me my profession and I said, "I'm a writer."

"Oh," he says, "then you're in the right place, aren't you."

"I am?"

"Of course. Everyone here is a writer," he said as he helped himself to the *babaghanoush*.

"Everyone!?" I looked for Naguib Mafouz at his usual table, but he wasn't there. "You're telling me that everyone here is a writer?"

"This is where writers come to talk and be together and enjoy each other's company."

"And drink and argue?"

"Don't writers in America drink and argue?"

"The good ones do."

He pointed out several and named them, saying, "He works for Al Arahm, the newspaper. He over there is a novelist, but I hate his work. That one is a fine poet," he said, pointing to the half-bombed Mahatma. "And that one is a whore. He should not be allowed to publish." A hell of a way for an Egyptian to talk about the late President Nasser.

"Do any of them speak English? I'd love to talk to them."

"No, not really, not this time. Just a few words. I'm the only one here tonight who speaks."

"Has anyone ever told you that you look like Omar Sharif?"

"Who?"

"Never mind."

The journalist left. And I sat bemoaning the fact that I had stumbled into the literary salon of Cairo and never knew it till now. All that cussin' and discussin' that went on for weeks was not about whose soccer team was better or about politics or who was sleeping with whom (well, maybe some of it was), it was about literature! The journalist told me they fight about the craft of writing all the time. If I had only known, maybe I could have joined in sometimes when the English speakers were present. Maybe I could have hobnobbed with my fellow scribes and taken away better memories, learned a thing or two. Maybe I'd have become "one of the boys" at the Look-Alike Bar. And, sitting here among all these familiar faces, swapping stories, propounding literary theories and sharing drink after drink maybe, just maybe, I'd have finally walked out of there looking like somebody!

2 3 *Marilyn*

So who doesn't want to be recognized? Be somebody? Even if only as a look-alike? What man would object to its being said at his funeral that, "He looked like Tom Cruise"? What woman would find offense in being compared to Marilyn Monroe? Can you look me in the eye and tell me that you would not like to be a legend in your own time? Even if the legend were something scandalous?

Toby, the silver-haired owner of the bar and decorated veteran of the battle of Leyte Gulf, set a pair of frothy drinks in front of my shipmate Mike and me. Mike was a golden-haired private-school dropout from New England. He was very fussy about his drinks. "O.K.," Toby said, "this is what I always served to Francis Ford Coppola whenever he came in. Makin' that Apocalypse movie took him so much time, he was in here so much drinkin' these, I decided to name it after him. I call it the Francis."

"The Francis?" Mike winced. "Couldn't you think up something a little more prosaic? Like the Coppola Cup, or a Double Apocalypse?"

"No. I like callin' it the Francis. It sounds dignified that way." Toby never used nicknames. Even my buddy Fred the Peace Corps guy was Frederick to Toby, with all three syllables pronounced.

Our drinks had the aroma of mango, the tang of pineapple, and a strong undercurrent of rum. As I sipped, I looked out through the dining room to the waters of Subic Bay. The sun was setting amid the great splashes and swashes and mottles of candy colors that are unique to the Philippine Islands sky. I once counted fourteen separate hues in the crazy quilt of a Philippine sunset. Purple, green, orange, six shades of blue, pink, and some colors I had no name for. They made the sky look like something delicious and fun to eat.

Toby's Beach Club Bar and Restaurant, and his four thatched and terraced bungalows, sat square on the beach of the eastern shore of the bay, about five miles out of Olongopo City. He was one of those American GIs who regularly fall in love with the East and stay around when their enlistments expire, or upon retirement. They marry a local woman, or at least set up housekeeping with one, and go into business as salvage divers, exporters, or innkeepers. Toby and his wife had had the Beach Club for many years. Actually, his wife had it all, as foreigners couldn't own real estate or a majority share of an enterprise in the Philippines. Legally, Toby was her employee. I was staying in one of the bungalows for a pittance a night.

"Hey, Toby," Mike said as he downed his Francis. "You've been here forever, you know everything."

"Sure," he said, running his fingers through his white muttonchop sideburns. "Waddaya wanna know?"

Mike looked at me. We both looked around the room to see if anyone might overhear. Then we both leaned inward over the bar, conspiritorially. Toby leaned outward over the bar, toward us.

"Toby," Mike said in a hush. "Have you ever heard of a place called Marilyn's?"

Toby gave us each a blank stare.

"Yeah," I urged, "Marilyn's."

"You know," Mike insisted, "the knobber shop, gobbler's gulch."

Toby still looked blank, so I said, "C'mon. You've heard the Fellatio Alger story. The whorehouse where only oral sex is available but it's, like, world class. They say the women even have to go through some kind of special training program!"

"I heard they even have a fellow working there, too!" Mike said. "They say he does more business than any of the girls! Hot damn!"

"Spill it, Toby! Is it in Olongopo City?"

"C'mon! What's the story?"

"O.K., look," he said, holding his hands up as if to stop us. "You guys been hearin' too many crazy sea stories. People tell you that just to pull your chain. That stuff's only fantasy. Besides, hey, if it were true, I'd be there spendin' all my money! Ha ha! O.K.? Here, let me get you two turkeys a couple more Francises. And if you ever do find a place like that, you be sure and tell me, O.K.? Just don't tell the wife, you know?" He smiled at the thought as he peeled another mango.

Mike looked glumly at the setting sun and said, "Well, maybe it isn't true, but it ought to be."

"Yeah."

Toby brought us two more Francises and reminded us that the martial law curfew was still in effect every night at midnight. Then-President Ferdinand Marcos didn't want his enemies skulking about after the witching hour. Toby warned us, "The last thing you want to do is get arrested around here. Could be bad for your health. And it's gettin' hard to bribe your way through after midnight because all the cops are gettin' in on the act. It's gettin' downright expensive. That reminds me, Richard, your girlfriend was here, that cute one with the stand-up bazooms. What's her name?"

"Erlinda."

"Yeah, O.K. She said to make sure you meet her in the

bungalow by curfew or she's gonna get jealous. And she says not to be a butterfly while you're out drinkin'."

In the Philippines a butterfly is a man who goes from flower to flower. It's even a verb: "to butterfly." Many of the women carry a switchblade-type weapon known as a butterfly knife. When pressed beyond endurance, they are known to clip the wings of the butterflies in their lives.

"Why is it," I asked, "that when I'm in port, and for as long as I'm in port, I'm the one who supports her, but she's the one who gets jealous. Something's amiss here."

"Don't you like her?" Toby asked.

"Well, yeah. She's the best girlfriend I've ever had here in the P.I. And the best dressed, too. A woman of style. But I just don't like having the butterfly knife of Damocles hanging over my head."

"Well that's what happens when you stay with 'em more than once or twice," the old sage counseled. "Suddenly you're their rice bowl and that's that. Besides, the women here just get attached easy, O.K.? Hey, maybe you like this girl more than you say. Maybe you think she might be something permanent?"

"It could happen. I'm not saying it will. But maybe, you know."

"If you don't piss her off too much. But I know; it's hard when you're a sailor, bein' gone all the time. During the war I was gone so much, my first wife got tired of it. She left me. So, O.K. 'Nuff said. You gotta get it when you can."

Mike broke in and said, "Well, the night is young, Richard. Let's go barhop our way along the bay shore. I'm not spoken for and I can butterfly all I like. You can watch."

We began a gradual progress east and north along the bay. At each noisy, colorful stop there were women who would approach our table and politely say, "Hello. May I sit beside you for a while?" Others were more aggressive and yelled from across the room or the road, "Hey, Joe. Let's go overnight!" In the Philippines all Americans are called Joe. "Hey, Joe. What do you want? I got it!" Through several miles of shoreline we traversed the sexual carnival that was Subic Bay. Whenever I seemed to be interested in a woman Mike reminded me of my "knife-wielding darling-true-love."

That's not to say that Erlinda was a hard or a violent woman. She wasn't. She was sophisticated and cultured beyond the norm, having come from a well-educated Manila family. She was warm and charming and carried herself with dignity. An inner strength came through in her every word and movement, and yet at the same time she was vulnerable and bruised. I was quite fond of her. My complaint was that she had little control of her passions. I had seen her vent her rage before, in public even, and I didn't care to again. I felt sure that if she went unchecked she would do some serious injury to herself or me or to whomever might get caught in the middle.

About ten miles from Olongopo we came upon a relatively quiet collection of a dozen or so buildings. Half of them were brothels and the others were bars and restaurants. A few sported colorful signs with splashy names like the Galaxy, the Stardust, and Stumpy & Gimpy's Muffdivers Inn. On the shore side, three buildings were wedged tightly together so as to all be near a small boat dock. The building in the middle looked particularly scrunched and the front was recessed, giving it an even more crowded look. A wooden walk descended from road level down a few feet to a little porch. An unpretentious sign over the door read "Marilyn's." Mike and I saw it at the same time. We stopped, very quietly, and simply gazed, smilingly, upon the sign.

"Do you think it's really?..."

"Sshhh. We're in the presence. I feel it. Sshhh."

Through the open door a light the color of candle glow shone warmly. A low hum of conversation enriched the air. Wordlessly, Mike and I took a single, tentative step forward. Mike reached with his right foot to the wooden walk and tested it. Nodding, he said, "I think it's safe. We won't be walking on illusion." Shoulder to shoulder we approached, slowly, quietly, indeed reverentially, till we came to the door and peered in. Small, round tables with matching chairs occupied the floor and a bar took up the far wall. Candles in hurricane globes burned on all the tables. To the left a stairway led up to the next floor and to the right was a little alcove for a band. Patrons collected in knots around the small tables. A larger group sat at three tables pushed together in a corner, drinking beer and punch.

Two waiters were working behind the bar perfectly dressed in starched white shirts, black bow ties, and cummerbunds. When one of them saw us he immediately put down his work and came forward to greet us. "Welcome, gentlemen. Welcome to Marilyn's. Please sit down and have something to drink. Do you want beer? Or we have a special drink, a punch. We call it mojo."

"Uh...beer, yeah, beer. Two beers," one of us muttered as we took it all in.

"Is this, uh...is this...Marilyn's?"

"Of course. Did you not see our sign outside?" The waiter took as much care in enunciating his words as he did in his fastidious appearance.

"I mean, is this, like, the real Marilyn's? You know, the one people talk about?"

"Ha ha," the waiter laughed. "There is only one famous Marilyn in all of Subic, and this is her place."

"You mean there really is a woman named Marilyn? An actual woman? It's not just the name of the place? It's all true? Everything we've heard is true!?"

"Well," he said, "I can't tell all that you have heard. But I'm sure pretty much everything is true. I have been working for her for many years. I know what I'm talking about. I hope you will like it here and come often."

A middle-aged American man, a civilian by his haircut, came wearily down the stairs, a smile on his flushed face. He lumbered across the room and sat down heavily with the patrons at the corner tables. Then a girl in a ponytail, short skirt, and blouse tied fetchingly beneath the breasts came bouncing down the stairs. As she passed our table she flashed us a white, toothy smile and waved hello. She went out through a door by the bar and called to the civilian, "Goodbye, Doug. See you again." Doug gave her a tired little wave and sighed the sigh of the content of heart.

When the waiter brought our drinks we told him how we had heard so often about this place but never knew anybody who had actually seen it. We went on to say that it was a real thrill to be sitting in a living legend, or something like that. "And you look so elegant in your cummerbunds," I said. "Everything about this place is just marvelous."

The waiter seemed immensely pleased with our compliments and enthusiasm. Then I asked, "Is Marilyn still alive? Does she live in town, or in Manila maybe?"

"Oh, she lives very near," he said. "Would you like to meet her?"

"Pinch me, Mike. I'm dreaming."

Our waiter, whose name was Mando, conferred briefly with his partner, then led us outside where we began walking along the shore. "Marilyn likes to meet new people very often," he explained. "She likes American guys very much. But first we have to stop at the Sari Sari store. If you are going to meet Marilyn, you have to bring her a present."

A Sari Sari store is a Philippine kiosk, or a tiny convenience store. In the towns every street corner has one. On the highways and byways there's one every mile or so. We stopped at one of two that serviced the collection of a dozen or so buildings and bought Marilyn the finest article available: a bottle of cologne. It was men's cologne, but it was all the Sari Sari store had. And Mando said it would be the thought that counted with his mistress.

We continued down the beach till we came to a well-lighted, walled compound. We stopped at a wrought-iron grill gate where Mando pressed a button and jabbered into a speaker.

"It's a villa!" Mike whispered with admiration. "A demi-palace! A palace for the queen of head!"

The gate buzzed open and Mando led us down a curvy, tiled walkway lined with ferns and flowers. An ornate bird-bath stood four high in the middle of a well-trimmed lawn. Laughter and party voices floated toward us from the main building as we approached it.

"What do you think is going on there?" Mike murmured.

"Whatever it is, I hope we're not too late."

"By the way, don't forget to get home on time tonight. Otherwise, you might turn into a butterflied pumpkin."

"Mike, did I ever tell you you're an asshole?"

"Yes."

"Just checking."

The front door of the main building opened and happy noises, color and light spilled out. The walls and ceiling of the large room were painted a pale coral. Majestic ferns and elegant potted palms made it lush with jade green. Rattan and wicker furniture with colorful cushions dotted the room and capiz shell lamps bathed it in velvety yellow light. I don't know what I had expected for occupants, but they were certainly not what I expected.

They were society folk. Local politicians, high-ranking U.S. naval officers, and civilian bigwigs from the nearby U.S. Navy base; businessmen, both Philippine and American; some people I took to be artists of some kind; musicians I had seen in nightclubs. Most of them were accompanied by their wives! One of the naval officers, a full commander (with his wife), was in a crisp, dress white uniform and I recognized him from a brief encounter in the past. The Mrs. wore blue chiffon and affected an ivory fan with little feathers hanging from it. The civilians schmoozed and the politicians conspired and the businessmen talked business. A man in a corner softly strummed a twelve-string guitar. Servants served drinks and tidbits. Dominating the whole scene was Marilyn.

She sat in an enormous rattan empress chair, or peacock chair, furnished with gaily colored floral cushions. A girl of about sixteen, dressed casually in faded jeans and a billowy t-shirt, stood leaning lazily against one side of Marilyn's throne. Now and then they whispered. Marilyn was smartly dressed in a finely woven cotton pants suit, expensive looking sandals and pearls. She looked to be about thirty-five to forty. It is an unfortunate fact that women in the Philippines tend to go to fat very early in life, and very quickly, too. I've seen women on the eve of their thirtieth birthday go to bed thin and wake up twenty pounds heavier. Or so it seems. I don't know if it's diet, climate, or heredity; I only know that it is. But Marilyn had beaten the odds. I don't know if she had been slimmer in her youth, but at the time when I looked upon her she was the size and shape of Marilyn Monroe. The luminous Monroe rendered in brunette and brown.

All the talk halted as we were conducted into the room. In the dignified strut of a majordomo Mando approached the throne and announced: "Marilyn, I have the pleasure to introduce these two American gentlemen. They have heard of you all the way from their home, and they would like to be your new friends."

The whole company broke into polite applause, smiles, and remarks.

"New friends, new friends!"

"How nice."

"Mabuhay!"

"Heard of Marilyn all the way from stateside."

"Great."

Marilyn smiled at us engagingly and turned her full attention to us. Mando gestured us forward. I was holding our cologne offering, so I approached and said, "Marilyn, I am Richard, and this is Mike. We've heard of you for such a long time. But we thought you were just a dream. Forgive us, and accept this small gift as a token from two of your admirers."

She took it in her finely manicured hands and read from the label, "Ah, Rawhide cologne. You're very nice to bring me this."

Mike found his tongue and said, "Well, that's all there was

at the Sari Sari store. But we'd have brought you diamonds if we could. Diamonds!"

"This will be very good for my nephew," she said, handing it to the t-shirted girl to take charge of. "And now come and sit by me and tell me your stories."

"Yes, yes," the courtiers all urged. "Tell your stories."

Mando, his duty done, had slipped quietly away, so Marilyn gestured to another cummerbunded servant who brought out two low footstools and set them at her feet. "Sit, sit, sit," she insisted with gestures of offering. "And bring them something to drink, too, Vincent. Bring them a mojo."

"Mojo, mojo," the people chanted.

We sat at Marilyn's feet, our heads on a level with her lap, and were soon served two icy highball glasses filled with a pinkish-orange punch that was rather the same color as the paint on the walls. It smelled of fresh pineapple and other sweet fruits, though I could not identify them. And it tasted just the same: delicious. "I don't taste any alcohol in this," I said. "Is it a soft drink?"

A ripple of knowing laughter shivered through the crowd.

"Soft drink!"

"Hardly!"

"It has a lot of rum in it," Marilyn warned us. "So you have to be careful when you drink it, because it can fool you a lot. I know. I'm the one who always makes it. And now, your stories. Please?"

And so we told Marilyn and her admirers our stories: where we were from, where we were going, places we had visited and what was important in our lives. Marilyn listened with a very attentive ear, and sympathetic and pleased expressions. She asked lots of questions. Whenever I made a joke, she laughed sincerely and touched me on the shoulder. The mojo flowed. I felt that I was in the company of someone special, a generous and commanding personality. It must have been something like Othello and Desdemona: he loving her because she loved his stories. Marilyn was a person I wanted to be close to. I wanted to put my head on her lap and let her sing me a lullaby. Or feed me more mojo.

When we had exhausted our stories Marilyn's followers gave us polite applause. Marilyn asked us, "Where are you staying now?" Mike named his hotel and I said, "In a bungalow at a place called the Beach Club, down the road a few miles."

"Oh, then you must know my friend Toby," she said with pleased surprise.

"Toby?"

"Yes, with white hair and big sideburns?"

"Oh yes. Toby. Yes, of course. Uh, we know Toby, don't we, Mike?"

"Toby," he nodded.

"He's a friend of mine a long time," Marilyn smiled. Then she reached down and patted and stroked me gently on the head, like a pet dog, smiling all the while. Noticing my empty glass she playfully scolded Vincent, charging him to be more attentive, and never again to let her guests hold an empty mojo glass. Leaning over to me and petting me again she said, "Would you like to hear my story now?"

"Marilyn's story!" one of the faithful cried out.

"Yes, yes, Marilyn's story," they all gushed, and yet again rendered polite applause.

"I never tire of it," the commander's wife said as she fanned herself coquettishly. The guitarist stopped his soulful strumming for the first time since we had arrived. Vincent topped off my glass and stood back in rapt respectful silence.

"Well, I was born a very poor girl on the island of Cebu," she began. "And when I was still just young I came to Subic to make my fortune. I tried to be a dancer, but if you know me very well you know I'm not very good. So I worked in the bars, I worked in the clubs. I worked every day and night. And I knew what my customers wanted." At this all the courtiers nodded and murmured their agreement. "So I practiced. And I became the best."

"The best, the best," the hangers-on added in refrain.

"And soon they were all coming to me. I began to earn a lot of money."

"Lots of money!"

"Ha ha!"

"Bravo!"

"I soon got to have too many customers and boyfriends. And I had money in the bank. So I opened my own place. The first was in Olongopo. And I hired the girls and I taught them myself. And I always treated them well, and paid them well. And they all became experts like me. I told them the secret to success is to always be the best. So I have been very successful. And now I have my other place here on the beach. I am a woman with two very successful businesses."

Marilyn was warming to her theme, smiling in satisfaction, and making pumping motions with her arm. A giggle wanted to escape from her, but she harnessed it and turned it into words, "I now have money and friends and houses and everything. And I got all this," she said stretching out the word "all," and making a grand sweeping gesture with her arm, "I got all this from sucking dicks."

"Ho ho ho!" her fans laughed with delight at the joke they had doubtless laughed at many times before.

"Bravo, well said!"

"Sucking dicks, ha ha ha!"

"I never tire of it."

"Commander," Marilyn called over the tumult to the senior officer present. "Do you know the big sign on the navy base that says 'What have you done for the fleet today?'"

"Of course, Marilyn. And what I have done is go to work. What have you done for the fleet today?"

"I sucked their dicks!"

And the people went into hysterics yet again. Mike seemed bemused. I couldn't tell how much rum was in the mojo, but by this time I had copped a mighty buzz and was laughing like a fool along with all the rest of her fans. As the hubbub died down, they all started chatting among themselves, the story over, and Vincent appeared at my side to fill my glass again. He smiled as he slipped away and I realized that I was resting one arm on Marilyn's lap. She stroked my head like a poodle once more and looked down at me with mirthful eyes. "Did you like my story?"

"Ha, it's a great story. Really good. But, hey. Tell me something, Marilyn. How do you know Toby?"

She considered for a moment, then decided to tell. "Well, he used to be my boyfriend."

"No."

"Yes. But his wife was jealous. So now...he's just...just my friend."

"C'mon. Don't be a tease. Tell me everything."

Cradling my head in the crook of her arm, she leaned down low and whispered in my ear with breath warm and moist, "He helps me when I'm training my new girls. I can't teach them everything with a banana or a squash. They have to know the real thing. I pay him a little bit. His wife keeps him on a short string; she doesn't give him very much. In more ways than one. But you need some more mojo. Vincent!"

It was now after 11 P.M. Those of Marilyn's admirers who were not houseguests began to make ready to leave in order to beat the curfew. Nobody wanted to have to pay a badly inflated bribe to the police or, worse, confront the constabulary troops: the federales. Mike had accepted an offer of a ride from one of the businessmen and was on his way out. I remembered Erlinda. Erlinda with her perfect bosom, her refined ways, her clever conversation, her high degree of lover's skill; and how delicious it was to awaken in the morning to her and the sound of the lapping bay surf. I had enough time plus ten minutes to make it back to her before midnight. And as I was low on cash, I lacked sufficient funds to bribe my way out of a tight spot.

"Stay," Marilyn said. "Stay."

"Stay?"

"Yes. Stay."

"Here?"

She laughed prettily. "With me."

We were standing now. She was reaching up to tug at my ear, still like her favorite pet. I looked at my watch. It read nine minutes to jail. "Stay," she repeated, like a mantra, running her fingers through my hair. "Stay." Eight minutes to spare. I had upset Erlinda once already this week. Sometimes when the women are angry they whip out their butterfly knives and say, "I'll give you a Filipino Haircut," with a slashing motion across the throat.

Seven minutes. I really liked Erlinda. I really, really did. I once fought another man over her. And she was worth it. When she was good she was very very good.

Six minutes. "Stay."

"I'm cutting this awfully close," I thought. "Just think of the story I'll have if I stay. In every bar I go to, and every other night at sea, guys will say 'Richard, tell the story of Marilyn, the queen of head!' They'll buy me drinks all night. I'll be famous in maritime circles. They'll all say, 'Oh, that's Dickie Sterling, what a salty guy he is. Get him to tell you a story.' On top of all that, I'll bet Marilyn can be brutally satisfying. Furthermore, I like her, I really like her. But I like Erlinda, too. And she's waiting for me. And so is Marilyn."

Five minutes.

2 4 *Test*

WOULD YOU CALL IT A STEP UP OR A STEP down, or something else entirely, to go from the BJ Queen of the Orient to the entertainments of a simple cook? I guess we'd all have to answer that for ourselves. It depends on the kinds of memories you want to collect. And to me, memories are the only things really worth collecting. But at any rate, I can tell you this much: it has come to pass that I've availed myself of the cook's attentions a lot more often.

I hopped on the overnight train from Bangkok to the end of the line at Nong Kai. But that was not my destination. I was heading to the place that's after the end of the line, in more ways than one. To cross the Mekong River from Thailand into Laos is to cross time and consciousness more than space. Crammed into the middle of the Indochina peninsula, it is a place the world passes by. Though the geography is vastly different—rainforest and tropical floodplain rather than craggy, inhospitable desert—it reminds me very much of Baja California. Few roads lead here; few airlines fly in. Nothing ever happens here, and nothing needs to happen. All is complete and satisfactory. The old French Colonial administration called it the "Land of the Lotus Eaters." I call it Baja Indochina: the "Land After the End of the Line."

Four million people inhabit Laos, a lush and fertile land the size of France. The first time I was here, a local expat described the character of the Lao people as lazy. "But look around," he said. "If it's green, it's salad. If it moves, it's protein. They just have to bend down and pick it up. You'd be lazy too."

I am here to learn how to cook the local fare. Lao cuisine is unique. It's as supple as water in its ability to accept new influences and ingredients, yet durable as time in maintaining its essential character. The blending of spices is an art receiving the same attention the Japanese give to flower arranging. Rich, smooth sauces and curries, grilled meats and fish, an abundance of salads, spicy condiments, and glutinous rice are its hallmarks. And the Lao eat more raw food and more wild foods than any other people I know. But cookery here is a private art. Secret recipes are common. Both high-born ladies and peasant women compete for local culinary fame, but they rarely reduce their recipes to writing. This is the only sophisticated cuisine I know of that is virtually devoid of cookbooks. I am hoping, eventually, to fill that void, lest a cultural treasure be lost.

I lunched today at the morning market. (They call it that even though it goes on all day.) There's a stall in the southeast corner run by a woman who has dubbed me Mr. Beer (or "Mistah Bia," in the local accent) for my taste for the brew at breakfast. Yes, at breakfast! Hey, it's hot here, the food is salty, and I don't have to drive, think, or operate machinery.

When I showed up today, the Mrs. took one look at me, turned to her daughter, and smiled "Bia," and the daughter fetched me a cold one. Madam then turned to making one of my favorites here in Laos: *som tam.* It's a spicy, tangy salad made from julienned green papaya tossed with chili, garlic, lime, tomatoes, and fish sauce. Then it's pounded a bit in a large mortar to release all the flavors and juices. It's very cleansing on the palate and a perfect foil for rich sauces or grilled meats. As this was going on, I turned my eyes to Madam's supply of skewered chicken, pork, fish, and stuff I couldn't identify. All had been previously grilled and needed only reheating on the charcoal brazier. I pointed to one in the shadowy corner that looked like the strips of marinated pork I had enjoyed on previous occasions, but as my good lady of the grill placed the skewer on the fire, I noticed little appendages on each piece of meat that looked rather like legs.

It occurred to me that what I had just ordered was tree frogs on a stick, a common item of diet here. I wasn't too alarmed, as I'd enjoyed stuffed frogs for dinner only the night before. But for last night's entree, the heads, guts, and skins had all been removed and the frog had been stuffed with a delicious forcemeat, rolled in spices and fried in a rich oil. Tree frogs on a stick, though, come to the table unaltered except by fire.

I thought of changing my order, but nobody at the market spoke English and I spoke no Lao. Also, by this time I had attracted a small crowd of goggle-eyed children who had apparently never seen a blue-eyed demon at the table, and I didn't want them to think I was a wuss. Besides, rats and bats on a stick are also common here; I figured I was getting off easy with frogs.

Madam's daughter turned the little beasties once more, then deskewered them onto a plate and set them before me. Frogs I was prepared for, but what I got was chicken feet! Marinated, grilled, scratch-at-the-ground chicken feet. The heel and toe, claw, instep, and ankle of the common barnyard chicken is esteemed a tasty treat throughout Southeast Asia. I have even seen them offered in the snack bars of movie theaters; I tell no lie.

I always knew that someday I would face this moment, but I never relished it. Funny, isn't it, that I who would eat anything should quake at the sight of chicken feet. I who have supped on soup made of ant larvae, quaffed bowls of blood, dined on dogs, and chewed through the guts of animals un-known. Not that I am an indiscriminate eater, mind you. My food must be artfully prepared and presented with care. But I've long boasted that I would eat anything on legs except a table and anything with wings but an airplane. Somehow chicken feet never appealed.

And now my gastronomic bravado was coming home to roost. This would be the test of my resolve. Madam set the "*som tam*" in front of me and her daughter brought forth sticky rice. Excellent Lao beer had been well chilled and poured into a frozen mug that had been resting under pounds of ice as though in anticipation of my arrival. The wide-eyed children seemed to hold their breath as though the thought had occurred to them that the big, sweaty *farang* might prefer the profane feast of a tender Lao child to the undisputed and civilized delicacy of chicken feet.

Their watchful parents ogled sidelong. I sniffed. The aroma of barbecued chicken was unmistakable. No toe-jam smells or athlete's-foot odors obtained. I looked closely at the curled digits and saw that few talons remained. Whether they had burned off on the grill or been extracted for herbal medicines I don't know. With thoughts of foot fetishes ajumble in my mind, I lifted one to my mouth, and as the children gawked, I gnawed. Dare I say it was finger-lickin' good? It tasted better than anything I ever bought from the Colonel. He should take lessons.

Of course there isn't much meat on a hen's foot, or a cock's either for that matter. You might get two swallows if you're a lady; one for a gentleman or a rogue. They're like pickled pig's feet: you nibble them for their flavor, not their nourishment. They provide much gustatory satisfaction with virtually no calories. And when you're finished, you can do as I did: use the toenails to pick your teeth.

2 5 *T e s t o s t e r o n e*

I THOUGHT AFTER THE FEAST OF CHICKEN FEET there could be no further gastronomic traumas for me. I'm prepared for anything, you name it. Human flesh? Make mine rare. Cup of blood? Pour me a double, dash of Tabasco and a twist. Snakes, snails, puppy dog tails, slugs and guts, and a hundred other things. I'm ready for them all if they are prepared with care and served with beer.

Such was my mind as I took a stroll along the left bank of the Mekong River. The sun shone silver upon the waters and butterflies floated lazily in the tropical heat. Thailand winked provocatively from the river's other side. I ambled along, slowly for the heat, and was thankful for a place where you can do anything slowly.

But as night follows day, thirst follows heat. I passed people selling coconuts brimming with milk for the thirsty traveler, soda, fruit juice, and even unchilled beer. My God! When it's ninety degrees in the shade and humid to boot, the thought of unchilled beer is almost as bad as no beer at all. I kept walking, almost hidden in the leafy folds of a giant banyan tree, and there on the riverbank I found a little watering hole.

It was really little more than a wooden deck, about ten by twenty feet, covered with thatch and tin, but set within the boughs of the banyan. It was a treehouse. The shady limbs of the great tree held the little house in a cool, dark embrace, giving protection from the midday sun while still affording a delicious view of the placid river.

I heard the friendly sizzle of food frying in good oil; that particular sound that beckons travelers and laborers anywhere. And I heard the clink of ice and the pop of bottle tops. I stepped off the bank and went inside.

"Mistah. Welcome, Mistah," a sarong-clad woman greeted me. "You drink bia, Mistah?"

"You bet!" I said, and took a seat at one of the low tables near the far railing so as to have the best view of the river.

The lady served me a cold one, and it foamed down my throat in icy relief. I slowly sipped the second one, and as I did I noticed a girl of about sixteen sitting across the deck and engaged in some household activity that looked like it might be stringing beans, and so I assumed it was. I smiled at her and she grinned in return. We exchanged numerous smiles until she finally gathered up her work, brought it over to sit beside me, and resumed her labor.

In a steep-sided bowl she had many dozen live, wriggling, trying-desperately-to-get-out potato bugs. Potato bugs, goddamn it, potato bugs! And she was preparing them as the specialty of the house!

She smiled at me again as she drew another bug from the bowl. Deftly and matter-of-factly, she broke the critter's neck at the back, leaving the head attached, and drew out the contents of his torso. Then she grasped his hind end, cracked the exoskeleton, and slowly drew out his viscera in a long, slimy string.

"You eat?" she asked, holding the carcass up to my face. It twitched.

"Oh," said I, "I eat anything, sure."

"You want?" she offered.

"Uh...Me no hungry. O.K.?"

"O.K.," she said, and cracked another neck.

Now, I've eaten insects before. Many times. I've eaten red warrior ants in Borneo where the people use them for their lemon/tarragon flavor to season fish. I've enjoyed numerous kinds of larvae, baked, boiled, and roasted in a leaf. Crickets? Jumping jimminy, ate 'em by the pound, roasted and salted like peanuts. And the noble locust, who looks more like his marine cousin the prawn when cooked, has made me a meal. Recommended by both the libidinous Nero and the abstemious John the Baptist, the locust is an excellent dish. But potato bugs! Oh, God, potato bugs! Eeeiiiww! There is nothing redeeming about a potato bug. He is the ugliest, yuckiest creature on Earth. He is the chosen weapon of wanton boys to throw at girls when they want to really gross them out. A potato bug is a six-legged pustule who, if he has any grace, is an offense even to himself! And I ate him.

I ate a whole bunch of him. I wasn't going to, but this French couple walked in and sat down near me. They were both shocked at the butchery being practiced by the bug-slaying girl. The Monsieur spoke English and asked me, with great distaste, what the hell was going on with the potato bugs. I explained as he translated to Madam. She blanched. And I mean she blanched real good, too. As though some wanton boy had just thrown one of the beasties at her. Monsieur didn't look any too healthy either, and I decided this was the time to do away with my last food prejudice.

"Madam. Cook *ke lai* for me?" I asked the girl, using the local name for a stinking, rotten potato bug.

"Yes, yes," she assured me. "One kilo?"

"Oh...what about a dozen to start?"

She called out to Madam and broke another neck, and soon I heard the furious sizzle of deep frying. The Frenchies looked unwell.

Madam set a plate of french-fried potato bugs in front of me. They were all on their backs, their little bug legs sticking up. A small cup of dipping sauce graced the presentation. A shaker of salt sat nearby. I sprinkled some salt on their fried bodies, tossed a pinch over my shoulder, and took a long pull of beer from my bottle. Then I grabbed a bug by the head and popped him in my mouth.

His spiny legs on my tongue felt alive, as though he would scurry down my throat. I bit down and he crunched audibly. The French caught their breath. The girl continued her casual slaughter and smiled.

"Good?" she inquired.

It was good! So help me it was! Mr. Potato Bug tasted and chewed like a shrimp deep-fried in his own shell until the shell becomes crisp and edible and its flavor permeates the meat. If I were a blind man you might have fooled me into thinking I was eating crustaceans.

"They're not bad," I said to the Gallic duo, and I crunched a few more as they watched in morbid fascination. Then I handed one to Monsieur and said, "Go ahead. Be a man, ha ha!"

I thought about wantonly throwing one at the little woman, but I restrained my boyish self. The challenge I had thrown down to the Frenchman was of the highest masculine order. The simple issuance of it effectively impugned his manhood in the now testosterone-charged air. Frenchy was in a fix: on the one hand, he didn't want to eat a bug—who could blame him?—but on the other, he would be damned among males as a wuss (at least in his own mind) if he refused the awful summons. And he would be doubly damned, as his humiliation would take place in front of girls. He sat upon the razor's edge, but I had faith in him. A Frenchman may be a cultural chauvinist with effeminate gestures, but he is no wuss. He can be a pain in the ass, look lengthily down his nose, and denounce things American as he consumes his Big Mac and Coke, but he makes an art of accepting the challenge. Melville shows us the cannibal harpooner Queequeg reaching across the table for beefsteaks with the shaft of his harpoon, but while outlandish, it was a thing done with grace for, he tells us, Queequeg did it *coolly*, and a thing done coolly, he writes, is a thing done with grace.

I saw the hot revulsion in the Frenchman's face begin to cool as he girded his gastronomic loins for the culinary duel. A tremble I had noticed in his hand was visibly abating. His wife looked daggers at me. In the hush, the bug girl audibly broke another neck. In the breathless silence, we could just hear the sound of the guts being drawn out in a long little slurp. My adversary hesitated. A part of me wanted to see him humbled, cast out, bearing the mark of shame, driven east of Eden and all that. But the better part of me would not see my fellow done so cruelly.

"Go ahead," I told him. "High protein, low cholesterol, no tropical oils. Lightly salted. And the sauce is piquant without being overpowering."

He took the proffered bug and boldly chewed it, savoring its shrimp-like taste. We exchanged that special masculine glance that is the gastronomic equivalent of the ancient warrior's arm clasp, a glance that says "Hail, thou bold fellow, and bon appetit!" Madam glanced at her husband in a way that said he would surely be a happy horseman that night.

Frenchy and I ate several bugs together. My work done, I paid the tab and tipped the bug girl. She wiped her gutsy hands and received it gracefully. On my way out I paused, turned and shot Frenchy a sort of half salute, which he returned. I think his wife gave me the finger. But it was subtly done—coolly, I might even say.

Once outside, I saw that the sun was dropping low to touch the horizon and set the waters of the Mekong ablaze with red-gold. I ambled down the dusty river road, a full belly and a full heart, knowing that I had dined, and done, well. "I wonder what tomorrow holds for me," I mused, "in a world of infinite gastronomic diversity." Who can say? Not I. But I can say this: A potato bug, artfully prepared and tastefully presented, is still a goddamn, gross, ugly, disgusting potato bug, and I'll never eat another one again! Ptooui!

2 6   *D e i r d r e*

YOU CAN NEVER GO BACK. I RELEARN THIS LESSON from time to time. If you don't stay connected to a place it can be lost to you forever. For reasons I'm not sure of I went for twenty years without returning to Hong Kong, a place that had had a grip on me for years. But now I have found that the Hong Kong of my youthful navy days has faded away. The demi-Shanghai, the outpost of empire, the steamy fleshpot is no more. Like Tijuana, she's grown up and got respectable. Unlike Tijuana, she's now big, she's thundering, she's powerful. She's a great shuddering machine and the ground trembles beneath her. She has become a giantess. Hardly anything of her remains on the human scale. They are not mere skyscrapers that shoulder each other on the harborside. They are behemoths, monuments, colossi, great monstrous temples to Mammon that dwarf the traveler. And all is clean and orderly and safe. The trains run on time. And the world of Suzie Wong is far, far away in mistiest memory. A lifetime ago I foolishly left a Hong Kong lady's apartment at 3 A.M. I found myself at the Kowloon docks, hiding in the shadows from a prowl of Triads (Chinese Mafia) going about their dark business. The Triads still operate, but nowadays I think that if they discovered me in the shadows they would help me to the ferry, purchase my ticket, and wish me long life and prosperity. Murder might put profit at risk, and profit is the greatest virtue in Hong Kong.

I go barhopping. But there are no more of the old scruffy bars. They are all neon lit, air-conditioned, and expensive. They have happy hours and promotional sales of this or that European beer. There are no more dens of iniquity. Cub Scout dens perhaps, but none of iniquity. If there are any whores left, they are those in public office. The waterfront teems with tourists, not with hordes of horny sailors thirsting for beer, brawls, and broads. The seamy side is buried under the foundations of banks and brokerages, and the former crown colony is now a Special Administrative Region of the People's Republic of China. They call it the SAR for short. In starkest truth, Hong Kong has become Manhattan's little sister, all grown up and possessed of Chicago's big shoulders and LA's air.

But not all is lost. The food is better than ever. Wine is abundant, if pricy. The entire world is here on a plate. The rooftops of Wanchai that used to accommodate brothels now sprout herb gardens to supply the trendy restaurants. And there are ballrooms with people practicing waltz and tango. But I confess that the shock of the change took some getting used to.

Indeed, upon arrival I was stunned. I felt robbed of an era in my life. Yeah yeah, I know, I shouldn't expect people to stay mired in sin and corruption just for my gratification. But intellect and emotions do not always comport with one another. At least mine don't. So I was pissed off, see? I was betrayed by the inexorable marches of history. I was dispossessed by progress. The book of my life had been suddenly and anonymously edited, and thrown back at me thus reduced. And I was sad. Deeply sad. And that special loneliness of the road that can descend upon us even at the best of times, fell with a special, ponderous weight.

My slumped shoulders would have revealed the burden as I trudged the streets of Kowloon looking for something, anything, comfortingly familiar. But of course the British and American navies rarely visit the SAR of the PRC nowadays. And the government frowns on every vice but greed. I found the venerable Peninsula Hotel to be now more shopping mall than hostelry, and its piano bar where I had met so many fascinating characters was closed till later in the evening. The Chung King Mansions didn't even look hazardous to health anymore. Just sad. The skyline was obscured by new construction, and the harbor filling up with reclamation. And then, up on Hankow Road, I saw it, gleaming in the night like a lighthouse in a gale, saying "This way to safe harbor and succor. Come hither." It was the Bottoms Up Bar.

You may know of this place from one of the James Bond movies. It's a subterranean lair of four small cellular hexagonal bars all keyed into a central hexagon which actually dispenses the drinks. Each of the five surrounding hexes is furnished with a small circular bar, in the center of which, on a cushioned pedestal, sits a half-naked woman. Each cell has its own color scheme and is decorated in garish 1970s blow-dried tackiness. To this day. And that, I found, was a great comfort. As was the half-naked woman in the first bar, the red bar. Her name was Deirdre. She was English. She wore what amounted to the original topless bathing suit designed by Rudy Gerlich in the 1960s.

"Is this your first time here? she asked, as I ordered a San Miguel beer.

"Hardly," said I. "I met my ex-girlfriend in here in 1974."

"Really? She was a patron of the bar then?"

"No. She was sitting where you are right now. She was English, too."

Now, my ex-girlfriend, Kelly, was a tall, slender, green-eyed redhead. Very athletic. Deirdre was dark eyed, about 5' 5", with skin the color of pale gold. She had a thick mane of auburn Titian hair that she casually tossed back from time to time. Her hips were full and her tummy nicely rounded. And of her...mammary endowment, I shall say nothing, but that they...caught the eye. I began to be cheered. What healthy man of the heterosexual persuasion would not be cheered with a great pair of bazongas in his face, I ask you?

There were other gentleman patrons in the bar, but Deirdre ignored them, except when they called for refreshment, and paid her kind attentions to me. I thought perhaps she was interested in this living link with the history of her place of employment. We chatted for a little while, and a warm glow began to infuse my soul. I drank in her company like balm. She was tonic for care. With each toss of her mane her bosom would ripple. And with the changing temperature as the air-con ebbed and flowed, I could see her nipples rise and fall.

At length I became aware that she also had a face. Of course I had known this, in the far reaches of my consciousness, as I had heard words emanating from it. But at some point I actually looked at it. And it was very pleasant to see. I resolved to look at it more often. Especially when she spoke.

By this time the Bottoms Up had become a portal to bygone days. I had spent many an evening in here. I had met beautiful women here, as well as cads, curs, and heroes. The BU (for such we called it) was a bibulous crossroads for all manner of persons in those olden golden times. I met a profane priest here, Father Frank O' Shannan, whom we later rescued at the fall of Saigon in 1975. "Bless you, Dickie," he shouted above the roar as I bundled him into a chopper, throwing a crash helmet in after him. "See you at the BU, laddie," he waved as the bird gained the air. And there was the blue-eyed New Zealand heiress on a world tour. Thrusting her alabaster face into mine she told me that if I didn't come immediately with her to her hotel suite she would, "ring up a male prostitute instead, and tell everyone about it." Her name was Victoria. I took her to the old airport the next day. That was before Kelly, or neither of us would have survived. Roberto Shultz, the Austrian-Argentine news photographer and regular in the red bar (Kelly's bar) once took an uninvited photo of Kelly's bare bosom. With great cursing and vituperation she made him expose the film under threat of breaking the camera over his head. He took it like a sport, though, and came back often. And then of course there was the divine and demonic Kelly, who alternately enraptured and enraged me.

With Deirdre's beguiling bosom and dulcet tones I had allowed myself to slide into a warm pool of nostalgia. I was bathing in memories and beer. I was spiritually naked and unarmed. "Buy me a drink?" she asked.

Out in the harbor there is a flag mast to indicate weather conditions. A signal known as a T6 is run up to indicate small craft warnings. A T8 is a typhoon advisory. A T10 means a full gale is a'brewing. My own personal T6 ran up the mast and snapped open in a now brisk wind. "It's only ninety-nine Hong Kong dollars," she cooed. Ninety-nine Hong Kong dollars at the time was equal to fifteen U.S. dollars. No wonder she was ignoring the other guys.

In the old regime this kind of solicitation was strictly forbidden. The BU was a respite from this kind of liquid pocket picking that was so rife in the bars of the Wanchai district. The BU was a civilized place. Of course a man, or woman for that matter, was perfectly at liberty to buy a lady a "Hong Kong Ice Tea," but her asking for it was clear out of the way. And it didn't cost ninety-nine Hong-Goddamn-Kong dollars!

"You buy," urged the lady manager, pointing to Deirdre. "You can buy her one." So they'd even descended to tag-teaming the lonely, helpless male. Hooked like a fish with beguiling bait they double up to reel him in. Betrayal in Hong Kong again. Betrayal of the worst kind!

Now consider my dilemma. In my lonely state, the mere presence of the half-naked Deirdre has been like a security blanket. The riveting charm of her riveting charms has buoyed my spirits immensely. And her conversational attentions have been welcome and sweet. And of course there is the physical compulsion of the evolutionary imperative: In her infinite wisdom Mother Nature so perfectly designed me that I always give the correct answer to any question put to me by a beautiful woman with her tits in my face. Of course that answer is "Yes."

"Do you think I'm pretty?"

"Yes."

"Are you a bounder and a knave?"

"Yes."

"Will you serve me like a dog?"

"Yes."

Truth to tell, fifteen dollars didn't seem so bad. I figured she would probably go through one drink in fifteen minutes, or four in a hour. At sixty bucks an hour, well, I don't think you can get psychotherapy for that. And in therapy you don't get tits. Or beer. And I've had psychotherapy before. I'm here to tell you, it's not nearly as good as tits and beer! But as the two women reeled in their line, the T6 came down and the T8 ran snappily up the mast. Now I was déjà vu and pissed off all over again. And their hook stung. I looked Deirdre squarely in the nipples and said, "Not tonight, sweetheart." I drained my glass, and getting up to leave said, "Hasta la vista, baby." Well, I didn't exactly say that. But I thought it.

A small triumph in a big world. So I had just said No to Knockers. It must have been the first time. Hmmm. Not really something for which to pat myself on the back, but still, I had left the BU with my dignity intact. Sort of. It would have to sustain me in my gloomy hour. I shortly found myself in front of the Peninsula Hotel again, and I determined to try the piano bar once more. It was open. And empty but for the bartender. Clark Gable introduced the screwdriver to Hong Kong in this very bar in the early 1950s. He taught bartender Johnnie Chung how to make it. I've met Johnnie any number of times in the past. He's mixed me many a drink, and he always remembers the nuances of how an individual bibber likes his liquor. He still works at "the Pen" but, now in his seventies, only part time, and not at night.

So now the duty barman, Edward, smiles as someone finally walks into his lonely station. Now he has a purpose. "Do you know Johnnie Chung?" I ask him as I survey the empty room.

"Oh yes. Johnnie is famous here. Though he is quite old, and doesn't work much. But he won't retire. He says he'll die on the job."

So maybe something remains of old Hong Kong. At least for a while. Until Johnnie dies. I order a martini, teaching Edward to make it just the way I like, hoping he will remember as well as Johnnie. Bombay gin poured generously over ice. Not too dry. Give it a good splash of vermouth. I like a cocktail, Edward, not a straight shot. Now shake it into submission. Shake it till it cries for mercy. Shake it so that when you pour it into a chilled glass a patina of ice crystals floats upon the surface. Now garnish. Ahh, we have genuine Spanish olives. Those were hard to find in the old days. We usually had to have a twist. Now taste. Mmmm. Perfect, Edward. Perfect.

I gaze into my drink, and listen to the silence of the empty bar. I think of Astaire and Sinatra singing "Set 'em up, Joe. Make it one for my baby, and one more for the road." I look up, and see that Edward has disappeared, off on some errand, no doubt. And so I am well and truly alone, and the silence is palpable. In my glass the crystalline patina has resolved itself into a shiveringly cold pool, and in its mirror surface I can see my right eye, startling in its clarity. I wink to myself in the gin. "I showed Deirdre," I assure the spiritous reflection. "And that smarmy manager. Fifteen dollars! If Gable were here again he'd say I did the right thing. Gable never paid to talk to some dame, not in any stage of undress. I'll bet there were plenty of dames that would have paid to talk to him!" I imagine him sitting there, right where he taught Johnnie Chung the elixir of the screwdriver. Women sighing over him. Gable would never be lonely. Would he?

I sip gin and vermouth. The coldly warming potion helps to bring Gable's image into view. I look surreptitiously about to see that no one is watching, then lift my glass to the King of Hollywood. "Fifteen dollars, Clark. But I showed her, Clark. She couldn't snag me. She was a looker, and a charmer, and I was sorely tempted, but I wouldn't let her take me like that. I hope you approve, Mr. Gable."

Edward returns to tell me that it's about closing time, setting my bill before me in a silver tray. "I won't be a minute," says I, and I start to knock back the remnants of the drink. I see that Gable is still sitting there, dangerously handsome. So I leave the last gulp for him. I pick up my bill. With service charge, ninety-nine Hong Kong dollars.

2 7 *Failure*

SOMETIMES THE BEST WE CAN GET IS THE COLD comfort of a hollow victory. And sometimes we just fail altogether. But we should never shirk from failure, never fear it. It cannot stop us unless we let it. And without it, how could we recognize success? How sweet could victory taste, never having swallowed defeat? It's still a grand game, life is, if you make it so. And don't ever let anybody tell you that you can't play another round.

Along the ancient spice route the timeless port of Mombasa lies halfway between India and Europe. Its origins are unknown, but Arab chronicles of the twelfth century list it as one of many small ports of the East African coast. It comes into the Western consciousness, though, with Vasco da Gama. Having rounded the Cape of Good Hope, he arrived here in 1498 on his way to India in pursuit of spices. Mombasa became the way station for those Portuguese adventurers who would come to dominate the Indian spice trade to Europe for a hundred years. Eventually, "His Majesty's Most Christian Army" would be displaced in turn by the Omani Arabs and the Sultan of Zanzibar, and they by the British in their turn, and finally by independent Kenya.

Here, at the edge of Old Town, the Portuguese built Fort Jesus, an imposing old pile of Iberian masonry bristling with cannons. From these walls they controlled the entry to the harbor, and the ships they stationed here kept open the sea lanes to the Malibar coast of India. Almost daily then the Portuguese carracks and Arab and Somali dhows arrived here laden with their precious cargoes of spice. And the trade went both ways. It was through here that historians believe the chili pepper was taken to India by way of Goa, that Portuguese enclave that endured till 1961.

Most of that trade is now carried on in container ships that bypass this old port. Yet still the pungent tradewind smell of spices sweetens the air. Still, cargoes of cloves and pepper are unloaded by sweating "headload workers" from the holds of little dhows in from Zanzibar. And I was here to find my way aboard one of those cockleshell boats and take passage from Old Mombasa to that fabled Isle of Cloves.

I arrived in Mombasa from Kenya's capital, the modern, British-built Nairobi, on the overnight train. A good ride with a good dinner in a circa 1950s dining car. The spotless table settings, efficient waiters, and the good food and cold beer boded well for things to come. The train even ran on time. I stepped off the carriage eager and refreshed at 7 A.M. on a clear, warm morning into the African gateway to the spice route. I was sure that everything would go my way. I shouldered my gear and followed the narrow lanes of Old Town as they twisted and turned, mazelike in their medieval convolutions, seeking some old hotel whose walls might talk.

All the town was alive with varied peoples in their traditional dress: Maasai and Kikuyu tribesfolk in smocks, beads, bare feet, and notched and pierced ears and carrying maces and staves, having left their long spears at home; Indians in saris, *khameeses* (flowing tunic and loose trousers) and turbans, dripping with jewelry; Somali women who use indigo to paint their hands and feet with extravagant designs of curlicues and arabesques. Most of them wear a variation of the chador, a long black drape that covers them from crown to ankle. Some of them leave their faces exposed, others just their eyes. Still others draw a heavy black gauze over their faces and wear a chador that covers even hands and feet. The billowy costume floats and flutters, making the woman look like a black ghost that moves effortlessly upon the breeze. What a contrast they make to their African sisters in their exuberantly colorful florals and batiks.

For all of its color and verve this is a dirty place, and it ain't cheap. The only budget hotel in which I felt my health to be relatively safe is called the Taj. Three stories tall with no elevator; the water runs only from 9-11 A.M. (most days); they clean house every day, but you'd hardly notice; it sits across the narrow street from a hostel for Somali refugees who alternately argue with each other and lament their fate. While staying at the Taj I picked up a cargo of fleas, and a tropical rash in a most indelicate location. I had had fairly good luck on my journey so far. I had reached all my destinations, made most of my connections. But the Third World travel gremlins were about to close in.

I took many of my meals in Mombasa at the excellent, cramped, crowded, little Big Bite restaurant on Maungano Road in New Town. Here I found cooks using spices like painters use colors. They speak little English but they were able to impart several recipes to me. My favorite was a hot sauce based on a spice blend and the juice of the Ukwaju, a native East African lemon. Also essential to the recipe is the pili-pili, or red chili pepper. It's everywhere in Mombasa. The Portuguese are remembered for two things here: Fort Jesus and the pili-pili. And when Fort Jesus is reduced by time and raindrops to a pile of dust, people will still be enjoying the pili-pili.

At the Big Bite I also met a charming English couple: Joanne and Tim. They're both clinical psychologists from London and were on a three-month romp through Eastern and Southern

Africa. "Got to get away sometimes," Tim said. "Or the patients will drive you crazy!" Their frequent absentminded
scratching told me they must be staying in a hotel a lot like
mine. I didn't ask if they had rashes.

"Ow's your 'otel?" Joanne asked me, inquiring about my
loathsome lodgings.

"Oh, uh, great," said I. "Running water two hours a day.
Sometimes."

"You 'ave running water?" she asked in surprise.

"Sometimes."

"They just bring us a bucket once a day. It's not really an
'otel, though. It's an 'ore 'owse."

"An 'ore 'owse?"

"A brothel," Tim explained.

"They 'aven't got enough 'orse, you see. So they've got
some empty rooms and they rent them out to tourists. It's a
good bargain."

"Do you ever get mistaken for staff?" I asked.

"No," Tim said. "Customers."

"Both of you?"

"Takes all kinds."

"I guess you should know," I muttered, wondering where
my quest was about to take me. I told them of my desire to
reach Zanzibar. "It's one of the great stops of the old spice
route," I told them. They declared that they would go to
Zanzibar, too. And that we should travel together as soon as
we could book passage on a dhow.

We celebrated our alliance with dinner at the Rekoda
restaurant on Nyeri Street in Old Town. The place is a little
hole-in-the-wall that spills out onto the street, draws cats and
dogs, and is the most popular cheap eatery in town. Here you
can get good examples of the unique Swahili cuisine, a fusion
of Indian, Arab, and native African tastes and styles. The most
ethereal dish was *karanga*, a braise of lamb, vegetables, chili,
tamarind, and other spices. Nile perch and freshly caught
seafish are rubbed with cayenne and turmeric and fried in

searingly hot coconut oil. Tomatoes find their way into nearly every dish here, as do other New World crops such as corn and beans and potatoes. They are rubbed with spices and fried or stewed in spicy gravies or soaked in spicy liquids and grilled over coals with meats and fish. I had been told that African tastes were bland. And in the interior they are. But here the people would mourn the loss of those things that brought Vasco da Gama to Mombasa.

Joanne and Tim and I went to the docks every day to find a dhow to sail us to Zanzibar. And every day the port captain said, "Come back tomorrow." And tomorrow and tomorrow and tomorrow. And finally we ran out of tomorrows, and looked for other means. But everything that could go wrong with Third World travel was going wrong. The gremlins were after me. Of the two hydrofoils that make the weekly run from Mombasa to Zanzibar, one was laid up for lack of parts and the other was simply "not running." There is a continuous railway between Uganda, Kenya, and Tanzania but no trains were running. Air Tanzania's "fleet" was reduced to one aircraft on which nobody who wanted to see Zanzibar and tell the tale would book passage. The buses are instruments of torture that take days to cover the three hundred miles, and more days to return, and I was running out of days. The three of us agreed upon a council of war to decide what to do.

We met in Tim and Joanne's room in the 'ore 'owse. The Taj Hotel was better. We began by commiserating over our disappointment, and my friends said they had decided to go to another island that they hoped would be nearly as pleasant. They showed me brochures and pictures. It did look nice. But there was no substitute for me. Since I saw Hope and Crosby in the movie *The Road to Zanzibar* I had yearned to visit the island. I was disconsolate.

Joanne reached into her backpack and took out a loaf of bread and some other items. "Would you like a peanut butter and jelly sandwich," she asked me. "I know it's something you Yanks are fond of."

"You travel with peanut butter and jelly?" I asked in amazement.

"We bought it 'ere."

"What kind of jelly?"

"Don't know, really. Fruit of some kind."

"Got milk?"

"Sorry. Only water."

That was no mean offer, as bottled water can cost as much as three U.S. dollars per bottle. (I said this place ain't cheap) Joanne made peanut butter and jelly sandwiches with a Swiss army knife and we ate them in silence, scratching ourselves and passing the water bottle between us.

"How could it have come to this?" I wondered, the sandwich sticking to the roof of my mouth as I awaited my turn at the water bottle. In all my years on the road I'd never failed to reach my destination. I'd always beaten the gremlins. It may have cost me saddle sores or bunions, bribes or bellyaches, even a heartache, but I'd always arrived. And now, here I was, with fleas and rashes, eating peanut butter and unknown jelly in the dirtiest little 'ore 'owse in the world with two head shrinkers on the lam from their patients! Such high hopes and lofty plans gone awry. What is it King David says in his famous elegy? "How have the mighty fallen." Damn!

There's nothing for it, though. I've just got to write this one off and keep on keeping on. O.K. then, I'm on the first train out of here to somewhere else. "Press on regardless!" That's what my old navy skipper would have counseled. Press on. I've had some good meals here, and I've collected some good recipes. I've had some good times, and now and then it was even pleasant to scratch. It's a disappointment, but it's only one stop along the way. Only one stop on a long, long road on which I could travel the rest of my life and never see it all. As long as the table is a place of joy and we can share a tasty meal together, there will always be another mile to go, to somewhere.

2 8 *Pictographs*

IN THE MIDDLE OF THE BAJA PENINSULA THE SIERRA de San Francisco mountain range rises almost straight up from the desert floor, climbing for a mile. No rolling foothills presage its existence. It lunges up like skyscrapers, stabbing at the air with crooked towers, snatching at clouds with twisted peaks. Here and there high mesas contrast with the crags. The mesas fall away into great slashes of canyons, as deep as the mountains are tall. From the distance, the mountain range has the appearance of a huge mottled castle or fortress town, its high battlements cracked and broken by monstrous engines of war.

Before Cortez landed on this peninsula in 1535, and long before the Aztecs ruled on the mainland, a wandering tribe had filtered into these mountains and stayed to live. They hunted deer and bighorn sheep, took water from the natural cisterns and rain catchments in the rock, and gathered the many edible seeds that the arid land yields. They multiplied, they throve, they split into rival clans and made war. They practiced magic and the healing arts. Then they vanished. They left behind few artifacts, little detritus for archeologists to find. Not even the Indians who lived here when the Spaniards arrived knew anything of the lost people. The only significant evidence that they had come this way is in their hundreds of pictures on the rocky walls.

They painted pictures in caves and on cliff faces and rock overhangs. They are giant pictures, in earth-tone colors. Men and women are depicted as much as three times larger than life on rocky pallets so high that it seems only giants could have done the work. Animals are usually life-size and they fight, they caper, they gather in herds. In one painting a huge serpent writhes along a cliff face for over a hundred feet. In another, a hemispherical outcropping of rock is cleverly painted to look like a shy tortoise. He faces a dragonfly of exquisite beauty. Every crawling and walking animal and every bird that lived in these mountains is represented. I have even noted sea creatures. A whale swims vertically up a mountainside that faces the sea. Elsewhere a yellowfin tuna lies near a ram. And almost always, at least one giant human form broods over the animals, as if to reaffirm Man's ascendance.

The first outsiders to see these paintings were the Jesuit missionaries looking to swell the ranks of the Catholic church. They wrote about them in their diaries, expressing satisfaction that, unlike the naked Indians they were dealing with, the painted giants appear to be clothed. The missionaries were able to keep the world at arm's length from Baja, so nobody else found out about the paintings. When the missionaries were expelled from Mexico, all outside knowledge of them ended.

The mission soldiers, artisans, and their families were not included in the expulsion. Left behind, and without the material support of the church, many departed the mission lands, leaving several missions completely abandoned. They moved to the high mesas. They established tiny hamlets where they subsisted by goatherding and farming. The world passed by, Baja California fading from its consciousness. The fortress of the Sierra closed up its gates, sealed itself off and held on tightly to its secrets.

Earl Stanley Gardner, the creator of Perry Mason, was a Baja bum. In 1962, he and his party were the first outsiders to penetrate the Sierra since the expulsion. They went to the high mesa settlement of Rancho San Francisco de la Sierra. The people living there took the Americans to a cave where herds of painted animals thundered past giant men. A few years later, Harry Crosby, a teacher in San Diego, learned of the paintings and set out on muleback to find as many of them as he could. With the help of local guides he found scores of them. Paul Harmon and I went to see if we could find them, too.

This trip was our second attempt on the Sierra. We had tried before to find a breach in the mountain walls but we had had no luck. That was the only time my modified four-wheel-drive, the Argo, couldn't take me where I wanted to go. We realized that only a mule could negotiate that terrain. To get into the Sierra we would have to go to the oasis of San Ignacio and hire mules, burros, and a guide. On our way there, with the Sierra on our left, I noticed something new in the land. A steep, narrow dirt road was snaking and switchbacking its way into the mountains. Plainly it was new, as construction gear lay about the road head. "I wonder how far it goes," I said.

We had plenty of supplies and fuel and it was early in the afternoon, so we turned onto the new road prepared to go whatever distance it might lead. Just before dark we arrived at Rancho San Francisco de la Sierra. We were a mile high and among people who had yet to see an electric light.

The next day we met a twenty-year-old consumptive muleteer named Francisco "Pancho" Arce Ojeda. We told him that we wanted to look for *cuevas pinturas*, painted caves. He said that he could guide us and would take care of hiring animals for us. "*¿No podemos¿ usar mi camionetta en su lugar?*" I asked. Can't we take my truck instead? He led us the short distance to the edge of the mesa. A deep canyon yawned, wide enough to swallow stars. The drop down was almost sheer. A switchback mule trail, inches wide, zigzagged to the bottom.

Pancho pointed to an area somewhere far below, smiled and said, *"Ahi, nos vamos ahi."* There, we're going there. *"¿Su camionetta puede volar?"* Can your truck fly?

"O.K.," I said. *"Mulas y burros."* He went off to make arrangements.

The next morning, as we got our gear together, I said to Paul, "Looks like we'll have to sleep on the cold, cold ground this trip, Pablo."

"Heh heh heh," he sniggered in a way that said "I've got a secret. Heh heh heh."

"What are you chortling about?" I asked.

He held up a nylon bag and in the voice of Curly of the Three Stooges said, "Nyuck nyuck nyuck. Air mattress, yeah."

"You S.O.B.," I said.

"Oh, wiseguy, eh? Nyuck nyuck nyuck."

We had everything packed, and I was filling my Spanish wineskin with Valpolicella when Pancho returned with three riding mules and two pack burros. We lashed the gear to the burros. I included my small icebox full of perishable food; I figured the ice would last at least two days. Some people would criticize me for not traveling light, but I insist on eating well, even on the trail. Paul pointed out that I should bring along a tarp since I "didn't have the foresight to bring along an air mattress." I told him to go to hell, but packed the tarp anyway. He quickly made it clear that he wasn't going to let me forget that I would be sleeping on road apples and he would be sleeping in comfort. "The comforts of the Argo have made you too dependent," he said. "You have to relearn self-reliance. Heh heh heh."

I took some brief comfort in the fact that Paul's mule turned out to be uncooperative. For instance, it wouldn't exhale enough to be properly saddled. Pancho and I had to work together on it. He shoved a knee into the animal's ribs while I gave a mighty heave on the cinch. "Ha!" I said to Paul. "Have fun on your mule." When we had all mounted and were just about to go, Paul's mule nipped at the flank of my mule, which then took off like bat out of hell straight into a cactus patch with me screaming, "Whoa!" I only had one foot in the stirrup and one hand on the bridle and spent the longest ten seconds of my life expecting to be hurled from the saddle into a prickly pear. Finally the beast stopped, realized where it was, and walked calmly back into line.

Pancho signaled and led the way. I followed behind him and the burros and Paul brought up the rear. We quickly reached the edge of the mesa and picked up the steep and narrow mule trail and began the harrowing plunge into the canyon. At times the trail was less that a foot wide and my shoulder brushed against the canyon wall. The most stunning moments were when the surefooted mules negotiated the outjutting hairpin turns of the switchback. Our bodies swung out in the saddle and seemed to hang in space above the chasm.

Occasionally the trail widened to two or three feet. In one of these wide spots we stopped to let the animals catch their breath, though we did not dismount. Except for Paul. He was mentioning something about his air mattress and I turned around to gesture sharply to him. That uncooperative mule of his finally exhaled. The cinch loosened, the saddle slid over, and one very chagrined Paul flopped onto the ground in midsentence about his damn mattress. I felt much better.

As the sun climbed, we descended. By noon the light was streaming down hot and fiercely bright. The canyon walls were almost devoid of vegetation. Only skeletal thorn bushes and gnarly roots protruded. They scratched at our faces and tore at our clothes. A streak of dried blood clung to my cheek. The hot light reflected off the bare, pale rock and glared in our eyes.

By the afternoon, the bottom was coming near enough to make out details of the terrain. I could see individual cacti and the larger boulders. As we made our final, winding approach, I noticed, ahead and below, in a narrow defile, a small cluster of thatched roofs and a patch of dark green. "Pancho!" I hollered up ahead to him. "*¿Que es?*"

"*¡Un rancho de mis primos!*" A ranch of my cousins'. Everybody in the Sierra, including his wife, is Pancho's cousin.

The patch of green was an orchard. Citrus trees, fig trees, pear trees, and grape vines were growing, seemingly, out of the rock. As we approached I saw that the orchardist had brought in the earth from afar. He had built a retaining wall about three feet high. For months, maybe years, every time he went to where there was dirt he brought some back, in his saddle-bags, in feed sacks, in jars, perhaps in his pockets, whatever he had with him at the time. Water trickled in through a sluice-way made of split and hollowed palm logs. Fruits hung heavy from the trees and the grapevines sagged with the weight of their vintage.

The five buildings of the rancho were made of whitewashed adobe. A corral held about forty drowsy goats, another a string of mules. The stiff palm thatch of the roofs hung well beyond the walls, forming large eaves that helped to shade the compound. Domesticated wildflowers made bursts of color in the courtyard. The narrow defile in which all was situated is called a *rincon*. Literally it is the Spanish for "corner" or "nook," but it has connotations of refuge and safety, as though being in the bosom of something.

We were invited to dismount and take the shade with the residents of the *rincon*. They were a very old couple, their middle-aged son and his wife, another woman a bit younger than the wife, and a boy of about fourteen. He seemed to suffer from something like Down's syndrome. He sat dully in a room in one of the cool adobes, staring at nothing, a metal bowl tied to his head. Occasionally he groaned or grunted and lunged with his head toward a wall. All in the Sierra are cousins.

The old man and woman were both infirm. They could no longer walk far, nor could they ride. And so they could never leave the rancho. They would die there. Their bodies would be washed and dressed and wrapped in shrouds by the younger people. They would be lashed to the backs of burros and taken to the high mesa for burial. A few years earlier they would have to have made the three-day journey to San Ignacio to find hallowed ground.

We sat on solid, old, wooden chairs in the patio, and conversed a little while in low tones; the *rincon* held no other noise to compete with our voices, and the acoustics were very fine. The señora served us oranges and lemons. I thought the lemons were to take with us, but she urged us to eat them. Not wishing to seem ungracious, I peeled and sectioned one as she watched, smiling. I thought I might have been in for a joke but when I bit into the fruit it tasted like lemonade with bitters. It was not quite sweet, but tart rather than sour. Its clean taste was like dry sparkling wine and as refreshing as cold spring water on a July afternoon. I greatly preferred the bittersweet lemons to the sweet, but seedy, oranges, and ate two or three.

The sun was in its long slide down and darkness would fall suddenly in the depths of the canyon. We took our leave and hurried on to find a campsite. About sunset we found a clearing, and while Pancho tended to the animals, Paul and I unlimbered what gear we would need for the night, rolled out sleeping bags, and built a small fire ring. We don't build any roaring bonfires in the desert. Fuel is too scarce unless you've brought your own. The practice here is to build a small fire and sit close.

We went looking for the twigs and sticks that would be our firewood. It was that late hour in the desert, just before dark, when the air is gold and the thin streaks of high cirrus clouds are tongues of flame. Shadows gather and disperse and gather again and the world is in flux, between two states of being, groping for its place. At the foot of a pile of huge boulders, Pancho stood in the shadow world, one foot in the daylight, one in the night. "*¿No lo veas?*" he said. Don't you see him?

He didn't point or otherwise indicate any direction. But our eyes traveled up the sloping pile of boulders to where its apex met the canyon's rock wall. Above that point, sheltered by overhanging rock, the ancient warrior stared down at us. He looked ten feet tall. Painted in brown, black, and red, his form was like a ghost. His hands were raised and he was shot with arrows, one through the heart, another through the gut. Animals and men danced around him. Then the night assumed its watch, and all became dark.

Clutching our bundles of sticks, we silently followed Pancho the short distance back to camp. We made a teepee of twigs in the fire ring and set them aflame. I found my wineskin full of Valpolicella and we all passed it around. We had said little or nothing since seeing the man of the arrows, but finally Paul and Pancho wondered what the painting signified and asked if I had any idea.

"No," I told them. "Nobody knows. We can only guess. The Catholics have a Saint Sebastian of the Arrows. His death was a sacrifice and he's considered a martyr. He's always depicted at the moment of death, with arrows sticking in him. Maybe this is some prehistoric version of something similar. Or maybe someone like Prometheus, another sacrifice, a suffering giant bound to the rock by Zeus for his unauthorized service to man. Who knows?"

"Maybe it was a warning to other tribes to stay away," Paul offered.

Pancho suggested that it might commemorate a victory in battle.

"How about a record of bad marksmanship while hunting?" Paul joked. "It says, 'Don't let this happen to you. Keep the safety on.'"

"Now that you mention it," I said, "some scholars believe the paintings were used as hunting magic. They theorize that game was chased or herded to these painted places, and that only here would they be killed or eaten."

"Then we're in their killing and feasting ground. A fit place for us to dine, I guess," Paul ventured.

"I guess. Whoa! Wait a minute," I blurted. "Think of the possibilities. If this is, indeed, a killing and a feasting ground, and the painting is of a man being killed and animals going free: then who is killing and eating what, or whom?"

"Ooh."

"Aye aye aye."

"Let's have another swig of wine and then some dinner," I said. The others approved, especially of the swig. I gathered my skillet and wooden spoon, my pantry box, spice box and icebox and a mesh bag of vegetables.

"*¿Que preparas?*" Pancho asked. What are you making?

"Cassoulet," I said with gusto.

"*¿Que es eso?*" What's that?

"Uh, mmm. *Frijoles frances.*" French beans.

Using my buck knife I cut up a Spanish onion, a green bell pepper, and some garlic. I didn't have a cutting board so I just whittled on them till they were all reduced to small pieces. From the icebox I took out three Italian sausages and four Oscar Mayer Smokey Links. I removed the skins from the sausages and cut the links into small slices.

I set the skillet on the fire, and when it was hot, put in the sausages, breaking them up with the wooden spoon and browning them. To that I added the vegetables and a little olive oil and sauteed them till tender. The Smokey Links went in next.

Having breathed the pure air of the canyon all day, the spicy, smoky smells that rose from the pan were especially potent. They wafted into our nostrils and found their way straight down to our stomachs, making them growl with anticipation. My salivary glands worked nonstop, constantly filling my mouth as all the good things sizzled in the pan. I took frequent nips from the wineskin and held the wine in my mouth. I rolled it around, my tongue kneading it, jaws almost chewing it. I swallowed it the way you might swallow ice cream: tongue pushing it to the back of the throat a little at a time. After swallowing, the remnant vapors traveled from mouth to nasal passages, reminding me for minutes of its excellent tart and fruity flavor and its undercurrents of cinnamon and black cherry.

Having lined up my remaining ingredients, I put them into the pan one by one. A small can each of kidney beans, lima beans, and white beans for substance; a spoonful of prepared mustard and one of brown sugar to duel with each other across the pallet; parsley, bay, and thyme for a traditional bouquet garni; Worcester and Tabasco just because; and stewed tomatoes and tomato paste to make a thick and savory sauce that would marry them all together.

The little fire was at a perfect pitch for simmering, so I stirred the pan and let it alone. We sat on the ground and passed the wineskin back and forth. We emptied and refilled it. When the beans were done we removed the pan and sat closer to the fire. We each took a spoon and a Sierra cup and scooped up our portions. We ate slowly, enjoying the chew of the meat, the mash of the beans and the spicy, tomatoey bite of the sauce.

The moon rose. With the help of its light, when the fire flickered just so, we caught fleeting glimpses of the giant Hombre de las Flechas (Man of the Arrows) staring down at us. "I wonder how often his fellows feasted under his gaze like we are?" I thought out loud. "I wonder if he wanted to be remembered? I wonder if he was a real man, or a god, or an abstraction?"

"Funny," Paul said. "All he is is a question. There are no answers in him."

We finished our meal and our wine, and as we would be rising at dawn, we prepared for sleep. There were many other paintings that Pancho was eager to show us. Paul kept alternating between "Heh heh heh" and "Nyuck nyuck nyuck" and "Don't lie on any road apples." I crawled into my bag to find that I was, indeed, lying on a road apple. I bolted up and retrieved it and threw it at Paul, narrowly missing him. "Oh, wise guy, eh. Nyuck nyuck nyuck," he responded. "And now the comfort king will prepare his boudoir." His face brimming with satisfaction, he opened his nylon bag and dumped its contents on the ground. It was a rolled-up inner tube.

"Heh heh heh. Good night, Pablito. Heh heh heh."

I slept very well that night, as I often do when on the road, even under uncomfortable conditions. I had the fire, the satisfaction of a good day's wonders, and the romance of the road. And I knew that several days later I would be sleeping between clean sheets in the Hotel las Casitas in Mulege. Javier, *el dueño*, would see me well served. His excellent kitchen would seduce me with something from the sea. And over drinks on the patio under the now waxing moon he would ask me yet again when I would "settle down" and lead a more "regular" life.

Most people live by the seasons. Their lives are cyclical. Christmas snows, spring thaw, summer heat, harvest moon. The red-letter days of the calendar. It's the way I grew up, too. And it was good. But since my first trampings and voyages I broke with the seasons. I now live by the road. When it's winter at home I'll come to Baja California. When it's summer at home I may head for the snows of another hemisphere. I'm never home for holidays. I've lost track of my birthdays. The only constant is this long, magnificent peninsula that we know as "the Baja." Here I come to restore myself, reorient, rest, explore again, and plan new journeys. Nothing repeats itself but this desert. Life is no cycle for me. It's an unending road, with no point of return. And as Paul has suggested, perhaps there are no answers to be found in it, but its questions always beckon.

2 9 *Vengeance*

 Man the hunter and Man the hunted, both predator and prey. Is that symmetry or symbiosis? Is it balance in nature? A kind of natural justice? Is this the ancient question of the man painted on the rock?

I landed in Nairobi after one of Air-India's signature uncomfortable flights. As soon as I had checked into the hotel I went looking for a feast, for succor, for relief from the pitiful rations and thin potations of the airline. I found a charming place in the second story of a nearby building. Like many restaurants here it had a little terrace overlooking the street. There I took a table and gazed out on the nightlife of the street below. I ordered a beer and the waiter asked me, "Would you like it cold or at room temperature, sir?" Of course I knew the drill. So I said, "I'm American," and just smiled. "Of course, sir," he said, returning the smile. "Cold it is." The waiter had just served me the first beer and as I sipped the soothing brew I perused the menu, my eye going from steak to *masala* to Nile perch. And there was a short wine list with some interesting local Kenyan entries as well as some Italian and French. "This place is going to be good," I thought.

As I relaxed from my grueling flight, from a distance the sounds of an angry commotion reached the terrace, though I paid it no heed. It came closer and I unconsciously cocked an ear to it while still paying most of my attentions to my beer. As a veteran of both war and riot this is a practiced response. The sound grew into a tumult as it rounded a corner some distance away. It was coming toward me and growing by decibels. Angry shouts now became discernible amid the blending of loud and hostile voices.

Before I could see the man, I heard his painful breathing and the soles of his shoes as they rapidly struck the pavement, echoing down the street. He burst into view some yards away, sprinting for the most important medal of his life, behind him a swarm of angry people bent on bodily harm. His knees were lifting almost up to his chest as he labored to increase his stride. His arms swung achingly up and back, trying to extract the last iota of speed and distance from each hurtful step. Having been a sprinter myself, I could see that he was not practiced in the art, his style was most inefficient. But he was trying for his life to improve it fast.

His face was a mask, frozen in panic. The crowd pursuing him was a mass of arms and legs, and voices and faces of rage. They caught him just as he reached the spot below my table. He hit the pavement with a sound like a side of beef being dropped from my second-story terrace. And the mob proceeded to beat the living shit out of him. As the waiter served me another beer, nice and cold, the harpies and the furies repeatedly kicked the man in the ribs, making a sound like a base drum. They stomped severally on his head, causing it to bounce up and down on the asphalt. They hit him with sticks and fists, and threw at him anything that came to hand. They grabbed him by his arms and legs, picked him up, and slammed him back to the ground. They spit on him and cursed him. People on the terrace, and people on the street gathered to watch and laugh. From the moment the mob overtook the man he made no struggle, but simply curled up and absorbed their violence and curses.

"What did he steal?" I asked the waiter.

"Something from a shop," he said, watching with interest.

When the crowd had spent itself they all cursed him one more time, then melted away. The man lay there on the street, also spent. Soon a friend, or accomplice, or maybe a Samaritan came along and helped him up, brushed him off, and he struggled home to recover from his occupational hazard.

I once heard a story about a Kenyan thief being pursued by a mob who ran for shelter to the nearest police station, preferring the uncertain mercies of the cops to the swift and certain justice of his victims. I read in the local newspaper of another thief who was caught by a mob that drenched him in gasoline and set him afire.

That night of the punishment of the thief I dined well on Nile perch and white Burgundy. But I dined very quietly, thoughtfully, and thankfully. Thankful for my good place in the world. For the relative peace and security in which I am privileged to live. I recalled that while on the cross Jesus was flanked by a pair of thieves, and he comforted them. I said a prayer for the thief on the street below. Later that night, when I returned to my hotel room, I found I had been robbed.

3 0 *Gratitude*

At home I always try to run six miles a day. Partly because I like to stay slim and in good shape. Never know when I might need to climb a mountain in Laos or flee from a riot in Ecuador or chase a pickpocket just for sport. And partly because I like the effort, to break a sweat, and to challenge myself anew each time. It makes me feel more alive. And as I age, it keeps me from aging too much. When on the road it's near impossible to keep my usual schedule, but I do what I can.

When in Greece I run with the Athens chapter of the Hash House Harriers, my favorite group of international "drinkers with a running problem." Our running is irreverent, noisy, and noncompetitive, with the express purpose of working up a thirst. Hollering our traditional cry of "On, On!" we once ran through the Plaka, the touristic theme park of Athens just below the Acropolis, where we scandalized a group of retired Czech civil servants on tour of the ancient sites. Next time we banished our naughty selves to nearby Cape Sounion where we tripped over marble fragments and found ourselves desecrating an archeological dig. The student volunteers on duty did a perfect impression of a riot in Ecuador, and so we fled, hollering our cry of "On, On!"

But in Greece you can never escape ancient relics, reminders of those who ran before. And if you are an athlete of any kind, and especially if you are a runner, in Greece you will be aware every day that you are in the birthplace of athletes and athletics as we have come to know them. Especially as we watch the modern Olympics and other professional sports. At our post-run thirst-quenchings of "the Hash" we speak of it. Ancient champions ran down the very paths we tread, though their prize was not a cold one. Theirs was just the satisfaction of the Contest, and if they won, the Glory. We freely acknowledge that the likes of Pericles and Cleander would wag the finger in a gentle admonishment of our juvenile antics. We don't even pour a libation to the gods from our plentiful supplies. The ancients always poured a cup of wine or a jug of beer onto the earth or into the sea as an offering of thanks to their gods. We sing bawdy songs instead. And that the ancients might have approved, were it to follow the libation. But we are sure of one thing. They would have disdained the modern Olympics.

Classical Greek athletes would have tolerated the Hash, maybe even joined us now and then just for the fun. But when it came to the Contest they'd get serious. The run was for higher purpose: for their gods, for the glory, for the pride of their city, for the sport. They did not aspire to represent soft drinks. Indeed they had to pay their own way. Nike? Hey, these guys ran barefoot. Their greatest reward was to be rendered in stone by a local sculptor, the statue to be mounted in the walkway to the arena. Those statues are still here at Olympia, and people speak in awe of Cleomenes and others as they regard their likenesses, after 2,500 years. Mark Spitz competed only quarter century ago, but do you remember him more for his medals or as a pitchman for razor blades? Do you remember him at all?

I traveled to the Peloponnese, the southern half of the Greek mainland, with my friends Clio and Domenic. Clio is

Greek-American, and she speaks the lingo. Dom is Sicilian-American, and he does not. And of course I am WASP from California, and speak Spanish, which does me no good here. But we are three musketeers, and it's all for one and one for all as we probe the hinterlands of ancient Laconia. Clio swims a little, but Dom and I are dedicated workout demons. Traveling together he and I skip rope, do calisthenics, run, and do all sorts of exercises in tandem.

We hired a car and drove from Athens to ancient Olympia in the western Peloponnese. It was a hot day. I thirsted for beer. I lost sight of the scenery. I confess I am in many ways a barbarian. I revere the ancients and the classics and the baroques, and even Elvis, but when I thirst, by Zeus, I thirst. In the late afternoon, when we parked in the wooded grove of Olympia, I was only mildly interested. A few of the columns I spied through the darkening trees competed for my attentions with a man in a kiosk selling beer and other necessities of life. As we walked to the entrance I was about to stop for a cold one, but Clio urged us on. "I have something to show you," she said. Dom followed, so I did, too, hoping for the best. Through the gates of the ancient sanctuary she led us, pointing out the displays of photographs of the heroes collected in the museum nearby. "All these men were champions," she explained. "Many posed for Pheidias," the sculptor who was famous for his renderings of athletes. "These are the remains of his studio," she pointed out, as we passed a clump of ruins.

"Can I get a beer now?" I asked. She only gestured, leading us on. Dominic, sensitive guy that he is, admired the stones, and flexed his rather large biceps at them in homage. I tucked my belt in a notch and wondered when I might quench my thirst. "Come on, boys," Clio said. And then pointed to the pedestal where once stood the statue of Phillip II of Macedonia, father of Alexander the Great. He had won a race here in the fourth century B.C.

On we walked. "These are the pedestals of the heroes, the champions, who were victors at '*Olympiacos*'" she went on to say. "On either side of us, down this pathway, into the grand stadium." We followed her, through the remnants of a tunnel. And we emerged into the stadium. This was the original. This was where it all started. This is where the heroes ran. This is where the Olympic flame is lit to this day, from the collected rays of the sun's undying fire. And how Greek we all are, you will think if you can look upon this. It could be any football field cum running track in any high school in America, or anywhere else. It's about a quarter mile course, I could see instantly. I've run a lot of courses; run a lot of races; won a few, lost more. If there's anything to which my eye is calibrated it's the quarter mile. For decades after the modern Olympics began the quarter mile was an American benchmark for speed. Glenn Cunningham measured himself against it as he healed from his almost fatal burns, suffered in an accident. He went on to break the four-minute mile. One-quarter mile every sixty seconds. Once around a track just like this one here at Olympia every minute.

And then there were all those ancient champions. Men who now reside in stone in the museum. Men like Phillip II, Cleomenes, Alcibiades, even Plato the philosopher was an athlete here. Here on this very ground. On this quarter mile ran untold ancient heroes, men who ran for nothing but the gods and the glory. They drank only water and they wore no shoes. And they set the tone and timbre and the standards for us the living today.

Without a word Dominic and I stripped off our shirts and began running. On the sloping, grassy grandstands the laurel-wreathed crowds were watching through time. Down the first hundred yards we passed the foundations of the judges' box. We waved to them as we sped by. We slowed just a little, for this would be only one quarter mile, and we wanted it to last. We came down to the curve. The sweat broke as we neared what we would now call the "bullpen" where contestants waited their turn. We waved to them. One of them laid a hundred drachmas on me. Another took the bet. We pounded the dirt in the footsteps of Phillip. Our arms were driving rods that Lysias would approve of. Plato would commend us for our form. In the summer heat the sweat flowed in rivulets, soaking even our trousers. We were both grinning like fools as we approached the seat of the priestess who presided over the ancient games. She waved us on with laurel, and our grins could no longer contain the joy, and we burst into laughter as we drove into a final sprint. We sucked in the sweetest air. A group of tourists from somewhere in Europe had arrived and were cheering us on. We were racing, laughing, exulting, sweating, alive. "It's a tie!" Clio shouted as we crossed the finish and the crowd erupted into applause, and what sounded like German. "Now you both have to pose for Pheidias!" she said.

I couldn't get the grin off my face. And I saw nothing and wanted to see nothing as we walked away into the gathering darkness. All was symmetrical and all was complete. One lap. One-quarter mile. One perfect unit of distance in one perfect unit of time. In the one perfect place. On the way to the car, as the kiosk man was about to close up shop, I stopped and bought a bottle of Mythos, the Greek national beer. I popped the top and held it up to my friends. "No thanks," they said, misunderstanding my purpose.

"The libation," said I.

I faced the stadium where the undying flame is lit. And I poured the Mythos out onto the soil of Olympia. An offering of thanks for the best quarter mile a man could run.

E p i l o g u e

"How do I get there?" I asked as we sat around the fire on the beach, swapping stories.

"Well, you can't get there from here," the old man snorted. "Best go to Catavina and hire mules. Then see Senora Rodrigues at Rancho Santa Ynez, she can tell you how to get there. But it's a hard ride through the desert, and there's no water along the way. Best not to go at all."

"There" is a place the Cochimi Indians called Cabujaka-maang, a place where spirits dwell. To the Spaniards it was the frontier Mission of Santa Maria de los Angeles. Today we know it as "The Lost Mission." At its founding by the Jesuit order in 1767 it was the terminus of a mule trail known as El Camino Real: The King's Highway. For its young padre Victoriano Arnez it was the very ends of the earth.

Three hundred miles below the U.S./Mexico border, nearly halfway down the length of Baja California, between Catavina to the west and Bahía San Luis Gonzaga to the east, there is nothing leading to it that could rightly be called a road, and the trail is not on any map. Snug in a neat canyon, it was the pretty little stepchild of the mission family that would eventually stretch, via El Camino Real, over one thousand miles to the town of Sonoma in Upper California.

Despite the old man's skepticism, I made it to Santa Maria. A few times. I made it because Arnez did. I made it because I stumbled upon him while searching Spanish mission records for something else, and I saw in him the fire, and I determined that I would know where it might take a man.

When Arnez set out from Spain for the New World, his passion was *"Mas alla, mas alla,"* farther, ever farther. He was afire with missionary zeal to go forth and harvest souls at the furthest reaches of navigation: the Californias. When at last he was assigned he took leave of his parents and rushed to take ship, only to find no room on board for him. After another year of waiting he secured passage on another vessel only to be storm-tossed and shipwrecked, nearly drowned and washed up on Portuguese shores. Another year of waiting. Finally, in 1765, he was able to complete the difficult and demanding six-month journey across the Atlantic, across the breadth of Mexico, across the Vermilion Sea, or Sea of Cortez, and to Loreto. Once there he and a newfound friend, Padre Juan Diez, another young missionary, were assigned to the then northern-most mission of San Borja. There they were to help the missionary, Padre Wenslavo Link, learn the Cochimi Indian tongue, and prepare themselves for their own mission *mas alla*.

By order of Father Superior Lambert Hostell, Arnez, accompanied by Diez, set out on October 14, 1766, to find some place at which to establish a new mission. As they were moving into unknown territory they were accompanied by ten soldiers and fifty Indian neophytes. They made an abortive first attempt at Calamajue, a barren and featureless place in the desert. Its bad water killed the crops they planted. The local Indians were hostile and the soldiers discontented. Worse, for Arnez, his friend Diez took seriously ill and had to be removed to San Borja.

Virtually alone now, without the company of his friend, with a dwindling troop of soldiers and a flock going hungry he set out *mas alla,* ever farther into the wilderness, to seek out some friendlier spot of ground. Half a day's ride to the north of sun-blasted Calamajue, in May of 1767, he found it. In a sheltered nook in the desert hills a shady grove of blue fan palms grew amid limpid pools of sweet water. Over the mountain that separates the place from the sea, the bay of San Luis Gonzaga offered secure anchorage for supply ships. The Indians told him that the place was called Cabujakamaang, and that spirits had dwelt in the grove forever. It was a stopping place in the Indians' annual migrations, and a place of ceremonies and communion with the other world. On a small prominence overlooking the palm grove, Arnez established and dedicated Mission Santa Maria de los Angeles, with due thanks to Maria Borgia, Duchess of Gandia, whose patronage had financed his efforts. The little mission of Santa Maria was now the terminus of the King's Highway. Victoriano Arnez had reached *lo mas alla*, the farthest of the far. He was at the hithermost reaches of the King's writ, as far from his native land and all that was familiar as a man could be. So hotly did his fire burn. So far did it take him.

Despite his efforts, the mission would fail, and he would be recalled. By 1800 the central desert was thoroughly and utterly depopulated by disease and despair. No one was left alive at Santa Maria. In 1818 the surviving northern missions were suppressed. In the land between San Ignacio and El Rosario nobody would come to live for nearly half a century. The track of the King's Highway began to fade from the ground. The location of Santa Maria with its spirit grove, even its very existence, faded from memory.

Faulkner would have called this a "magnificent failure," I thought to myself as I surveyed the adobe remains of the church and the small residence. But it was doomed to fail. All the land for miles around is hostile to human life. I came here in my four-wheel drive, and even with that advantage I had to use my winch several times to extract myself from sand traps and rocks. Arnez came here on foot. I can hardly imagine the struggle. So I walked a few miles of his trail. And I marveled that he would come here at all. And yet he came. He had to. His passion compelled him. To deny it would have meant the death of his spirit.

I have come here one last time to honor him. I want to tell his spirit that the fire did not die here when he was recalled. My passion, my fire, has brought me to this very same spot to which his brought him. I want to tell him that all fires descend from the same Promethean spark. That my passion, my fire, is his as well. "I'll pour a libation for you, Victoriano," I say into the silence. "I've brought it with me. A most special kind."

In my wanderings throughout the world I carry journals of travelers who have gone before me. In Mexico I have carried the journal of Bernal Diaz, Conquistador. He rode with Cortez from the very start of the Mexican Conquest. He knew the Generalissimo, and he knew his beautiful Mayan interpreter, advisor, and mistress: Dona Marina. He knew the near erotic thrill and the soul-shaking horror of the great enterprise. And he knew and admired the man he always referred to as "the Great Montezuma."

Among his records are many processes, techniques, and recipes. Thus Diaz on treating wounds when the usual dressings were unavailable: "After the battle, we sealed our wounds with grease rendered from the fat of an Indian we had killed." And Diaz, the watchful saucier, upon witnessing Aztec human sacrifice and cannibalism: "They kicked the bodies down the steps. There were butchers waiting below to cut off the arms and legs. These they kept for their fiestas, when they got drunk and ate the meat with *chimole*," a salsa made of tomatoes, chili, and cilantro.

The domestic and the culinary were always of great interest to Diaz. He often was present when Montezuma sat down to dine, and he recorded what he saw. He was vastly impressed that Montezuma's cooks prepared as many as "thirty kinds of dishes for every meal, done the way he liked them, and they placed small pottery braziers under them so they wouldn't get cold." He was fond of dishes of birds. And he was exceedingly fond of hot chocolate. Diaz reports that the great Montezuma drank as many as forty cups a day, and that because of this he was able to service as many of his concubines as he liked on any given day.

Ever the close observer, he noted the recipe, and passed it down to us. The great Montezuma liked his cup of hot chocolate flavored with vanilla, sweetened with honey, and spiked with a good dose of red chili. The conquistadores picked up the habit, too, and Diaz and some others stayed in Mexico carving out huge haciendas and quaffing chocolate in the manner of their admired late foe. They kept the original recipe but expanded on it a bit by adding a splash of "vino de Tequila." But basically they drank what the emperor had drunk. And so I'll make a libation of it for a man I'll never meet, yet consider a brother.

I've spent two days and nights here at Victoriano's mission, meditating on many things, drinking wines grown in vineyards planted by his contemporaries, and preparing for the moment of my homage. The morning of my departure I rise and begin to break my camp and pack my gear. I unload some oak wood and pitch pine that I've brought and construct a pyre on which to pour the libation. For tinder I use the paper-like remnants of dead cardon and other cactus, and dried palm fronds. Next is the pitch-pine shards, for oak will need fierce heat to make it burn. Then the thick oak sticks, and lastly a heavy oak log that will burn hot for many hours. I must have this done and be gone by midday, for I'll need all the light of the afternoon to cross the broken terrain between here and Senora Rodriguez's rancho, and the road that will take me back to Mulege. And I want my last vision of this place to be the fire at its brightest.

There are four sweet water pools in the palm grove, and I select one for a tub and have a bath. The water is tepid, which is perfect for the desert. I wonder as I soak if Victoriano availed himself of this luxury. Clean and refreshed, I dress, and prepare the libation. Over a camp stove I make hot chocolate, sweetened with honey and vanilla, and spiced with red chili. Then I dose it with a goodly dollop of tequila. I taste. Add a little more tequila. And a little more.

When all is ready for my departure I touch a flame to the tinder. The cactus remnants billow black creosote smoke until the pitch pine begins to crackle. Its flames are almost white hot and the oak sticks soon ignite. Big golden flames rise and rise and soon the fire is roaring and the heat sears my face. I pour into the middle of the fire. First steam, and then the tequila flame rises furiously amid the mother flame. "It never died, Victoriano. It brought you here. It brought me here. It will bring others. Watch for them, by and by."

About the Author

Richard Sterling is a writer, editor, lecturer, and insatiable traveler. Earlier in life he was a Silicon Valley engineer, but stability and respectability lost out over wanderlust. Since taking up the pen he has been honored by the James Beard Foundation for his food writing, and by the Lowell Thomas Awards for his travel literature. He is based in Berkeley, California, where he is often politically incorrect.

Other Books by Richard Sterling

Travelers' Tales Food: A Taste of the Road

The Adventure of Food: True Stories of Eating Everything

*The Ultimate Journey:
Inspiring Stories of Living and Dying*

*The Fearless Diner: Travel Tips and
Wisdom for Eating Around the World*

World Food: Vietnam

World Food: Spain

World Food: Hong Kong

World Food: Greece

Unofficial Guide to San Francisco

*The Eclectic Gourmet Guide
to San Francisco and the Bay Area*